The Religious Metaphysics
of
Simone Weil

SUNY Series, Simone Weil Studies
Eric O. Springsted, Editor

The Religious Metaphysics
of
Simone Weil

by
MIKLOS VETÖ

translated by
Joan Dargan

State University of New York Press

Published by
State University of New York Press, Albany

©1994 State University of New York

For information, address the State University of New York Press,
State University Plaza, Albany, NY   12246

Production by Christine Lynch
Marketing by Dana E. Yanulavich

Library of Congress Cataloging-in-Publication Data

Vetö, Miklós, 1936–
    [Métaphysique religieuse de Simone Weil.   English]
    The religious metaphysics of Simone Weil / by Miklós Vetö :
translated by Joan Dargan.
        p.   cm. — (SUNY series, Simone Weil studies)
    Includes index.
    ISBN 0-7914-2077-9 (alk. paper). — ISBN 0-7914-2078-7 (pbk. :
alk. paper)
        1. Weil, Simone, 1909–1943.   2. Metaphysics.   I. Title.
    II. Series.
    B2430.W474V4813   1994
    194—dc20   93-40293
                                                                          CIP

10 9 8 7 6 5 4 3 2 1

Contents

Series Editor's Preface

When Professor Vető's *La Métaphysique religieuse de Simone Weil* appeared in 1971, it was, indeed, the first methodical exposition of Simone Weil's thought, despite the fact that Weil's striking originality had been noticed as early as 1946 with the first posthumous publication of her writings. As the first, and still one of the few books that give us any sort of thorough conceptual map of Weil's thought, it has been invaluable to a generation of scholars. For its clarity and thoroughness it still remains one of the best sources to consult when wending one's way through the thickets of Weil's thinking. For these reasons above all we are therefore especially pleased to be able to make this book available to the English-speaking reader.

I would be remiss, however, in letting the matter stand at that. Within the last few years, increasingly the question of how to interpret Weil, after one has gotten the concepts at all in order, has been at the forefront of Weil scholarship. One important view, particularly prominent in the English-speaking world, argues that Weil's originality lies in her ability to address and incorporate important classical philosophical and spiritual questions without subscribing to the metaphysics by which previous generations had attempted to address them. This is not Professor Vető's view. Rather, he contends that Weil was a classical metaphysician. As such this book continues to have critical interest in an ongoing debate, a debate that is of importance as the nature and character of Weil's thought continues to challenge our thinking.

ERIC O. SPRINGSTED
Series Editor

Preface to the American Edition

Ever since Simone Weil died a half century ago, she has been a figure in the pantheon of contemporary thought. Shortly after her death, her parents, out of devotion to her memory, arranged for the publication of *La Pesanteur et la Grâce* (*Gravity and Grace*), and the immense interest provoked by this selection of her thoughts led to the rapid publication of most of her writings. The stunning texts and the unique personality of their author became established in a postwar world avid for new spiritual resources and fascinated by the witness of an exceptional being. With the cultural trend toward more openly political and social preoccupations in the sixties, there was some loss of interest in this *philosophia perennis* offering a very classic spirituality. With the return swing of the pendulum and the renewal of interest in things spiritual, there is a massive revival of interest in Weil as a philosopher and religious writer, and as a social and political thinker as well. This consolidation of the cultural position of the author of *Attente de Dieu* (*Waiting on God*) is reflected in the foundation of several Simone Weil societies and by the publication of the critical edition of her *Oeuvres complètes*.

Weil is read in Europe, America, and Japan; there is nothing to suggest that people will ever stop reading her. She is read because of her lucid and harmonious prose, her vigorous writing that blossoms into magnificent expressions. Weil is read because of the overwhelming authenticity of her spiritual experience. She is read because hers is a philosophical thought in which attentive reading of the great minds of the past culminates in a coherent and original metaphysics and ethics. She is read above all—whether one be religious or not—as the writer best able to formulate and reformulate the essential points of Christian doctrine all the while practicing an ardent and fruitful reading of Hellas and India. And ultimately, in light of the intellectual history of this century, it is impossible not to admire the intellectual honesty of this militant syndicalist who never compromised with totalitarian imposture.

The meteoric appearance of Simone Weil has from the beginning inspired secondary works, but usually in these writings praise and occasionally invective take the place of conceptual analysis. Rapid overviews take precedence over systematic exposition, and biographical study gives way to hagiography. My book was the first methodical study of Weil's thought, and if it has been followed by a number of works of high intellectual content, it remains even today the only methodical, conceptual reconstitution of Weil's thought.

The translation presents a practically unchanged book. Of course, there are things I would have said differently if I had to say them today for the first time; and if I still believe Weil's philosophy descended essentially from Plato and Kant, I would have insisted more on other sources, especially on the hidden but very perceptible influence of Rousseau. I have made some very small corrections and left out much of the bibliography rendered superfluous today by the publication of the *Oeuvres complètes*, now in progress, and by Patricia Little's bibliography. But otherwise, for the most part, I have not changed anything. The image I formed of Weil, the path I took through her work are, to be sure, only one possible image and one possible path, but they have a coherence and specificity that would be ill served by rewriting. Having served a generation of readers of French, this book is now made available to the English-speaking reader.

Acknowledgments

The initial version of this book took shape under the sympathetic eye of Iris Murdoch, the novelist and philosopher, who unstintingly offered me encouragement and critiques. David McLellan and, at a later stage, Gilbert Kahn and my wife contributed many critical observations and suggestions, especially on form, and also on content. To them I am grateful.

I am printing some unpublished passages with the kind authorization of André Weil. And finally, I wish to evoke the memory of Selma Weil, who followed my work with interest and facilitated my access to manuscripts. In spite of illness and age, she lovingly and efficiently prepared her daughter's works for publication. Those who did not know Simone Weil in her lifetime were able at least to experience the radiance of her genius in her mother's presence.

Translator's Note

The present work is a translation of *La Métaphysique religieuse de Simone Weil* (Paris: J. Vrin, 1971). I wish to thank Eric O. Springsted for his unfailing advice and encouragement; Miklos Vetö, for his careful review of an early draft of the manuscript; Martin Andic, for welcome corrections and for the painstaking (and undoubtedly painful) work of identifying the English equivalents of the original French references; and St. Lawrence University, for its generous support of this endeavor. In the interest of stylistic consistency, all translations from Simone Weil are mine.

Abbreviations[1]

French Texts:

AD	*Attente de Dieu*
CO	*La Condition Ouvrière*
CS	*La Connaissance Surnaturelle*
CSW	*Cahiers Simone Weil*
EHP	*Ecrits Historiques et Politiques*
EL	*Ecrits de Londres et dernières lettres*
En	*L'Enracinement*
IP	*Intuitions Pré-chrétiennes*
LP	*Leçons de philosophie de Simone Weil*
LR	*Lettre à un religieux*
OL	*Oppression et liberté*
P	*Poèmes*
PS	*Pensées sans ordre concernant l'amour de Dieu*
S	*Sur la Science*
SG	*La Source Grecque*
1	*Cahiers I*, 1951 edition
2	*Cahiers 2*

---

[1] [Editor's Note: One of the admirable qualities of Professor Vetö's work is its exhaustive use of Weil's texts. In order that the English reader be able to take full advantage of this, all references are first given to the French text and then, noted by a =, are given the English textual equivalents. There are, however, some texts—only a few to be sure—that have not been translated and hence are not given English references. We have also sought to use the now being published *Oeuvres complètes* when possible for French references.]

3   *Cahiers 3*

OC   *Oeuvres complètes* (Citation given as:
        Tome.volume.page)

English Texts:

F   *First and Last Notebooks*

FW   *Formative Writings*

GTG   *Gateway to God*

IC   *Intimations of Christianity among the Ancient Greeks*

LP   *Lectures on Philosophy*

N   *The Notebooks of Simone Weil*

NR   *The Need for Roots*

OL   *Oppression and Liberty*

SE   *Selected Essays (1934–1943)*

SL   *Seventy Letters*

SN   *On Science, Necessity and the Love of God*

SWA   *Simone Weil: An Anthology*

SWR   *The Simone Weil Reader*

WG   *Waiting for God*

Introduction

Very little of Simone Weil's writing appeared during her lifetime, and when her works began to be published post-humously, fascination with the figure made by this exceptional young woman to a great extent accounted for the interest of readers. The first writings on her thought—and not only the first—reflected the grip of this fascination with her life. In most of these writings, biographical or, rather, hagiographical concerns predominate, and elements of the strange, the tragic, and the picturesque are to be found to the detriment of solid and methodical investigations into ideas.[1] Naturally, Weil's importance resides as much in the witness of her life as in the stunning fragments of her work, and this author would certainly be the last not to admire the fascinating greatness of this life: her unrelenting struggle with violent headaches; her heroic year in factories; the months she spent working in the fields; the episode of the Spanish Civil War; her preoccupation with the refugee camps; and the tragic consummation of her life in a sanatorium near London. I am persuaded that anyone unaware of the circumstances of her life has no chance to truly understand Weil's thought, but I have assumed such familiarity here. I have no ambition to write a biography; my sole desire is to shed light on the admirable connections in Weil's thought alone, nearing insofar as possible the perfect intelligibility she always pursued as an ideal.[2]

Weil's renown was established especially by *Attente de Dieu* (*Waiting for God*) and *La Pesanteur et la Grâce* (*Gravity and Grace*); the latter is often thought to present the real quintessence of

Weilian thought. If *La Pesanteur et la Grâce* does indeed contain many of the most admirable texts from the *Cahiers* (*Notebooks*), these texts comprise only a fifth of the total. I am convinced that in order to understand the profound internal logic of Weil's thought, it is necessary to begin with the *Cahiers* and *La Connaissance Surnaturelle*, which sketch out almost everything to be developed later on in definitive form. But these works contain even greater treasures: the whole scale of possibilities the definitive works will draw on, while fully developing only several of these.[3] And finally, in a rather paradoxical way, the study of these diverse and heterogeneous "thoughts," which open to view the genesis and elaboration of all her ideas, will keep us from taking Weil as a writer without doctrinal claims, as a mere writer of aphorisms. Weil certainly never intended to leave an exposition of her "system"[4] for the excellent reason that she had never thought of constructing one. That is why, moreover, it is so often thought that her writings primarily contain scattered aphorisms; that there is no sense in trying to reconcile her many paradoxes, because they are not meant to be reconciled, being not at all the expression of a systematic and coherent thought; that they are only vaguely tied together through a few of their author's basic ideas and feelings.

This conception making of Weil an extravagant moralist or a "mystical spirit" reveals a fundamental lack of understanding. Obviously, no one would think of denying there exist irreducible inner contradictions in her thought and that even her attempts to prove, or merely illustrate, her ideas sometimes end in failure. The simple fact that the substance of her work is made up of fragments and general but still implicit ideas reveals the presence of insoluble difficulties. Nevertheless, despite the apparent chaos, Weil's thought is a coherent whole, and my sole claim is to decipher its organic connections.

Weil was above all a philosopher, but while keeping to one side of contemporary schools, her thought, which betrays a certain heteronomy of philosophical, religious, and, occasionally, openly scientific ideas, hardly corresponds to the traditional conception of metaphysics. Descartes was the thinker who influenced her thought most, after Plato and Kant; but toward the end of her life, she would not hesitate to affirm that, to her mind, the founder of Cartesianism was not a philosopher in the authentically Platonic and Pythagorean sense of the word,[5] and to conclude that "ever since the disappearance of Greece, there has been no philosopher."[6] We shall see that this severe and exclusive judgment will not prevent Weil from returning to the Kantian bases of her speculation. But the reference to Platonism as a criterion of true philosophy draws attention to the central characteristic of that thought: the harmony between reason and mystery that make the developments in the *Cahiers* so fascinating. Reason and mystery both have just claim to complete authority in their respective domains, and it would betoken a lack of honesty or courage to appeal to the one before exhausting the resources of the other.[7] Mystery ought not to be invoked before the power of reason has been wholly engaged in the understanding of the world and the mind has been presented with an inextricable difficulty. Even then, recourse to faith will not be able to "solve" the problem but simply change the level of investigation. One has the right to have contradictory attitudes toward the same object. Since they are mysteries, dogmas must be met by faith; but, being susceptible to rational exposition, they can and must be grasped by means of the instrument of doubt.[8] The natural faculties of the intelligence must fulfill their role before opening the door to mystery (cf. 2:214 = N 280). "The notion of mystery is legitimate when the most logical and rigorous use of the intellect leads to an impasse, a contradiction one cannot avoid, in the sense that one term forces one to pose the other. Then the notion of mystery, like a lever, carries the intellect to the other side of that door it is impossible to open, carries it past the domain of the intellect, above it. But in order to go past the domain of the intellect, it is necessary to have travelled through it to the end and to have travelled through it on a path marked out with irreproachable rigor. Otherwise, one is never beyond it, but only beneath."[9] The domain of reason is made up of mathematics, natural sciences, psychology, history, and so forth; the domain of mystery is God and his relation to humanity. Discursive intelligence is out of place among "the things of God" (cf. *CS* 81–82, etc. = F 132–33), whereas there is an illegitimate use of mystery in wanting to draw God into domains he has nothing to do with: the events of history and natural processes.[10]

Weil is, however, far from faithful to the "distinction" she establishes between these domains. Believing she has found "projections" of Christian dogmas within the structure of the universe,[11] she often says that it is only a question of symbols, but she ultimately treats these symbols as facts.[12] She is also strongly inclined to make the boundaries of so-called "natural reason" merge with the views of her religious intuition. Thus against the theologian she can invoke the rights of reason, mystical intuition, and the comparative history of religions, while gesturing in the direction of philosophers she would appeal to the respect due revelation and spiritual experience. And yet, despite the simultaneity, if not the mixture, in it of religious, philosophical, scientific and political elements, her thought is far from heterogeneous, for all these diverse elements are integrated into the intellectual experience of her personality and find their completion in her daring speculation. The result is an integrated, profoundly coherent whole, but it obeys only the laws of its own internal logic, irreducibly determined by the spiritual experience of its author, a profound vision of a world where "the supernatural is present everywhere. . .under a thousand different forms; grace and mortal sin are everywhere" (*AD* 132 = WG 132).

Weil's gifts for observing and analyzing the secret motives of human actions have made her comparable to the greatest moralists of all time, and yet, after presenting a masterpiece of psychological description, she will typically conclude by making remarks of purely metaphysical or theological interest.[13] She is never satisfied with mere psychological explanation or definition, because for her human acts and desires are always situated in the context of our relation to God. And this relation, the only thing of real importance to humanity, being determined by the Fall, she tries to understand what is and what ought to be with the Fall and its consequences as her point of departure. The Fall, as we shall see later, is not a religious or moral event merely. It modifies humankind in its very being; indeed, it inaugurates a new dimension of the "worldly" being which, for its part, inevitably tears divinity itself apart. Thus anthropology, ontology, and theology will reveal themselves as interdependent and determined by the Fall. From this moment on, there is in being a region of opacity—humanity sins and suffers—and God is torn apart. Humanity, the instrument of this corruption, will have to be the mediator of a complete cure. Weil seeks the science of this cure, this "medicine" in Plato's sense, and analyzes its conditions, stages, and symptoms. Therefore, in exposing the foundations of her thought, I am going to concentrate my attention on the conceptual study of conversion (in the Platonic sense) and its metaphysical and theological context.

Further, this exposition will have two limits, one of which is my desire to refrain from discussing her social thought. A very considerable part of Weil's work—*L'Enracinement, Oppression et Liberté, Écrits de Londres et dernières lettres*—addresses primarily social and political issues, but the present study is devoted to the conversion of the *individual*, to the *individual's* return to God. One might say that the only paths Weil judges adequate to the attainment of this conversion remain absolutely inaccessible to the immense majority of human beings; but, unfortunately, "Human life is made in such a way that many problems that pose themselves to all human beings without exception are insoluble outside sainthood."[14] All this does not at all mean that the subject of her most important writings does not concern "the average person," for any perfection, virtue, or sense of God whatsoever found in the life of a human being is a fragment of an intuition of the paths of conversion. Although a "well-ordered society" (*En* 256 = NR 302) ought to contribute greatly to the spiritual development of an ever increasing number of individuals, social conditions are only the context of this development. While these cannot be neglected entirely, they cannot find a place in this work. The second limit of the work is chronological: it is devoted to Weil's mature thought.

There is an obvious tripartite division in her written work. The first period (1925–31) is marked by her years of preparation at the Ecole Normale Supérieure at the Lycée Henri IV and by the years spent on the Rue d'Ulm and at the Sorbonne. During this time, Weil acquired a very solid knowledge of several great philosophers and wrote some fine essays, two of which were published in 1929,[15] and her thesis (1930) for the Diplôme d'Etudes Supérieures: "Science et Perception dans Descartes" (*OC* I. 159–221 = FW 21–88). All of these writings are characterized by a highly complicated and dense style, extremely tight reasoning, and a regal and authoritative tone. The reading of these works should be completed by that of the notes, fragments, and unpublished essays which are a very important source of information on the genesis of her thought. Among this mass of works, many of them school exercises, the magnificent long essay on "Le Beau et le Bien"[16] stands out, allowing a glimpse of the extraordinary gifts of Alain's young pupil. That single work apart, all she wrote in this period is not truly important, its chief value residing in its stylistic beauty and in striking definitions and formulas.

Works written in the second period (1931–39) already often showed a great maturity of thought and expression. We will refer only to the articles "Reflections on War" ("Réflexions sur la Guerre") (1933), "The Power of Words" "(Ne recommençons pas la Guerre de Troie") (1937), "Cold War Policy in 1939" ("Réflexions en Vue d'un Bilan") (1939),[17] and especially the great study "Reflections on the Causes of Liberty and Social Oppression" ("Réflexions sur les Causes de la Liberté et de l'Oppression Sociale") (1934),[18] which Alain considered a work of "first importance," one that is "Kant continued."[19] This study is surely a permanent contribution to the analysis of work and human activity in general—and yet its heroic and stoical conclusions are surpassed by the pages of the *Cahiers*, *La Connaissance Surnaturelle* (*First and Last Notebooks*), or *Intuitions Pré-chrétiennes* (*Intimations of Christianity among the Ancient Greeks*). From a biographical perspective, the 1930s are divided into two parts, the first of which (1931–35) begins with the syndicalist activity of the young professor and culminates in the experiences of the factory year. The second (1935–39), at least insofar as her interior development is concerned, would be attached to the last years of maturity, but the interior changes engendered by her spiritual experiences[20] do not reveal themselves in her writings. Weil did not seem to want to confide them to her personal notes, nor does her correspondence show any sign of religious preoccupations.[21]

The third period, that of her maturity, is inaugurated by the study "The *Iliad* or the Poem of Might" ("*L'Iliade* ou le Poème de la Force") (1939–40)[22] and lasts until her death.[23] Despite all the respect due the articles mentioned above, along with the great study on liberty and oppression and the fine letters of *La Condition Ouvrière* and those written to "a student" (1937),[24] were it not for the writings of her maturity, almost no one would read those of the preceding decade. Without these writings, Weil would be a brilliant but minor essayist and a once promising philosopher. Nothing more.

The works of the last years of Weil's life concentrate essentially on religious subjects, leading many readers to claim the existence of a break between the youthful writings and those of her maturity. But this "break" is only superficial. On the one hand, the political and social interests of the 1930s are fully maintained in *L'Enracinement*, *Écrits de Londres et dernières lettres*, and the final pieces in *La Condition Ouvrière* and *Oppression et Liberté*, just as they are present in countless texts of the *Cahiers* and *La Connaissance Surnaturelle*. On the other hand, a study of unpublished manuscripts reveals that most of the philosophical subjects on which she wrote in the 1940s were at the heart of her preoccupations as of the 1920s; the problems of necessity, time, attention, purposiveness without purpose are already present in her first student essays. The present work, as stated before, addresses only the ideas of her maturity and does not closely examine what is contained in the early writings only to be taken up again in the later works with great depth and beauty. But throughout all the chapters of this work I will try to reinforce or illustrate my exposition by referring to these early writings.

The underlying reason for the inability of most critics and readers to conceive that there is no break between the first and last works is that they can or will not accept that this young anarchist, agnostic, and practically Marxist professor is the same person who was later "captured by Christ" (*AD* 38 = WG 69) who thinks that "God alone, and absolutely nothing else, is worthy of our interest" (*CS* 74 = WG 126), who asserts that "crucifixion is the end, the accomplishment of a human destiny" (2:195 = N 268), and who asks, "How can a being whose essence is to love God and who is located in space and time have any vocation other than the Cross?" (2:195–96 = N 268).

Those who knew Weil well cannot help but sense the unity of her thought and try to explain it by the continuity of her deepest moral aspirations.[25] In that they are perfectly correct, given that intellectual speculation in Weil really always obeys ethical passion and spiritual experience. This continuity can, however, be shown in a very satisfying way through the development of a particular idea in her work, as we will see in the chapters on the role of beauty and time and the self. A truly complete discussion of the genesis of Weil's ideas ought to entail a substantial part devoted to her "sources," to the philosophical systems that determine her first reflections and the stamp of which one cannot mistake even on her mature writings; the framework of the present study excluding such investigations, I prefer to "situate" her thought in relation to the two metaphysics whose influence on hers was decisive, those of Plato and Kant. As for the Gospels, the Epistles of Saint Paul, and the dogmas of the Church, if they give Weil the central subject of her preoccupations and the images or notions with which to express them, they contribute little to the development of the speculative structure of her thought. In any case, she treats her sources with such liberty that often she will only retain a given term, all the while emptying it of its original content.[26] Weil is, moreover, very conscious of the daring of her interpretations, and she ultimately declares in a commentary on the *Symposium* that "Plato never says everything in his myths. It is not arbitrary to continue them. Not to continue them would be much more arbitrary" (*IP* 48 = IC 112). Thanks to such an identification with the author, the commentator thinks herself authorized, if not compelled, to continue the exposition of what to her mind the text contains; this is the reason I consider the *Intuitions Pré-chrétiennes* and *La Source Grecque* an integral part of Weil's work, and a very important part.

The systematic exposé that follows bears on the metaphysics of conversion insofar as it is developed starting from strictly ontological bases. It begins with a statement of the concept of *decreation*, the metaphysical expression of the mystic way. It continues with a description of the different aspects of the mystic process and concludes with an outline of the state and action of those who have attained perfection.

Chapter 1

The Notion of Decreation

The basic vision of Weil's metaphysics is the sinful condition of humanity. She undoubtedly wants to see everything in relation to God, but she is a theologian only insofar as she must locate and base discourse on the redemption of human existence. The key idea of this metaphysics of conversion is decreation; the term is itself significant. The privative *de-* points to the passion for reduction and annihilation erected as moral imperative, the strictly metaphysical context of which is indicated by "creation." The word itself is a neologism invented by Péguy, who used it, moreover, in a diametrically opposite sense.[1] Weil herself never provided any exact definition. Although certainly it was a question of more than a simple attempt at terminology, she was not very decided about its use and hesitated even over its spelling. Sometimes "decreation" is a single word, but more often one finds "de-creation" or the verb "de-create."[2] What is certain is that it is the only term than adequately expresses her fundamental intuition:[3] that of the self-annihilating vocation of human beings (2:206 = N 275), a vocation stated in the ancient commandment of the *Theaetetus* on the imitation of God and which finally—as we shall see— is founded in the very essence of God. But "how" to imitate God, or rather "which" God to imitate? By way of answer Weil only outlines theories of a "distinction" within divinity. This distinction is profoundly influenced by her experience of Christ, but it bears only rather superficial marks of the Christian doctrine of the Trinity. At bottom, it is a matter of a vision of reality containing in its totality only two true perfections,

11

necessity and love, which will thereby become the two faces of God. The act of creation itself will reveal this duality.

To create is certainly to give proof of power; it is a matter of establishing existence, communicating being, and, moreover, establishing eternal laws. But all that is but one implication of creation: God, being powerful by definition, can act as he will, create everything he wishes, call non-being to existence. Non-being is very malleable; it offers no resistance. Even the problem in the most formal sense of some modification in its relation to God is not posed, for, as St. Thomas says, "before" creation non-being was in no relation to God. The true problem does not lie there: it is to be sought in the idea of divine perfection, in its necessarily flawless essence to which nothing can be added and from which nothing can be subtracted. "Before" creation, God was "all in all"; now there is something "outside him." "Before" creation, the Eternal reposed in the luminous and unalterable halo of its perfect actuality; "now" it is bound by a thousand twisted threads to that swarming of beings we call the universe. How is this possible? The answer to the "how" implies the one to the "why."

For God the act of creation was not an expansion of self, but much more a renunciation or abdication.[4] This universe is an abandoned kingdom;[5] its price is the withdrawal of God, and its very existence is the cause of separation from God (cf. CS 222 = F 260). Theological reflection customarily opposes creation and passion, but at heart they are one. The Book of Revelation expresses this profound truth in the passage on the Lamb sacrificed since the beginning of the world,[6] which the Cahiers echo in declaring, "The crucifixion of God is an eternal thing."[7] If creation is a sacrifice on God's part, then it is not a means of growth, but on the contrary the very form that his love takes on in order to give, and to give himself, to his creatures. Thus it is not the power of God that spills over into creation, but his love, and this overflow is a veritable diminution.[8]

The sacrifice of creation, the fact that the Lamb has been sacrificed since the beginning of the world, appears as a primordial rent between the two divine persons;[9] thus the "space" that God left in the world is located not so much outside God, but instead "between" God and God. This metaphor will enable Weil to dramatize the obstacle creation represents for the loving union between the Father and the Son. It therefore remains to be established whether it is all of being that interposes itself between God and God in this way, or just one of its ontological levels. The solution to this choice cannot fail to reveal the basic lines of this entire metaphysics.

As abdication, sacrifice, and renunciation, God is love. He is God the Son, having nothing to do with might and power,[10] having no part in the events occurring in the material universe. His only presence in the world is facing a human soul, where he remains standing like a beggar imploring it to do and to love the good (cf. *CS* 92 = F 141). This basic humility forms a radical contrast with the most striking image we could have of the Father: majestic and terrible power. However, power has another meaning also which is, indeed, the true meaning: it is *necessity*, that is to say, the *fascinans* and *tremendosum* the intelligible harbors in its breast. Thus the power that is the very sign of a radical transcendence ultimately explains what is as it were crushed in its presence. It seems obvious that all discourse bearing on God must designate him—implicitly or explicitly—in relation to reality, that is to say, insofar as he is its cause; thus the two different faces of God will be opposed as two causes, two different causalities. Plato in the *Timaeus* (48a) speaks of the good cause and the necessary cause, while Kant distinguishes noumenal causality and phenomenological causality. In Weil, the necessary cause of the *Timaeus* will be subsumed and merged into the causality of phenomena: its violence, its opacity, its blind resistance will be integrated into the great mathematical clarity of the structure of appearances. The good cause of Plato will, however, welcome and recover the Kantian causality of noumena whose perfect rigor and severity will be as though softened by the love expressed through the "persuasion" spoken of by Plato.[11]

Weil was always fully convinced that all reality was completely determined by necessity,[12] and it is basically to exonerate divinity from all responsibility in the cruel mechanism of this world that she found herself led to posit God as Power separated from Love. On another level, one might also say that she wants to defend God against his own power by depicting him as liberty, love, or "the good beyond being," perhaps beyond even his own being. At the same time, she means to keep God in the perfect shell of absolute and intelligible necessity, or rather, it might be said, she wished to be able to deify necessity. Thus the powerful intellectual fascination that the implacable determination of the material world always exercised over her emerges reinforced by the religious duty of adoration of the creator, of which this fascination basically had always been an intuition.

Necessity appears above all mathematical in nature to this Cartesian thinker (*IP* 160 = IC 192–93). It is a network of immaterial and powerless connections that are nonetheless "harder than any diamond" (En 243 = NR 288). These are pure and abstract relations that compose the very essence of all that is real, for it must be understood that "Reality is only transcendent."[13] Seen from this angle, necessity loses all its numinous or moral connotations and offers itself to the contemplative eye or the intellect of the scholar like the crystalline clarity of the intelligible, the level at which purity and reality ultimately coincide. Alas, that sublime spectacle appears quite different to the human being exposed to risks and at the mercy of contingent existence. If the acceptance of necessity as destiny is the virtue characteristic of the Stoic philosopher, that same destiny will appear to ordinary mortals as pure arbitrariness. The sage will speak of its majestic impartiality, but the ordinary person will only be able to accuse it of cruel indifference. But can one bring such accusations against an impersonal force, a simple network of relations? Is it the diamond's fault if it is hard? Can one reproach statistical laws for not making distinction of persons? These questions are as old as the universe; if they are being asked here, it is uniquely to draw attention to a certain ambiguity in Weil's thought in the way she envisions the relation between God and necessity.

If necessity is the fundamental meaning one can attribute to the power of God, then the very transcendence of the latter seems compromised. God is no longer the source of reality; he is as it were reduced to being its intelligible structure. But Weil hesitates to draw such a conclusion. She says instead that, while in creating the world God had withdrawn himself from it, he delegated his power to necessity, "entrusted" it with his material creation.[14] Necessity is the limit that God imposes on Chaos;[15] it is the master of this world but continues to bear the divine signature (*CS* 308 = F 339), being a principle of order. Whether it be mediator (*IP* 151 = IC 182) or compromise (*CS* 269 = F 301) between God and matter, necessity as truth of being will always represent the divine essence, and for this reason Weil has fewer difficulties leaving its true relation to God in obscurity. For her, transcendence manifests itself by relation to existence and to evil, not to essence and ideality. God is source and archetype, not master, of truth; thus the idea of his continuity with the network of essences, an idea left, moreover, imprecise, does not present anything problematic. But is there a continuity between God and necessity inasmuch as the latter is master of the life of rational beings, that is to say, of the misfortunes and perils that blind destiny metes out in such abundance to mortals? Must one think that even in this guise necessity may be attributed to God?

Weil always rose up violently against the notion of Providence insofar as it was taken to mean direct intervention of the prime cause in the functioning of secondary causes.[16] However, her unshakable conviction, on the one hand, of the necessary character of everything that happens in the world, and on the other of the fact that this necessity is but the face of God turned toward the universe, forces her to admit "a providential order" (independent of human goals) (*IP* 31 = IC 97) in the world; she goes so far as to say that, "Necessity is one of the eternal dispositions of Providence" (*CS* 307 = F 336), that "God. . .wills necessity" (2:193 = N 266), indeed, "God makes himself necessity" (2:75 = N 190). Still, be it only the faithful servant of God or his fundamental attribute, necessity presents itself in continuity of essence with God. In other words, being as such, whose truth is necessity, cannot represent that obstacle interposing itself between God and God. All the reality of the being of the Universe is concentrated in these forceless, diamond-hard relations; the very reality of being is thus too directly tied to God to be able to oppose itself to him. The material universe through its intelligible structure having been as it were "subsumed" into an aspect of God himself, it is only in light of the special meaning Weil attributes to "creation" that one can understand how "the abdication constituted by the creative act" is able to rend God from God. Despite a confusion and ambiguity that, it must be admitted, go beyond the purely terminological level, the internal logic of Weil's thought seems to suggest that for her "creation" is only the creation of autonomous beings, and that only those invested with free will are creatures. A note in *La Connaissance Surnaturelle* clearly identifies "creature" with autonomous being and "creation" with the world of these autonomous beings: "*Genesis* separates creation and original sin because of the requirements of a narration made in human language. But the creature in being created preferred itself to God. Otherwise would there have been creation? God created because he was good, but the creature let itself be created because it was evil. It redeemed itself by persuading God through endless entreaties to destroy it" (CS 70–71 = F 123). This is taken up again later: "Is not this gift of free will creation itself? That which is creation from the point of view of God is sin from the point of view of the creature."[17] Question and answer are explicit: in creating human beings, God gave them the gift of free will, which entails autonomy. It is only autonomous existence and not being in itself that separates God from God. Both human beings and matter are between God and God, human beings as a screen and matter as a mirror; but it is the screen only that is an obstacle in the exchange of love between the Father and the Son through that perfectly transparent mirror that is material creation (CS 48 = F 102). Material things, by the presence in them of necessity, are in perfect continuity with God. This continuity will be broken only at the moment when autonomous beings assume an independent, and thus separate, existence: it is a crime to be other than God,[18] a crime shared by all those who will use their free will, thereby dissolving the bond creator-creature (3:192 = N 539). If this is so, then we see the obstacle between God and God more clearly: it is the realm of autonomy.[19] "Evil is the distance between the creature and God," and if it disappears, creation itself will disappear also (2:303 = N 342).

At this point we have completed a sketch of Weil's ontology. Between the two pincers of Love and Power-Necessity, autonomy asserts itself. In other words, *truth or being is separated from the good by evil*. The idea of decreation will thus be introduced as an ontological requirement: that which ought not to be should remove itself or be removed. In more "religious" terms: "If one thinks that God created in order to be loved, and that he cannot create something that is God, and that he cannot be loved by something that is not God, one meets a contradiction...all contradiction is resolved in becoming. God creates a finite being who says I, who cannot love God. By the effect of grace, little by little the I disappears, and God loves himself through the creature who becomes empty, who becomes nothing" (2:289 = N 330-31).

At once ontological requirement and religious commandment, the dissolution of sinful existence is the idea through which the metaphysics of man will reveal itself as being at the very center of all metaphysics. That which is to be dissolved is the evil third, that malignant excrescence on the body of the real, that unjustifiable violence that rends the beautiful harmony of the good and necessity. Autonomy is evil, and "its name is legion." The autonomous condition itself is called *existence*. It is existence that, through decreation, must be reduced to *being*. Being is real and perfect, while existence is but a faulty shadow; only by driving the shadow away does the real acquire its plenitude: "De-creation as transcendent completion of creation: annihilation in God that gives the annihilated creature the plenitude of being of which it is deprived so long as it exists."[20] Whatever Weil may understand by the good or the necessary, what interests us here is the description of that which is neither one nor the other and which constitutes precisely our earthly condition. In order to abolish that condition—Weil would harshly say—it is necessary "to live while ceasing to exist so that in a self that is no longer the self God and his creation may find themselves face to face" (3:80 = N 464). The "self" corresponds to "someone." When one ceases to be centered on the self, one renounces being someone; one gives complete consent to becoming something (CS 223 = F 261). Being someone, one affirms one's self and therefore one is a screen between God and his creation. That screen is abolished to the very extent to which one uses up one's individuality,[21] one's personality, to which one no longer speaks in the first person.[22] The word "person" has acquired in modern times a respectable connotation, but it is, at bottom, identical with the ego or the I, terms directly suggesting egotism, egocentrism, a certain violence and rapacity.[23] "The person in us is the part of us belonging to error and sin," says a note from London,[24] but this succinct formula only takes up again, in an abridged form, the substance of an earlier definition: "The ego is only the shadow projected by sin and error which blocks God's light and which I take for a being" (3:10 = N 419).

Creature and existence, enjoyment of individuality and of free will, person or personality, "I" or ego—all of these express a fundamental intuition of the status of the human being; but they really only designate *one* of its components, even if the others are as it were buried under the shattering weight of the latter. Before looking more closely at what is so buried, we must consider the manner of this burial itself. The two notions which come up continually in Weil's writing to designate personal existence are *crime* and error: "man begins not with ignorance but with error," wrote the young student beginning her advanced studies (OC I. 161 = FW 31). This means that human unknowing is not a simple lack of knowledge but the unmistakable perversion of knowledge itself. For the convinced Socratic thinker that she was, error meant "fault always in the moral sense of the word."[25] The most important of our errors, our fundamental error in the sense that it is the basis of our very existence, is to seek within perspective. Every finite being is subject to the law of perspective, which is distortion in a double sense. To be subject to perspective does not simply mean that there is an inevitable gap between the way in which the world is "in itself" and the way in which it presents itself to us. To have a perspective means to have a point of view, that is to say, to be at the center of a field of vision (cf. CS 29 = F 84). Human beings who live in space and time cannot avoid finding themselves at such a center of vision; what is of gravest consequence is that they eventually consider themselves centers on the moral and metaphysical level as well. The effects of physical perspective obey strict general and normative physical and psychological laws, while moral and metaphysical perspective is particular to each individual. Physical perspective is an innocent and superficial manifestation of the fundamental fact that each human being accepts himself or herself as a center of reference irreducible to any other. To be a center of reference means to interpret the universe as a function of one's desires, beliefs, and ambitions.[26] Such an interpretation cannot fail to be terribly deficient, for "people, being finite beings, apply the notion of legitimate order only in the immediate neighborhood of their heart" (*IP* 73 = IC 133). On the other hand, perspective blurs the very sense of reality (2:143 = N 234) in forcing us to appreciate other beings only according to their importance with respect to ourselves. One is as it were riven to one's point of view, one is chained by one's perspective, and thus one is incapable of "going around" what one is looking at to convince oneself of the truth and manner of its existence.[27] Such is the genesis of knowledge in an autonomous being whose intelligence, exposing the relations of the real, imitates the poor butcher of the *Phaedrus*, incapable of cutting along the joints of a chicken.

Knowledge and method are universals; to be deficient in these is the sign of our individuality. When a child carries out an addition and makes an error, the latter bears the stamp of his or her person.[28] Truth is impersonal; of course, one strives to discover truths, but when these are present, they alone exist and the self is nowhere to be found (2:335–36 = N 364). While the distinctive trait of the person is to affirm himself or herself by existing as fully and forcefully as possible, the very nature of the intellect, that faculty executing the correct operation, "consists of being a thing that is effaced by the very fact that it is being exercised."[29] In fact, it is not the intellect but the imagination that acts in the heterogeneous knowledge secreted by autonomous existence. Pure intellect is without center; all reality is for it equivalent. It deciphers things; it does not interpret them. It is quite different with the imagination, it being only the *eikasia* of the Line (cf. 2:272 = N 319) or that imagination "of wrong constructions" spoken of in the *Regulae*. In this domain Weil was resolutely pre-Kantian; for her, the imagination is never creative, it only "fabricates." It secretes illusions, the essential one of which is the dream of autonomous existence itself. It is through the imagination that the immediate passage from error to crime is accomplished.[30] Much more than simple constructions of images, dreams, and illusions is involved. A passage from the *Cahiers* is very enlightening: "To conceive the notion and possibility of evil without imagining it... is what is meant by Ulysses bound and his sailors with their ears full of wax" (1:174 = N 110). To see and hear the Sirens while being bound means to know them rationally without involving one's own self, that is, while keeping a certain distance. The imagination is inseparable from the desire that would have pushed Ulysses toward the Sirens if he had not been so firmly tied; it is a central, essential element of that very desire leading me to remove the distance between myself and some external thing or person.

Ordinarily one understands by the imagination the discovery, or rather the invention, of new things; that is to say, an imagined thing has the "vocation" of becoming a real thing. For Weil the imagination takes on another meaning. It changes its objects into *imaginary* things; it deprives them of their autonomous reality. Present in the imagination as objects of my desire or as obstacle to my will, things or persons are no longer beings that are sufficient unto themselves. Existing only in relation to me, they have become as it were unreal; they serve only to maintain that precarious balance we call personality. Once that balance has been shattered by the blow of external reality, all our desire tends toward reestablishing it.[31] Often one does not have the means; one is not determined or strong enough to eliminate the deadly presence of the external obstacle. Then "the void-filling imagination" rushes forth to supply the self with lies, consolations, little tasks to carry out (cf. 2:89 = N 199). In general, that is not enough to keep us occupied for very long, and it remains only for our anger to come back in and take our revenge within the imagination, where it may rage without hindrance (cf. 2:80 = N 193). But if occasionally we have the power to translate our hate and our destructive desires into action, we will not hesitate, for the object of our passion no longer has any true existence in our eyes. At the moment when we violently hate (or desire) a being, the fire burning in us has already consumed that person; he or she is already ashes even if retaining external form, and the least movement will make him or her collapse. The ego will tolerate no obstacles in its path and, thanks to the imagination, obstacles are as it were emptied of content, pulverized in advance. An imaginary act is necessarily an unreal act, for it meets only shadows (cf. 2:287 = N 329). To kill someone, for example, is an act whose "essence is imaginary" (2:132 = N 227), for if murderers knew that their victims really existed, they would not be able to thrust their knives into them. Not to see obstacles is the terrible secret of the carnage of the victorious warrior (*SG* 21 = IC 34) and of the misdeed of the criminal (cf. 1:174 = N 109); victims are in their eyes only shadows without substance, inert and inanimate objects. Thus an imaginary act is sinful because in being unaware of them, one violates the boundaries of another being.

We have finally reached the point where personal and autonomous existence, that is to say, the self, appears in its true sense: the negation of the other. The imagination, in giving us a fictitious point of reference, arrays us in an "imaginary royalty" (2:109 = N 213), makes us set ourselves up against the sole true center of reality. It is the absolutely diabolical center in the human being,[32] for it incites us to usurp the place of God,[33] and once seated on one's throne one will without fail be unaware of others. Indeed, it is here that the terrible consequences of distorted perspective emerge: we are incapable of recognizing that others have as much right to esteem themselves centers as we do.[34] The world is essentially the coexistence of beings, and "All crimes, all grave sins are particular forms of the refusal of this coexistence."[35] The first prescription of the metaphysics of man for Weil is to acknowledge that coexistence, to protect it, and, if necessary, to reestablish it. When we meet a being who, through suffering and affliction has been reduced to the state of an inert and passive thing, we must stop and turn our gaze toward that person, as did the Good Samaritan of the Gospel. Exerting and exerting oneself in behalf of an unfortunate person without expecting any reward, without any personal motive, one accepts being diminished in favor of the independent existence of a being other than oneself (*AD* 106–07 = WG 146–147) One is no longer at the center of the world; one gives from this moment on one's loving and active consent to coexistence with another being; one "preserves" the other. This preservation is the work of the "impersonal decreated person" (*CS* 77 = F 129); it implies the acknowledgment, in the universe, of relationships that are independent of us—the acknowledgment, that is, of reality as such. An error in the understanding of these relationships, like the mistaken addition of the child, bears the mark of the self, as does the act which destroys another being. In the action of the decreated human being, recognizing and preserving the veritable relations between beings and things, there is no trace of the "I" (2:65 = N 183); these actions are an imitation of the intellect, something that effaces itself by the very fact that it is being exercised.

If the very meaning of autonomy is the refusal of co-existence with other beings, then we have defined human beings as a function of their relations with their neighbor.[36] We shall see that this characterization is not limited to the self, that is, to that which ought not to be, but to those two other levels that will reveal themselves as representatives respectively of necessity and of the good in humanity. For the moment let it suffice to point out that through her view of autonomous existence and imperious commands to destroy it, Weil marvelously explains Christ's integration of the second commandment into the first (cf. 1:216 = N 281). If one accepts that beings have an existence independent of our imagination, then one imitates the sacrifice of God in creation: he renounced being everything and made room for other beings.[37] To act in this way signifies that "[w]e participate in the creation of the world in decreating ourselves by ourselves" (2:257 = N 309). If nevertheless—and such is the character of sinful existence—one despises and fails to know one's neighbor, it is because one rejects God by putting oneself in his place. Or rather: one wants to imitate "divinity through power and not love, through being and not nonbeing."[38] To imitate God through power is the claiming of the imaginary kingdom, called the Fall of man or the sin of Adam by Christian theology. By abandoning their natural place at the periphery, human beings place themselves at the center, and this revolt against God implies at the same time the will to dominate one's fellow man; whereas if they remain at the periphery out of loving respect for the Lord, human beings will keep the right perspective in order to be able to respect and love others. This love of one's neighbor is an emanation of love for God. And it is precisely our love for God that conditions the love we bear our neighbor, in that it is nothing other than imitation of him as Love; it is the same attitude of sacrifice and abnegation whether it concerns God in relation to humanity or humanity in relation respectively to God and neighbor. Thus the very "program" of human life is given by this note in *La Connaissance Surnaturelle*: "I am the abdication of God. . . . I must reproduce in inverse sense the abdication of God, refuse the existence which has been given to me."[39] But why then has this existence been given?

This hard and desperate question has been asked countless times, and the answer Weil outlined can hardly contain truly novel elements. She repeats that God gave us autonomy (*AD* 136 = WG 179–80) and the power to think in the first person in order that we might be able to renounce it out of love;[40] he "forgives us for existing at the moment when we no longer wish to consent to exist except to the extent it is the will of God" (*CS* 226 = F 263). Indeed, God perpetually begs back the existence he gave us.[41] But why did he give it to us? Why did he provoke this gaping flaw in the interior of his self by creating human beings? Why did he let himself be torn throughout the whole length of space and time? Why did he choose to suffer the otherness of human beings and their profound evil will to sink more and more deeply into it? These "whys" must remain without answer, for they try feverishly to uncover the "cause" of this madness of God that is the creation of the world (cf. *IP* 148 = *IC* 182); in actual fact, the creation had no cause. God created because he loved the world; thus the world is the fruit of his pure generosity (cf. *IP* 128 = *IC* 166). As for the structure of the material world, it flows infallibly from God in the form of Necessity, and as Aristotle rightly observed, they are coeternal. And the presence of the good, of the infinitely small, supernatural point in the soul, is owing solely to the inexplicable generosity of the God who is Love. But the question of autonomy remains entire: even if one no longer dares formulate it in terms of "why," we must at least ask, "where does it come from?" One thing is sure—as Plato said—God is beyond cause. But—the question keeps returning—must not what is finite come from the infinite? Can the contingent repose and found itself upon itself? Weil searches and hesitates. She uses images: "We are in relation to God like a thief permitted to carry off gold by the goodness of the person whose home he has entered. . . . We have stolen a bit of being from God to make it ours. God has given it to us. But we have stolen it."[42] Through such metaphors there emerges the outline of a profound doctrine on evil and human finitude. We shall come back to it. For now, let us be content to treat a less ambitious question. If one is incapable of giving a satisfactory answer to the *why* of autonomous existence, at least its practical use (even in the Kantian sense of the word) can provide an area for research.

For Weil, the assumption of our autonomy[43] was certainly a "happy fault," for it is the very means of its own destruction, the very dimension of its own dissolution. Moreover—and the following is only something very traditional—autonomy is the test of the love we bring to God. Without free will—affirms tradition—one could not truly *choose* the love of God. Not truly traditional, at least according to the letter, is Weil's conviction that the only good use one can make of autonomy is to suppress it entirely.[44] Being always the expression of a choice, of the choice between good and evil, it is "a notion of the lower stage" (cf. 2:341–42 = N 368), for the decreated human being should be beyond the possibility of choosing evil.

That there may have been some underlying self-destructive passion and will to expiate in Weil is a fact that might shed light on the empirical genesis of her ideas on decreation; but the essential thing, from the philosophical point of view, is that she resolutely condemns self-torture or suicide, the latter being only an "ersatz of decreation."[45] What concerns us here is the passivity and obedience of this entire process; we can only consent to our destruction by making a primarily negative use of our will (2:396 = N 404). It is its only good use, for "humanity. . .was created with a will and the vocation to renounce it. . . . Adam. . .was in a state of sin by virtue of the fact that he had his own will."[46] It is one's own will[47]—with the help of the imagination—that says "I" in us; it is precisely the "I" that must be destroyed from within.[48] Certainly the external destruction of the ego, the scorn of the surrounding world, suffering, the agony of death, are always means of decreation, on condition that we consent to these in some manner. What really matters is that the process of the destruction of the "I" begin from within, because a purely external destruction of the "I" is something "nearly infernal," having nothing to do with decreation; it can even completely ruin all hopes for it. When the blows of external destruction are very strong and the process of "killing the I" is still only at its beginning, the destruction of the ego will be partially completed from the outside in spite of the cooperation of the individual, and this entails an imperfect decreation (2:295–303 = N 336–342). This is the case when death arrives before the "I" has had time to kill itself.[49]

Despite the violence that can accompany the death of the ego, it is basically nothing other than the exposure of its nothingness, of its non-being. We must know that we are not, and at the same time we must want not to be: "Our sin consists in wanting to be and our punishment is believing that we exist. Expiation is wanting not to be, and salvation for us consists in seeing that we are not."[50]

This profound intuition of the nothingness in human beings is already expressed in all its power in the pages of her *Journal d'usine* (*Factory Journal*), and here we will not hesitate to use descriptions that can be considered elements of the empirical genesis of a metaphysical idea. The continual headaches from which Weil suffered and her general physical weakness allowed her to know from experience the distress and fragility of the human being, in particular during the year she devoted to harsh physical labor (cf. *AD* 37 = *WG* 68). Fatigue, pain, worries, various fears, the impression of her absolute subordination, the insane rhythm of the work—all these engendered "[t]he feeling that I possess no right, whatever it may be, to whatever it might be[51]...that I didn't count, that (*CO* 141 = *SL* 38)...I counted...for zero" (*CO* 136 = *SL* 33). This feeling of not counting for anything, of having no importance of any sort can enter into the very heart of a human being (*CO* 144), and Weil relates that one afternoon while taking the bus she had suddenly had a "strange reaction," and that she asked herself: "How is it that I, the slave, can get on this bus, use it for my twelve *sous* just like anybody else? What an extraordinary favor! If someone had brutally made me get off, telling me that such convenient modes of transportation were not for me, that I had only to go by foot, I think it would have seemed entirely natural to me. Slavery had made me completely lose the sense of having any rights."[52]

"Not having any rights" implies that one does not count for anything; to Weil, this state was not the result of some degradation but rather the very expression of the truth of our condition.[53] A whole gamut of definition on the negativity of human existence is located in the wake of the idea of autonomy, and one can thus easily have the impression that the nothingness in question is the third component of the human being. Indeed, the *Cahiers* say quite explicitly that "one is nothingness as a human being, and more generally as a creature."[54] The context of this passage, which speaks of Lucifer, removes all doubt as to the meaning of "creature"; it concerns autonomous beings—human beings and angels. Still, this reduction of autonomy to nothingness would be a too facile subterfuge for being rid of it, and Weil would then be only too faithfully continuing the narrow and lazy tradition of mediocre Platonists. We can rely on her texts; they will help to show how different the dialectic at work in them truly is.

Decreation, which is at heart self-knowledge, reduces the human being to nothingness, but curiously this reduction implies an "intensification" of our reality. Looking at negative integers, there is diminution going from minus ten to minus twenty in terms of absolute quantity, but the succession of numbers shows a gain. To approach zero is thus to grow. As for us, "[w]e are born far below zero. Zero is our maximum" (*CS* 327 = F 354). We are born below zero because of original sin, and we will reach zero only thanks to decreation. There is therefore a profound difference between zero, that is to say, nothingness, and negativity. Essentially one is nothing, but as a sinner one becomes "a negative being" (2:202 = N 272). These two texts explain the profound logic of this entire thought: from the viewpoint of the ontology of the two attributes of the real, autonomy is only apparent, thus unreal.[55] However, that does not at all compromise its profound actuality and the powerful opacity it turns so resolutely toward God. That human beings are zero or nothing means that we are as it were transparent in relation to God, that we oppose no resistance to him, that indeed we are in continuity with him. One must not lose from sight that the negative labels that would-be Platonists attach so easily to this world are ultimately metaphors intended to designate the *direction* of things in relation to the absolute. Nothingness—in the strict sense of the word—in such a language is that which, offering no resistance to God, is in perfect transparent continuity with him. These two modes of continuity will reveal the two other components of the human being.

The necessity that represents God as Power in the universe is the structure, the meaning, and the very essence of this world, of which our body and our mental faculties are only parts (*En* 244–45 = NR 288–90). The world is completely subject to the domination of necessity, and with the world the human being also, as a material being. The nothingness of humanity reveals itself above all through the flawless docility of its belonging to that network of forceless, diamond-hard relations closing around it on all sides. From the beginning, the "practical" and "theoretical" meanings of necessity, master of the world, support each other in Weil. On the one hand, in such a representation of the universe she finds the intelligibility and order she cherished most of all. On the other, a quasi-mathematical outline of the world,[56] the regularity of the events infallibly succeeding each other in the universe, the impossibility of escaping the order of the world in which the material being finds itself—all this harmonized quite well with her basic vision of the nothingness and enslavement of humanity, of our irremediable weakness and absolute subjection to external necessity. The intellectual vision of determinism, united to the moral vision of human nothingness, led her to unmask with indefatigable vigor the lies and errors human beings entertain in their relation to necessity. The dreamer and the tyrant believe it is their slave; in deprivation, suffering, and affliction, it seems an absolute and brutal master; finally, in a methodical activity there seems to be a sort of balance. Necessity offers human beings sometimes obstacles, sometimes means toward the attainment of their goals. It would appear that a sort of equality exists between human will and universal necessity.

But all these attitudes are only illusions. The balance of methodical action is unreal, because "[i]n the state of intense fatigue, human beings cease to adhere to their own actions and even to their own will, perceiving themselves as a thing that drives other things because it is itself driven by a constraint" (*IP* 145 = IC 180–81). As for blind violence, it only seems to be such, being seen from our erroneous perspective (*IP* 149 = IC 183–184). And, insofar as the dreamer or tyrant is concerned, each passing moment can inflict the cruelest refutation of his illusions.

In any event, human beings are subject to necessity, and Weil never tires of repeating that our vague desires to free ourselves from it are doomed to failure; enslavement is written into the very essence of our condition. This obviously does not mean that one is thereby acquitted of responsibility for leading an autonomous and sinful life; for if, as part of the material world, one cannot extract oneself from its laws, as a free being one always retains the power to consent or not to consent to evil. The double Kantian causality recovered and penetrated by the language of the *Timaeus* should have helped Weil to explain this parallelism, but she does not manage to clearly state the relation between necessity and liberty (cf. 2:337 = N 365). Let it suffice to say that her fundamental intuition is that humanity is always subject to necessity; it belongs to us only to choose the order of the necessity of which we will be part. The choice ought to be conceived as extending over our whole life: "Our sin consists in wanting to be" (*CS* 175 = F 218); that is, one permanently chooses autonomy,[57] for autonomy itself, inasmuch as it is expressed in physical attitudes and actions, is but a form of necessity, of the necessity according to which unfolds the existence of the ego in expansion. But what is the role of necessity in the metaphysical scheme of human beings? Human beings share the destiny of all material beings that have their whole reality in intelligible laws. Possession of a body and mental faculties is due only to the interpretation of this necessity through perception, because basically one is only network, relationship, law, relation. Inertia, impotence, the fragility of our flesh, which escapes continually from the requirements and commands of the ego, are all the striking expression of this docility to universal laws, the very essence of matter. However, this intelligible and passive essence is completed and complicated by an active intelligibility, called intelligence or intellect. Without wishing to use the traditional arguments on the rational soul conceived as the highest level of the intelligibility of the human being, we may affirm that the principal representative of the sphere of the "necessary" in Weil's anthropological scheme is intelligence.

In intelligence, which is but its supreme form in this world, necessity seems to fold back upon itself. It becomes like its own mirror in which it is understood in all its limpidity. Noisy agitation becomes calm, pulsation and vibration cease, events divest themselves of their passional attributes, and the relational skeleton of the world is brought to light in its mathematical nakedness. At this moment, intelligence contemplates necessity peacefully and is subject to it only in the way the eye of the reader is to the printed text he or she is in the process of decoding (cf. *IP* 146 = IC 181). It is like a mirror, the virtue of which lies in its not having any part in the image it is reflecting, in its not having any dimension of its own, in lacking any substantiality of its own, in not having any opacity. All this, of course, only paraphrases the beautiful formula on the intellect that is effaced by the very fact of being exercised. This brings us back to the notion of dissolution of perspective and self-reduction to nothingness.

The recognition and acceptance of the right of others to exist in the same way as we ourselves exist must be preceded by knowledge of the fact that they *are* and of the fact of *what* they are. Objective knowledge of an external reality is possible only insofar as one sets oneself aside, that is, insofar as one is reduced to nothingness. This means—at least in the case of pure intelligence without relation to supernatural love—abandonment, the suspension of perspective. All true activity of the intelligence bears on the mathematical necessity constituting the very order of the world, that order "through which each thing, being in its place, allows every other thing to exist" (*IP* 151 = IC 185). Necessity is therefore the worker and guarantor of the coexistence of beings, and Weil is able to say that "[t]he understanding of necessity is an imitation of creation" (3:104 = N 480). In effacing itself, intelligence allows pure truth and the reality of things to appear, thus bringing itself into conformity with the image of that withdrawal of God permitting the universe to function independently of him. The most important truth thereby allowed to emerge is that of the existence of others; a relation of intersubjectivity is therefore affirmed even with respect to intelligence. However, the recognition of the other at this level still remains completely formal; it is not really possible that the other in no way infringes upon the goals and aspirations of the ego in expansion, that is, when it presents itself as an objective and neutral fact and not as a true self. To a certain extent, the intellect anticipates the decreative vocation of love, for, in paying attention at least temporarily to a difficult Latin translation or a complicated mathematical problem, the goals of the ego are forgotten (cf. *AD* 71ff. = *WG* 105ff.). As Plato saw clearly, all intellectual activity in the narrow confines of its very exercise is pure and purifying; it necessarily implies that one set personal interests and desires aside, and so the demons of autonomy are exorcised for a while. This same idea will be vigorously affirmed in a certain number of texts where Weil links the intellect to that which is supernatural in humanity.[58] But she is much more likely to speak of it as being "at the intersection of the two worlds" (of necessity and love: *IP* 147 = *IC* 182) or as an indifferent and impersonal faculty. The reason for this hesitation is to be found, in our opinion, in the ambiguous way the intellect emerges in action.

It seems absurd to speak of an "objective" application of the intellect when it bears on God or others, for intersubjective relationships exclude the very idea of a certain neutrality. Thus intelligence appears either stifled by the imagination or invigorated by love. As for its use in the domain of necessity, it can be only neutral and disinterested, for this domain is the world of objectivity itself. Obviously, it is this use that explains its essential role; only there does it act without the help or hindrances of an external faculty. Intellect is essentially only a function; indeed, it is function itself. It has no substantial or existential extension; intellect therefore most properly corresponds to the definition of man as nothingness or nothing. Intellect adds nothing to the beings it contemplates; and it does not contemplate them from a particular point of view, because it is characterized by non-perspective. From non-perspective one can contemplate and study the mathematical structure of necessity, but understanding its true nature is conceivable only when one has adopted divine perspective. Transported into the perspective of God, the soul knows the sphere where God resides as love, while pure intelligence searches the network of intelligible relations where God is present only indirectly as power. Already, it is true, non-perspective implies a decreated attitude, for it puts the ego in parentheses; but intelligence, being founded in the necessary, that is, in the material in us, is incapable of prolonging the attitude of detachment when the fatigue of the body or the opposition of the ego becomes too powerful. From simple non-perspective one inevitably falls back on an individual point of view, while once transported into the perspective of God, it seems that one has gone definitively past a certain threshold.[59]

If we can adopt God's perspective, it is because there is in human beings a supernatural faculty, something in us corresponding to God as Love. Through the intellect I understand that I am nothing, that is, nothing more than others, each one of whom is a simple point on the immense periphery of that circle whose center is God. However, this understanding is not yet a true realization of the existence of others; such realization will imply a truly decreative movement. The intellectual deciphering of my place and of the place of others in the network of necessity remains a neutral and purely theoretical operation; it cannot effect the passage to the recognition of other beings as ends in themselves. Above all, as mere intelligence myself, I am not such an end; I have only a *structure*, but I do not yet have a *meaning*, and the same is true for others. The intellect does not suffice for understanding that which is beyond "natural necessity," because it is only at the "intersection of the two worlds." On the other hand, seen from non-perspective, *I certainly count for no more* than others, but at least *I count for as much*. From God's perspective, where I, decreated being, reside, I transcend the relations of justice and the objectivity of coexistence; I live from now on in abnegation, in sacrifice, in the gift of self. It is not a matter of simply putting my personality in parentheses, but of dissolving that voracious existence I call myself. Intellect does not have this power, because it is ineffective once one passes from the transparent domain of necessity to the opaque shadows of autonomy. Thus true recognition of others is consenting to their existence, and this implies a withdrawal and a renunciation of self. The non-decreated human being is aware of the existence of others only to the extent that they are statistical givens, shadows without substance, or means of self-satisfaction and self-expansion, but such a person does not believe in the reality of their existence in the same way that he or she believes in his or her own.[60] We truly know the reality of other beings when what we love in them is their freedom and not the nourishment we find in them.[61] At this supreme level where knowledge is faith, it is no longer distinguished from love.[62] Love is the whole and unreserved consent to the existence of another.[63] This love is inexplicable; it is spontaneous and generous. Opposed to free will that calculates according to the objectives and interests of the ego, this loving consent is freedom itself (3:133-34 = N 500), and it corresponds in human beings to the sacrificial generosity of God as Love.

That one can consent without reservation to the existence of the other implies that, if need be, we are ready to accept in his or her behalf a diminution of our very being. The preliminary condition for such an acceptance is consent to the laws of necessity and all they imply—that is, to our enslavement, our fragility, and our extreme destructibility. It is a folly—says Weil—the "folly proper to man, just as the Creation, the Incarnation, the Passion constitute the folly proper to God" (*IP* 148 = IC 182). The Creation, the Incarnation, and the Passion are three aspects of divine decreation; its essence is consent to the reign of necessity over matter and to the reign of freedom at the center of each soul.[64] Once we consent to the laws of necessity, we will realize its true nature: "In everything that exists, in everything that occurs, [man] discerns the mechanism of necessity and savors the infinite sweetness of obedience."[65] Deciphering this secret meaning of necessity is possible only once one has been transported into God's perspective;[66] there, necessity appears as pure obedience. The wild and impersonal majesty of sea and mountain, the infallible perfection of the trajectory of the stars, the implacable cruelty of the destiny striking human beings—all of these eventually appear to the soul that has passed through to "the other side of the curtain" as one immense network of obedience.[67] These universal laws of necessity in their cold power are the very sweetness of the consent the material world offers daily in silent sacrifice to God. At this point it can be seen that even what belongs to the sphere of God as Power is as it were penetrated and illuminated by the good, because material things consent at each moment to the order of the world (cf. *IP* 151–52 = IC 185–86) and thus "renounce being everything." One can therefore say that necessity itself, *as necessity,* imitates the good by its obedient renunciation:[68] "The whole universe is nothing other than a compact mass of obedience. This compact mass is strewn with luminous points. Each of these points is the supernatural part of the soul of a rational creature who loves God and consents to obey."[69] So appears the sketch of a supreme synthesis of the two attributes of the real, for finally it can be seen that "the pair of opposites constituted by necessity in matter and freedom in us has its unity in obedience" (*IP* 152 = IC 186). The only being to whom this synthesis applies in its whole meaning is the human being. Human beings alone in the universe are the compound of these two opposites; therefore, once the upsetting third part that is the ego has been erased, the harmonious duality of the real will appear in the manifestation par excellence of our decreated status, obedience.[70]

To be always obedient, and to be so in all circumstances, was Weil's highest aspiration. Even as a young student she comes across the idea of *amor fati* in the *Meditations* of Marcus Aurelius; the duty of acceptance with respect to the divine will, whatever it may be, became established in her mind as the first and most necessary of all duties (*AD* 35 = WG 65). However, the stoical attitude of which she speaks in her *Journal d'usine* (*OC* II.ii.218 = FW 226) still only expresses the acknowledgment of a certain necessity and respect for obedience (*CO* 152 = SL 48). It is only a few years later that respect for obedience changes into a violent love that leads her to write to Father Perrin that, "[i]f it were conceivable that one could damn oneself by obeying God and that one could be saved by disobeying him, I would desire obedience all the same."[71] But this desire bears on something that is already "granted" to us, for in a certain sense one cannot escape obedience. All is obedience in this world of which the human being is only a simple fragment, and basically there is nothing in us that can fail to obey God (2:98 = N 205): "The human being can never go beyond the confines of obedience to God. A creature cannot not obey. The only choice offered to the human being as a free and intelligent creature is to desire this or not to desire it. If he or she does not desire it, he or she nevertheless perpetually obeys as a thing subject to mechanical necessity."[72] Thus there is no choice[73] for humanity, or if there is one, it is only between different chains of necessity.[74] The choice is to consent or not to the fact that we are obedient. Afterward, "the human being. . . remains subject to mechanical necessity, but a new necessity adds itself to it, a necessity constituted by the laws proper to supernatural things. Certain actions become impossible for him, others are accomplished through him, sometimes in spite of him. . . a human being does not accomplish the same actions depending on whether he or she consents or not to obedience, in the same way that a plant, all other things being equal, will not grow in the identical way depending on whether it is in light or shadow. The plant exercises no control, no choice in the matter of its own growth. We are like plants that have as sole choice whether or not to expose ourselves to light."[75]

All the same, it must be said that the essential thing for Weil is not so much the fact that a new necessity will appear to the obedient human being, but rather that obedience must be conscious and assumed.[76] One must obey necessity and not coercion, the relationships of things and not "gravity": one must obey as spirit and not as matter.[77] Obedience must not follow from a particular effort, but must simply express an ontological status, that of the decreated state.[78] The certainty of the intellect is its obedience to necessary relationships (*CS* 25 = F 81), but it is only a formal anticipation of the obedience of the decreated person. It is true that once one understands the intelligible laws that define a situation, our action ought to follow them naturally (2:22 = N 155–56), but autonomy prevents such a coincidence between acting and knowing. It is necessary first that the individual will learn the lesson offered by intellect every day, that it too become a thing that is effaced by the very fact of being exercised. It is only through this transubstantiation of the personal will[79] that the imitation of

God is perfected; the screen of the ego dissolved, there emerges "that which in humanity is the very image of God... obedience."[80]

This "divine part of the soul" (2:369 = N 386) has three principal aspects: love, liberty, consent. For want of being able to adequately express the ontological status of the "secret point of the soul" (*PS* 110 = SN 185), Weil is reduced to employing a handful of metaphors.[81] Let us not try to force analysis of these terms: when she is in a predicament, she seeks refuge with Meister Eckhart in the term "uncreated" (cf. *CS* 85 = F 136): the uncreated part of the human being is like the Son of God or else it is his presence in this world.[82] We cannot wrest from Weil's fragments the "exact" sense of the continuity between the uncreated and God. It is very clear, though, that the uncreated is the opposite of the created, that is, of autonomy, and so the best definition one can give to decreation is to say that one is decreated "by making the created pass over into the uncreated."[83]

Weil's anthropological scheme thus presents itself in the form of a triad. In one sense, a human being is more complete, or rather, more complex than God, for while God has only two attributes, a human being has three. The necessity of God is reflected in humanity as matter. At first glance, its role in the great drama of creation is neutral; it is only the location. However, it is related to the good under two aspects. On the one hand, it reminds us every day of our belonging to the material world and thereby instills in us the feeling of our subjection. On the other hand, in its culmination as intellect it surpasses itself and offers us the possibility of decreation by revealing to us the truth of our non-being.

The Love of God is represented in humanity by the "uncreated," where lies freedom, exercised through love and consent. All decreative effort serves to remove that jumble of autonomy that paralyzes human beings, for it is through autonomy that we "miss" our vocation of being the image of God. Through consent we as human beings participate in the good, while the material in us is only neutral.[84] Evil comes from the distance that separates us from God, all the while making us creatures; it comes, that is, from autonomy. It exists only in autonomy; indeed, it is autonomy itself.[85] One now understands why Weil can speak of the "unreality of evil."[86] It is not a question of the "lazy" solution to the problem of evil put forth by so many theologians with complacency. When she taxes evil with unreality, Weil does not conceive of it as a pure privation; she is simply attributing to it a mode of being other than the good, one whose power is such that it goes so far as to rend God from God, to keep him in a state of painful waiting for reunification with himself.[87] From these scattered and hesitant notes there emerges a hypothesis, one that would satisfy the two indispensable criteria of all metaphysical reflection on evil: safeguarding its existential positivity and basing it on a properly ontological level. On the one hand, there is nothing more positive than the personal existence of each human being in its opaqueness and its expansion of the self. On the other hand, this positivity, despite its radical contingency, is a fundamental and irreducible ontological power. It is true that Weil seems to remain very Platonic when she designates the finitude of man—for her, the only true finitude—as evil. It thus appears for an instant that what is given with one hand is taken away with the other, for autonomy, insofar as it is evil, is that which ought not to be, that is, something that has no true place in the real. However, it is precisely by virtue of the fact that evil is that which ought not to be that its origin cannot be traced back in being and reveals an absolute independence. Finitude as evil is an ontological category as radical as infinite good and necessity. It is contingent, but it is not conditioned, and it is as free as freedom itself. These ideas surely represent a certain deepening of Platonism, but they cannot escape the fundamental objection one must make to the anthropology of the *Phaedo*. If the soul is the good in humanity and attachment to the body is evil, and if one becomes good by placing oneself on the side of the soul, evil by espousing the cause of the body, the fundamental question still is not answered: exactly what is it in us that consents to good, what chooses evil? Plato tries to avoid a too visible and discontinuous dualism in representing man in himself as a sort of master-slave relationship in which the soul, the master, is that which is truly real, and the body, the slave, is only a shadow. The fact nevertheless remains that the human being has no personal center whose liberty would be intact in relation to the soul and the body. For Plato it cannot be otherwise, for he could not guarantee individualization at an ontological cost, and he especially wants to avoid a neutral freedom beyond good and evil. It is, moreover, the basic reason for the difficulties experienced by any metaphysics of value in conceiving such a finite subject that would be a center transcending the opposition of the factors of "good" and "evil," or of "high" and "low" parts. Weil is an exception to the rule only to a certain extent. She resolutely clears away the rules and subterfuges by which one habitually sends responsibility for sin and error back to something not "essential" in human beings. The fact still remains that consent and love are the source of decreation, and it is a difficulty that cannot be resolved by the attempt to attribute freedom to the supernatural level with the justification that one is free only for the good.[88]

That being said, one cannot dispute the fact that Weil succeeded in giving independence to finitude, even if it was at the cost of designating it as evil. It remains to be seen that she attributes another radical power to humanity, that of serving as mediator between God and God. Nevertheless, representing that mediation as the work proper to humanity is not unambiguous, for Weil's thought is hardly clear as to the ontological relation between God and the eternal part of the soul effecting mediation. In referring to it, we have intentionally chosen the vague term of "continuity," the same one we used for the relation between necessity in the universe and God as Power. There are doubtless a certain number of passages that deny all independence to the soul, but we do not think these interpret the internal logic of Weil's thought the most faithfully. In the end, decreation can and must be accomplished in this world, and the human being—once ego has been destroyed—will continue to "live while ceasing to exist."[89] As the last notes say, "Having abandoned all sort of existence, I accept existence, whatever it may be, only in conformity with the will of God" (*CS* 333 = F 360) and "out of love for creatures" (*CS* 182 = F 224). At the time of this "new birth," Christ "enters" into the soul and substitutes himself for it (*CS* 182-83 = F 224). These striking metaphors ought not to obscure the fact that, to our mind, Weil says nothing fundamentally different from New Testament doctrine. Her writings are a late and distant echo of the Apostle's exclamation: "It is no longer I who live, it is Christ who lives in me."[90] Difference from God will not disappear; it only replaces opposition. The very idea of the role humanity can play in the ontological and spiritual drama lived by a divinity rent by its abdication—a role Weil insists so much upon—would be inconceivable without a true ontological independence of the uncreated in human beings.[91] This rending, as we know, is due, moreover, to the interposition of autonomous creatures who in their turn can erase it by abdicating their existence (*CS* 72-73 = F 124-25). This conversion is, in the best Platonic tradition, a "recognition" of our true being, for the essence of humanity is description and prescription at the same time. Intellectual understanding of what one is *ideally* will eventually mature, thanks to consent, into an ontological realization. Understanding that "zero is our maximum" and that God alone is center is fulfilled in the "realization" of our nothingness, that is, in reduction to non-being.[92] Therefore, to know that God is and to know that I am not are one and the same thing (*CS* 205-6 = F 243-45), or as a text from Marseilles puts it very succinctly: "Self-knowledge is love of God" (2:217 = N 282). One cannot really know oneself, and therefore consent to being, without love of God. The love we bear God is the key to the mystery of decreation (2:213 = N 282). As Aristophanes says in the *Symposium*, love is the healer of all ills (*IP* 32 = IC 108), for it cures our fundamental indigence, that duality piercing through our condition (cf. *IP* 44 = IC 109), the supreme form of which is the opposition between existence and the good. All the same, this duality can be surpassed only by union with God, and the true sense of love is therefore love of God. But if our love of God heals the wound that separates him from himself, then it is not only the healer of human ills; it is the healer of God himself. To analyze the meaning of this healing mediation in strictly metaphysical or theological terms would not make much sense. If anything is to be avoided, it is succumbing to the temptation to find Hegelian parallels for the *Cahiers*. If God "needs" human mediation, it is not because humanity is the necessary moment in which the Spirit returns to itself. What God "needs" is our love, and he "needs" it because he has wished it so, and in the way in which true love desires reciprocity: in the fullness of free generosity.

Chapter 2

Attention and Desire

We have said that, like Plato, Weil does not ultimately found her metaphysics of man upon a subject transcending the various components of the human being, all the while unifying them. Still, the mere fact that it is the same being who passes from the status of autonomy to that of decreation, and that this passage is the decreative process itself, forces the philosopher to look for anthropological elements that would explain an indisputable continuity. The condition for all decreation is contemplation of external reality, and decreation itself takes place when contemplation is based on consent. Attention[1] and desire, respectively, are the human faculties that channel these two basic attitudes.

Weil was already fascinated as a student by the concept of attention, which seemed to her to reunite intellectual and moral virtues: the discipline of "objective" knowledge of the world with the power of self-mastery.[2] Her first important work, the long essay on the causes of social oppression, is essentially a treatise on the human slavery originating in the mind's incapacity to oversee all levels of human activity; a human being accomplishes gestures or series of gestures mechanically while his or her attention is "elsewhere," or, more often, is absent.[3] Once one's attention has been suspended, one lives in a sordid mixture of vegetative functioning and fragmented dreams; one is cut off from external reality and only plunges into the self. At this point we discover how superficial and fragile our personal existence is. What we call personality is a curious contradiction: the self exists only to the extent it draws

41

its very substance from the external world it so passionately denies. The whole sphere of the self is maintained by a centripetal force greedily sucking in reality, and the more one nears the center, the more powerful is the force. However, the center is nothing in itself; it is only aspiration. The self is a violent contraction paralyzing and crushing the beings and things it encounters. Such an attitude serves the purpose of destroying the world, leaving there a trace of the self; it never helps us to understand the world. Even at the most simple level, the faculty of attention is the opposite of a contraction; it must not be confused with a muscular effort. When students are told to pay attention, they will often only knit their brows, hold their breath, tense their muscles. It is tiring physical exertion, but they have not really paid attention; they have only tensed their muscles. If attention is an effort, it is only a negative effort[4] whose sole purpose is to leave us free, empty, and open to penetration by the object (AD 76 = WG 111). To be attentive means to be open, supple; one must "seek nothing, but be ready to receive the penetrating object in its naked truth" (AD 77 = WG 112). Such is the paradox of attention: it must not be concentrated upon anything in particular, for the very condition of its effectiveness is that it be exercised empty of content.[5]

Indeed, the identification of attention with attention emptied of content is basically a truism. One pays attention to something one does not know or does not know well. One knows only that there is "something," and one wishes to know "what" it is and "how" it is. If knowledge were complete, one would not pay attention. That is why attention that would endeavor to learn something is always an empty attention waiting for something to appear, reveal itself, become manifest.[6] One can encounter the same situation when using the faculty of attention in contemplating a work of art or in praying, if the prayer is not simply a prayer of petition. One can have already seen the painting several times and be familiar with it, and one knows also that God exists. Nevertheless, whether contemplating the painting again, or turning to God in prayer, the faculty of attention is always empty. One might recall that the painting was beautiful and rapidly glance at it before deciding to give it attention, but it is neither the memory of it nor the glance that gives the impression that the painting is beautiful. The "beauty" of the painting emerges only after a certain time, when we have paid attention to something external and real, the image of which we retain before our eyes, but which was not perceived as "beautiful" when we began to pay attention. At that moment, only a desiring emptiness was preparing to welcome the beautiful; it is the same for any prayer that is more than a simple request. In prayer, we pay attention. We know that God exists, that he is one, good, all-powerful, eternal. We remember that, paying attention to God through prayer, we have had a certain experience of God, a certain "real knowledge" of him; but knowledge of the concept of God and the memory of an actual knowledge of the past do not necessarily entail a present actual knowledge of God. We must begin to pay attention in emptiness and then, perhaps, our knowledge will become actual.

The essence of attention is not, however, the gain it brings us but rather the fact that it is an operation making us turn toward the outside while emptying our mind of the self's own goals.[7] At this point we see how artificial was our "classification" of the intelligence as the culmination of the necessary and thus as something distinct from love and consent. It is quite possible that the *operation of the intellect itself* be of the world of the necessary, but the *attitude* making us apply the intellect must arise from another level. Even if one pays attention only for brief moments or in view of selfish and impure ends, there occurs a certain suspension of the ego inadequately explained by purely natural data. In our opinion, it is in this sense the several texts in which Weil insists on a great nearness of the intellect to love and consent must be interpreted.[8] There where she explains these two faculties as being in close relationship, the common element connecting them is not the intelligible, but rather the good. Intelligence and love are connected not because they both bear on the intelligible, but because they are brought to maturity—both of them—by the good. A commentary on the *Phaedrus* says that the sign of "the divine origin of the soul" is "the aptitude to form general ideas" (*SG* 116 = SN 121); that is to say, thanks to the supernatural element in our soul, we are able to suspend our ego, forget our desires and needs, and turn patiently toward the outside. Seen from this angle, the searching gaze of the intellect is but *one* of the expressions of attention at work in each authentic contact we succeed in establishing with the external world.

On the subject of attention Simone Weil ultimately develops two different, if not incompatible, views we can call "vertical" and "horizontal."

The essay on Pythagorean doctrine distinguishes between "intellectual attention" nourishing the intellect and a "superior attention" that is love and free consent[9] and is related to the supernatural.[10] In this view, the level of attention varies according to the object it is applied to, but the faculty itself shows a continuity. There is no human being who is completely deprived of the power of paying attention. From time to time, attention pierces through the imagination hiding from the view of autonomous human beings the reality of things and of human beings; the soul embarked on the steep path of decreation is only, so to speak, exercising the faculty of attention. That this faculty should be entrusted to all human beings is the proof of their capacity and their vocation to reject autonomy in favor of freedom and decreation. In this way, as a critic notes, "[a]ttention would be the permanent *human sign* insuring the ontological continuity between the old man and the new man."[11] This continuity, in this view, has a horizontal sense; it is exercised as intellect at an inferior level and as love at a "superior" one. Still, what can be considered as inferior from an absolute point of view remains nonetheless the highest degree of perfection a human being might be able to demonstrate in a certain area of his or her life; thus, "[a]uthentic and pure values. . . in the activity of a human being are produced by one and the same act, a certain application of the fullness of the attention to the object" (3:58 = N 449). This faculty is the "sole source of perfectly beautiful art, of truly new and luminous scientific discoveries, of philosophy that truly approaches wisdom, of love of neighbor that is truly helpful;

and, when turned directly toward God, it constitutes true prayer."[12] In each of these domains, it is through the faculty of attention that the human soul is opened to the exterior and grasps what is truly real there.[13] But attention does much more; it creates or recreates reality in a certain way. Without wanting to consider here the obvious relation between artistic creation and attention (cf. Chapter 5), we can state as a general law that the creative faculty of genius in all areas of human existence is based upon extreme attention (cf. 3:45 = N 441). Human beings do not create out of nothingness but rather out of the matter reality offers to their action; they merely actualize the beauty, truth, and life surrounding them on all sides as unrealized possibilities. Attention is like the sorcerer's wand; applied to all these frozen potentialities, it fills them with reality, with being (cf. 3:174 = N 527). In the sphere of scientific or mathematical knowledge, the mind confronts necessary relationships; if it cannot modify these, it still remains that they cannot be realized without its help. In the domain of whole integers, one and one remain one beside the other and will never become two unless an intellect carries out the addition. Only intellectual attention can grasp relationships, and when it is relaxed the relationships are as though dissolved. Therefore, "[t]his virtue of intellectual attention makes of them an image of God's wisdom. God creates by the act of thinking. We, by intellectual attention, certainly do not create, we produce nothing; still, in our sphere, we do in a way incite a certain amount of reality."[14]

In relations with the other, the faculty of attention is always exercised through the acceptance of, and consent to, the existence of others; it is thus "the rarest and purest form of generosity."[15] The parable of the Good Samaritan shows how "supernatural" attention is a process creating reality. Those passing by the inert and bloody body of the assaulted man hardly notice him, whereas the Samaritan stops and turns his gaze toward him. The resulting actions are the automatic consequences of that moment of attention; this faculty is creative (*AD* 107 = WG 146–47) and constitutes love of neighbor itself.[16] Finally, it is well known that spiritual life is identical to a certain form of attention; God cannot be pulled down to earth, one must wait for him in silence.[17]

Attention thus perfectly represents the meaning and direction of decreation. If personal existence only empties of its content the external reality encountering the self, in decreation it is one's own self that is emptied of substance (cf. PS 109 = SN 185) by giving back to the real through attention that which we have taken from it. The self is always conscious of the mortal threat attention represents to it, and it will deploy many fervent efforts to counter it in its exercise. In one of the most profound passages in all her work, Weil notes that "[t]here is something in our soul that is repelled by true attention much more violently than flesh is repelled by fatigue. That something is much closer to evil than flesh; that is why whenever one truly pays attention, one destroys some of the evil in the self."[18] Evil is therefore, as Hegel noted, going back into the self, and the good for us consists in being robbed of our personal existence, with the help of the incomparable instrument that is the faculty of attention. Through attention one leaves the shell of autonomy and is wrenched from personal perspective; it is therefore not paradoxical to say that "the utmost ecstasy is the fullness of attention" (3:156 = N 515). Making a void in ourselves implies making a fullness in the world, but this exit from ourselves is not truly ecstatic unless it is permanent, that is to say, when attention is transmuted into *waiting*.

To pay attention is to bear witness to the humility that betrays our powerlessness to influence or change an event or an external fact on which we in some way depend. From the pupil who fixes her gaze on a page covered with equations the sense of which escapes her, to the war captive kneeling before the raised sword of the conqueror, there is a whole gamut of forms of attention expressing the fact that we are subject to the external world. Attempts to escape external power having been revealed as vain, we can only "remain still, implore in silence."[19] In the domain of knowledge, attention is the supplication of the intellect emptied of all its troubling attachments so that the truth of reality may be revealed to it. That is why waiting, that habitual form of empty attention, will, far from being a state devoid of thought, be the very spasm of the receptivity of the intellect.[20] At the other end of this scale of forms of attention, the spasm extends to all our physical and moral being when the imminence of death by the conqueror's sword chills the heart and empties it of all its attachments (*CS* 44 = F 98–99). The only hope remaining is that his glance meet our own, now become in its totality humble supplication. There where effort and ruse are powerless, the gaze saves in establishing contact with the external forces that would otherwise ignore or crush us. This is above all true in spiritual life, for it is only through the gaze praying out of hope and faith that we can turn toward God,[21] since, in the end, it is by this gaze that we imitate him, and we can only meet him by imitating him. "God is attention without distraction" (*CS* 92 = F 141), that is to say, he is waiting; and we can imitate his waiting in two ways. On the one hand, the greatest perfection proposed to us is to adopt the docile passivity of material things,[22] that is, their obedient submission to necessity. Their "patient waiting" become our own, we conform to the image of God as necessity. There is still, however, another way to imitate the decreation of God by waiting: it is to follow the example given by his presence as Love in the world. God waits for his beloved, the human soul; he is "standing, motionless, nailed to the spot for the perpetuity of time. . . . The Crucifixion of Christ is the image of this fixity of God" (*CS* 92 = F 141). Our waiting is therefore the imitation of divine waiting and, indeed, it is the sole reason for, and justification of, our existence. By imitating the waiting of God, by participating in it through humility,[23] we will eventually fulfill it,[24] for if God awaits my attention it is above all because my consent alone can erase the screen of my autonomy separating him from himself.[25]

If attention is the faculty through which, humble and obedient, we turn and listen to external reality, *desire* seems to be the channel proper to self-expansion. And yet, in her important study, "Reflections on the Right Use of School Studies with a View to Love for God," Weil states that attention can be directed only by desire (*AD* 75 = WG 110). This definition will become clear once the essential structure of desire has been explained. Desire is perhaps the most paradoxical faculty given human beings. Desire is primarily "an uncontrollable force thrust toward the future" (2:28 = N 159). It thus contains that which cannot be tamed, at the very heart of self-expansion. At the same time, the basic spontaneity of its leap does not keep it from always being oriented toward a very precise goal.[26] Like the ego it represents so faithfully, desire wants to devour the world, all the while calculating with great application each of its aggressive operations.[27] Still, the fact of being a universal appetite that can be directed only toward one particular object is the secret of its exercise and effectiveness; but this opposition between the universal and the particular contains still other meanings and potentialities. Desire is unlimited in principle but limited in its exercise, because there is nothing infinite or unlimited in this world where its objects are necessarily found (1:140 = N 88). However, we do not want to accept the bitter truth of this limitation, and we want to conceal it at all cost by acts or dreams, deluding ourselves and others with the illusion of omnipotence (1:159 = N 100). Through each of our desires we aspire to conquer the universe, but in fact we will only be plunged further and further into personal existence. The relation between this unlimitedness and each of the finite desires it maintains and nourishes serves to transform desire in revealing its relation to decreation.

The paradox of desire is that it constitutes the very foundation of our being,[28] but each time it manifests itself, that is to say, turns toward an object, it makes us commit a crime or exposes us to degradation. We cannot not desire, for "[m]an is assuredly made of desire."[29] But each time we desire, we end up defiled and frustrated, since "[n]othing on this earth is truly an object for the desire I have in me."[30] Desire seems to be lost in a strange contradiction: on the one hand, its universal impulse makes its particular orientations so powerful; on the other, the necessity in which it finds itself of being scattered and converted into the contingent and imperfect inevitably debases it. But what really is the meaning of that impulse, or rather can it validly be identified with desire? Weil certainly did not think so; even if the general and elementary form of desire in autonomous existence is only the uncontrollable violence of a desire of the ego, this blind impulse can be only the perversion of true desire, whose essence is a movement toward the good. Here also she harks back to Plato, who made Diotima say that "all desire is for the good and for happiness. . . . For human beings there is no other object of love if not the good. . . . In short, love is that through which one desires to always possess the good."[31] It matters little that Plato seems to identify the use of the faculty of desire with love; the essential thing is that desire be always *desire for the good*. Desire as desire for the good, that is to say, of absolute good, is beyond all particular objectives, which ought to be pursued only with a view to the Sovereign Good. But thanks to the "reversal effected in human things by original sin" (*IP* 85 = IC 143), desire has fallen beneath particular goods, in that "evil infinity" that is the ego (cf. 3:60 = N 451). Not merely a perverted application of desire occasionally lost in harmful occupations, but rather its veritable transformation is at stake. Human beings in their finitude cannot not continually direct their desire toward particular goods, but we redeem ourselves if we aspire toward them only with a view to the Good (cf. 3:122 = N 493). However, exactly the opposite occurs in autonomous existence; instead of being absolved by their constant reorientation toward the Sovereign Good, particular desires find their justification in the very fact of being particular. Therefore, instead of being effaced as a particular beneath the cloak of the universal, the particular becomes universal *as a particular*. In this way the oriented character of desire gains its dimension of generality, meaning the illegitimate universalization of the individual as an individual in his autonomous existence. Now we can see that, if one wants to reestablish desire in its truth, it is not enough to uproot it from its evil applications; it is instead its system of perverted universality that must be overhauled.

A purification of desire itself must be undertaken, a project not without a Kantian overtone of formalization and which must at the same time be shown in relation to both the object and subject of desire. The unceasing effort to surpass a particular thing as object of desire continually "generalizes" desire until, all that is particular having been transcended, there remains only "desire without an object."[32] To reach this stage, it is not enough to abandon concrete objectives in which the orientation of desire is accomplished; any and all orientation must be suspended. In other words, it is not enough to uproot things from our own self-expansion; it is also necessary to bring to a stop that voracious imagination that changes the things of the world into simple functions of our personality (cf. 3:215 = N 553). Fed by the imagination, that central faculty of the self, our desire is necessarily limited; only the disappearance of the self will restore to it its original vocation for the unlimited and the infinite. Only once "the sword of obedience" cuts through our orientation toward the world of particular objects (CS 111 = F 159) will our desire be delivered from all subjective limitation and become "desire without wish" (3:216 = N 554). The convergent aspects purification of desire takes on are becoming "objectless" and "wishless"; but, after such a radical formalization of the term "desire," does it retain a real meaning in Weil's world? She herself would reply that to be without wish does not mean indifference and that to be without an object does not imply a loss of contact with external reality. Quite the contrary; the same commandment that orders us to leave our desire "non-directed" prescribes that it be "kept extended" (3:272 = N 593), and one abandons concrete objects of desire only with a view to being better able to follow the supreme object, which is the will of God. It is in wanting the will of God that we accomplish the true purification of our desire, for we put desire back in its proper sphere where it may henceforth act upon reality. In this way desire becomes "a lever that brings us away from the imaginary into the real, from time into eternity, and out of the prison of the self" (AD 168 = WG 217).

Desiring something as willed by God means "[a]sking for what is, what truly is, infallibly, eternally, in a way completely independent of our request" (AD 168 = WG 217). But this "perfect request" must not be limited to what is; it can be extended to whatever occurs in conformity with God's will. And, since "whatever it may be, the future, once brought to pass, will be brought to pass in conformity with God's will" (*AD* 169 = WG 218), we must desire everything that happens, since everything occurs according to the will of God as Necessity. As a result, the "will be" is delivered from contingency and receives reality in the same way the "is" possesses it.[33] Finally, the same thing holds true for the past; we must desire all that has happened because God allowed it to happen. Its purification now brought to completion, desire is replaced by perfection. It has just transposed "time into eternity," where the three dimensions of past, present, and future merge in the unity of the "is."[34]

The purification of desire by attaching it to the will of God is obviously a way of expressing the obedience that lies in consent to necessity. Thus, by perfect desire one imitates God the Almighty; does this not also include another kind of imitation of God, of the God who is Love?

In the many passages where Weil identifies the good as the true object of desire, she only repeats a central maxim of classical Western philosophy, and she will again take her inspiration from Plato when taking up discussion on the faculty of desire itself: "The search for the Good in Plato. We are composed of a movement toward the good. But we are wrong to seek the Good in a given thing.... The good is only in our movement itself."[35] The reference to Plato excludes even the possibility of attributing to this definition a heroic or Faustian meaning. There is no question of celebrating force, endurance, human resistance. Nor is one invited to admire the sublime impotence of an effort endlessly fragmented against the adverse forces of this world. Quite the contrary; the fact that the good resides in our very movement reveals its supreme effectiveness. Our quest and our search for the good attain the good simply in desiring it. The reward for each particular desire is a future object, while in the desire for the Sovereign Good the "will be" takes on the very color of the "is." As long as we desire a particular object while wishing for it, we desire it for ourselves with a view to possessing it. Once we have generalized the object and withdrawn the wish, the very idea of the personal possession of what we desire is abolished. There therefore remains of desire only the act of desiring, which is fulfilled by its very exercise. Desire for the good is therefore already in itself the good: "It is with respect to false goods that desire and possession are different; with respect to the true good, there is no difference" (CS 110 = F 157).

The exalted language of these mystical descriptions makes us too easily ignore the powerful presence in them of an important Kantian moment. Already the "formalization" of desire only takes up the famous prescriptions of the *Foundations of the Metaphysics of Morals*, and we find again, clothed in Platonic garb, that one existing good thing, Kantian good will. The *Cahiers* explicitly state this; the sole truly absolute, eternal thing is "my will for the good. Pure and inexhaustible good is in that very will only" (3:120 = N 491). This Kantian presence, suddenly revealed at the very heart of the idea of the good, reminds us once more that the entire ontology of decreation is to a certain extent an interpretation, and a very original one, of the great distinction between the phenomenal and noumenal worlds. Weil insists on the fact that God as the Good is not being, that he is beyond being; she will go so far as to say he is "nothingness" (cf. 3:120 = N 491). Obviously, this is not a veiled attack on divine transcendence, but rather a very conscious effort to protect and save it by situating God, at least under one of his aspects, beyond being, a concept at once too cumbersome and overly imbued with everything that is opaque and violent in the reality of this world. Nowhere are Weil's formulas more beautiful and striking than where she speaks of the detachment of desire from "false goods" with a view to turning it toward "absolute good." But what exactly is "absolute good," and does such a thing exist? "The argument" takes the form of a monologue:

> But, it will be asked, does this good exist? What does it matter? The things of this world exist, but they are not the good. Whether the good exists or not, there is no other good than the good. And what is this good? . . .
> It is that which whose name alone, if I attach my

thought to it, will give certainty that the things of this world are not goods. . . . Is it not ridiculous to abandon that which is for that which perhaps is not? Not at all, if that which is, is not the good and that which perhaps is not is the good (CS 284–85 = F 315–16).

Why should being be connected to the good? Why say of the good that perhaps it is not? "The good certainly does not possess a reality to which the attribute of the good might be added. It has no being other than being the good."[36]

All this only clarifies the definition of reality we have attributed to Weil: the good is separated from being, that is from the true, by evil. Still, insofar as evil is concerned, the Platonic terms referring to the world of appearances do not manage to conceal the fact that it is essentially that-which-ought-not-to-exist, that is to say, something integrally related to the concepts of duty, moral law, and the categorical imperative. Without attempting an exact translation of personal existence into Kantian terms, it is clear that it corresponds to imperfect will acting according to impure motives. So long as one uses one's autonomy (one must not be deceived by the non-Kantian use Weil makes of the term), one brings into being, that is, into the domain of the theoretical, a deviation from the good. When one acts as a decreated being, the good is incarnate in deed, always according to the infallible and precise laws of the phenomenal world. There is no incompatibility or even original discontinuity between theoretical and practical laws; although things may be other than they should be, the guilty party is humanity, whose imperfect will does not conform to the moral law. Human beings alone can come between the realm of ends and the realm of nature, and the categorical imperative requires of us nothing other than to end that intrusion.[37]

Analysis of attention and desire having brought us back to the ontological context of decreation, it is on this level that we must conclude our study of these faculties, if there can be a conclusion. We have defined them respectively as the faculty of the apprehension of being and the faculty of the search for the good. But once it has been seen that, on the one hand, attention at its highest level is love and consent, and, on the other hand, desire without an object tends only toward what "is," all possibility of a clear distinction seems to vanish. Obviously, as long as one remains on a descriptive plane, it is possible to distinguish the passivity of the eye of the soul keeping distance in contemplation from that uncontrollable force through which desire attacks its prey. However, once the systematic requirement hidden beneath the scattered fragments composing Weil's work becomes apparent, the edifice of evident and simple definitions begins to crumble. One single thing remains solidly established: there exists an ecstatic faculty in human beings apparent under the double aspect of attention and desire. Two sorts of ecstasy are accessible to us: the ecstasy of expansion and appropriation, and the ecstasy of contemplation and abandonment of self in free generosity. As long as one remains within the domain of the first kind of ecstasy, one is in the world of particular and selfish desires. Once contemplation has entered the scene, attention appears to replace desire. It would be desirable to be able to say that the presence of attention is limited to the space at "the intersection of the two worlds" and once one has adopted the perspective of God, a particular purified desire channels one's contacts with external reality. That might be the case if attention were only inert and passive intelligence, but we have seen that, rather than become depleted in the narrow limits of knowledge, it "is the unique source of perfectly beautiful art . . .of truly helpful love of neighbor, and, turned directly toward God, it constitutes true prayer." We need only admit that even if there is a profound difference between particular desire and attention, once desire has been "purified," no more real divergences between these two faculties are to be found, save in what is related to their "formal object."[38]

These developments lead us back to the formula stating that attention is "the permanent *human sign* insuring the ontological continuity between the old man and the new man," with a view to modifying it. Attention expresses only a presence of the "new man" in the "old man," and not a permanent state linking them as successive stages in our evolution. The real continuity is represented by desire as an ecstatic faculty, because it alone links together the appropriative voracity of the self and loving acceptance of the Cross by the decreated soul. Have we now found the indifferent center that transcends good and evil, spirit and flesh, the new man and the old man, all the while connecting them? Perhaps, but surely not in the form of a personal subject; at most, one can identify a formal impulse tending toward the external, one that might take in radically heterogeneous "contents." How then to interpret this basic continuity? Is it a question of a fundamental indifference merging and unifying good and evil, or more precisely, the good, evil, and being? Such a conception could only be repellent to Weil and contradict her often expressed ideas on the essence and vocation of the human being. A different interpretation must be retained, even if it reveals a certain ambiguity. Rather than speak of an indifference basic to the human being, it would be better to speak of the omnipresence of the good within us. It is "the ruse of the good" that is at work in every blind impulse; it is the good hiding from evil and replacing it gradually from within.[39] Is expansion, that is to say, the wrong form of ecstasy, not the essence of evil? Yet love uses that same ecstasy, turning it completely around, to destroy egotism (cf. 1:158 = N 100). In this way, in the best tradition of Christian Platonism, the good is found at the very root of evil; and if it is not the whole of its being, it at least constitutes a formal element of it.

Chapter 3

Energy, Motives, and the Void

Were the reader of the *Cahiers* tempted to adopt the hypothesis on the "ruse of the good," he or she must still not forget that one "participates" in the good through non-being, and not through being.[1] The formal impulse at the base of all desire and apparently of the ontological continuity of human existence is the pure possibility of the good; "possibility" is to be understood here in the sense of "receptivity," rather than "potentiality." The impulse does not ripen of itself into desire for the good; on the contrary, it seems to reveal instead an innate tendency to expand into covetousness. At most one can state that it is an environment given to freedom by necessity, enabling freedom to come to terms in and through it, if it is nonetheless, as usually happens, not appropriated by autonomy, of which it is the channel. The impulse in itself is neutral, being the element derived from necessity without which good and evil would have no *being*. Most often Weil calls it *energy*.

Energy is the vital substratum of all our activity. It is essentially one but is qualified according to the part of the soul it serves. Weil therefore distinguishes *supplementary* (or voluntary) energy from *vegetative* (or vital) energy. Vegetative energy is useful only to maintain and preserve biological life, whereas supplementary energy is the powerful channel of the multiple desires of an autonomous individual.[2] The mysterious and complicated relation between necessity and autonomy is illustrated perfectly by the metamorphoses undergone by energy according to the changing interpretations the imagination gives to the goals pursued in human activity. So long as I labor at a work promising pleasure and remuneration—and all this in proportion to the effort given—I mightily exert myself, I renew my strength, I am vigorous, bursting forth, resourceful. If, however, I find myself to be completely rewarded before the work has been completed, I can no longer hope for any subsequent satisfaction; my mood will change, and my impulse will flag. I will still have to finish the work, for otherwise I would have to return the money paid to me, but the thought of giving myself trouble simply with a view to preserving what I already possess now does not engender any real enthusiasm. For so long as I exerted myself with a view to rewards to come, supplementary energy rose easily; now that my preoccupations bear completely on preservation, supplementary energy slowly becomes vegetative. This is obviously not a real mutation of energy, because preservation here bears on a goal deriving from autonomy. Still, it is clear that conservation as such, whatever its direct object, is in the final analysis related to life, to biological life itself. This state in fact appears very manifestly in one of Weil's examples. Sent to a concentration camp where one must carry stones from point A to point B and then from B to A, and must do so every day without interruption, one pursues no particular goal. The source of supplementary energy dries up with the disappearance of any of expansive autonomy's goals. One carries stones simply because one fears death and thus uses energy only in order to preserve life (cf. 2:54 = N 176). Transition and communication between vegetative and supplementary energy, that is to say, between necessity and autonomy, therefore exist. But what is the relationship of these realities to the third human level, the level of "free consent"? This is indeed the central question on energy, an idea that Weil treats simply to complete the analysis of the decreative process. Expressed in terms of energy, decreation means the suppression of supplementary energy and the perfect subjection of vegetative energy to supernatural freedom:

> One must destroy that intermediate, uneasy part of the soul...in order to expose the vegetative part directly to the fiery inspiration that comes from beyond the heavens. Strip oneself of everything above vegetative

life. Bare vegetative life and turn it violently toward the heavenly light. Destroy everything in the soul not attached to the light. Expose naked to the heavenly light the part of the soul that is practically inert matter. The perfection offered to us is the direct union of the divine spirit with inert matter. Inert matter seen as thinking is a perfect image of perfection.[3]

This is simply a translation of the decreative process into striking imagery. The "intermediate part" of our being is of course the self, fed by supplementary energy. It hides the part that is practically "inert matter" and is a particle of the domain of necessity. When its autonomy has been decreated, the soul becomes the perfect site for the encounter between God and God. The faculty of free consent achieves that perfection by exposing to divine light that part of soul remaining after the destruction of the self.

Only through these descriptions of energy does it become clear why decreation must necessarily progress through the ordeals of physical suffering, why religious life is necessarily ascetic. Always at stake is the establishment of a regime starving supplementary energy and transposing it into vegetative energy: pain, fatigue, hunger, and anguish are, so to speak, cut into two parts. The autonomous part cannot accept pain, whereas the eternal part consents to it.[4] Their "confrontation" takes place in time, which is itself transformed. Time, in its characteristic structure of orientation toward the future, is the very milieu of autonomy nourished by supplementary energy. If, however, pain and privation place us in a situation where the direct interests of biological life are threatened, the goals of autonomy fade. One has then been torn away from the future and attached to the present; depleted supplementary energy now gives way to vegetative energy. The latter, guardian of biological life, aims only toward the suppression of physical suffering, but it is taken in hand by consent and forced to endure the ordeal; that is to say, it is used with a view to an end other than the preservation of life. In such moments time grows heavy and concentrated, and an effort of a quarter-hour's duration seems like a whole eternity.[5] We have reached a critical moment in any religious metaphysics, the moment of the "passage" at the intersection of heaven and earth. And the passage cannot be explained.[6] The ordeal evidently entails a preparation having its own mechanism (cf. *CS* 253 = F 287). Supplementary energy must be spent in the "apprenticeship of pain"[7] in order to reach the moment when, the self having been abolished, the very flesh of the human being is exposed to the burning demands of supernatural love. This is the instant when "[t]he soul splits into an unlimited part and a limiting part. The compound on the finite plane has disappeared. In this microcosm the original chaos is reproduced, the original water upon which the spirit is floating. One part suffers beneath time, and each fraction of time seems an eternity to it. One part suffers beyond time, and eternity seems to it a finite thing" (*CS* 182 = F 224).

Despite an apparent lack of distinction between the biological and the autonomous, the meaning of the imagery, especially in the continuation of the passage, permits no doubt. The "redemptive suffering" of the eternal part of the soul "justifies" the "guilty part." This justification is accomplished in the moments of the reproduction of the original chaos in which the recasting of the human compound is carried out. The abolition of supplementary energy has repercussions for vegetative energy, from this point on "stimulated" by "a vital inspiration come directly from beyond the heavens" (*CS* 261 = F 294).

Now all the theological import of what had originally seemed a psychological and metaphysical description is revealed. If the abolition of supplementary energy is indeed the death of the "old man," the transubstantiation of vegetative energy appears to refer to a glorified body. Indeed, from the start, the long passages in *La Connaissance Surnaturelle* treating the role of energy in decreation allude to the sacraments.[8] They are taken up again in highly condensed form in a very late text where they are used to explain the soul's attitude toward the reception of the sacraments (*PS* 140–42 = GTG 68–70). There is nothing surprising in this; the culmination of the quarter-hour's ordeal is the transubstantiation of vegetative energy. A new human being is born, one who is only matter attached to God by free consent: "After that, there is a new creation the soul consents to not in order to exist, for it aspires not to exist, but solely out of love for other creatures, just as God consents to create" (*CS* 182 = F 224). A harmony between the supernatural faculty of desire and the bio-psychological faculty of energy is newly established. "The ruse of the good" has won in the end.

That impulse Weil calls energy is the bio-psychological substratum of our life and activity, qualified according to the relationships between self and matter in us. When the basic needs of biological life are met, autonomy governs us. Supplementary energy is the channel of autonomy, causing it to flow by offering it ever renewed objectives, or "motives." The term itself, Kantian in origin, expresses the essential characteristics of a representation inciting the self to go toward a goal or initiate a movement.[9] Anything can be a motive for a human being, anything useful in maintaining and expanding his or her personal existence.[10] Since our energy is subject above all to the imagination,[11] and only to a very limited extent to pure intelligence, it is not astonishing that base motives engender the most energy and make us endure the harshest ordeals. The reason for this is that "base motives require no attention, and...subsequently fatigue does not keep them from being present to the mind. On the contrary, fatigue, in paralyzing attention, causes elevated motives to disappear."[12] The original goal of supplementary energy is to lessen or eliminate distance and hurl the self upon something, whereas the goal of attention is to keep that distance. In general, in a non-decreased person there is no source of energy for goals other than those of the self. No doubt each human being has in his or her life more or less brief and intense moments of realizing the existence of another and trying to act for the other's good. In such cases, the goals of the self can be momentarily forgotten but, at least when the depletion of energy for an extrapersonal goal rejoins the limits of vegetative energy (this is indicated by fatigue and exhaustion), the "highest motives" dissipate and "the coldest egotism" appears (2:220 = N 283). This is true of the average person subject to multiple attractions, whose imagination is unmoored, and who, all the while ardently working toward self-expansion, is not ruled by any "absolute" objective or intention.

It is not the same for the soul that, according to the words of Socrates in the *Republic*, is subject to "a governing passion." Such a passion can go beyond the limit of vegetative energy and continue to make efforts toward extrapersonal goals. Still, this is not decreation, but rather a sort of alienation of the self. This is what occurs in the great passions of human life—blind loyalty to a leader, an ideology, a collectivity, or in the kind of love Weil calls "cannibalistic": the other is not loved as a good but as something necessary to the lover's life.[13] The ambitious person struggling to acquire social prestige puts the supernatural love in him or her on the shelf, so to speak; but at least his or her autonomy is safe, and it always holds the possibility for decreation to the very degree one remains free to renounce it. But the person possessed by a governing passion has abdicated even to autonomy, has alienated some of the ego in favor of something external, and until the self has been destroyed (and sometimes even afterward), he or she is incapable of becoming engaged in the process of decreation.[14] The reason for this is that decreation requires an uprooting of vegetative energy, but "[c]ertain human beings can invest so much energy in an object outside themselves that, so long as that object exists, never, even very close to death, are they reduced to the wrenching away of vegetative energy" (*CS* 193 = F 233). A sacrifice accomplished under such conditions, even if it is the sacrifice of life itself, has no decreative value; only the death of something already alienated is at stake. All that is sacrificed is supplementary energy leading to vegetative energy.[15] The tragedy for such a person is to have become closed off to the call of the supernatural by the very depth, heroism, and determination of his or her will. A guilty lack of "discernment" (cf. 1:220 = N 141) is at issue; nothing in the world ought to justify a total gift of self, for this world is ever the kingdom of the ego, whose highest ideals are only egotistical motives, supremely present wherever passions relate to the group, that is, to the social self.

The interpretation Weil gives to the significance of alienating passion is the eloquent proof of the seriousness with which this creature enamored of obedience treats human freedom. Indeed, a freedom that could "experiment" without risk of irremediable compromise would be less freedom than a natural force. Such a freedom is apparently indestructible, but in fact it is not really free in its relation to the world or in relation to itself. No doubt it finds itself intact and unchanged again after each of its undertakings, and so the world has no hold over it. It can play with anything, penetrate anything, get mixed up in anything with impunity, without its having the least effect on its exercise or constitution. But in this case it is unthinkable that it could maintain respect for, or attach a price to, a world of wax, giving no resistance or reaction. And then, could one really have any hold over anything so malleable and transparent? All being possible to it and nothing entailing any consequence whatsoever, freedom would endlessly evaporate in a world devoid of substance. Moreover, this impossibility of being affected by its own action, this inability to be compromised by itself, remove from freedom any hold over itself; incapable of involving, losing, alienating itself, freedom would endlessly escape itself. What an absurdity!

Weil, however, understands that without the very real possibility of self-alienation, there is no true freedom in this world. And indeed nothing fascinates freedom so much as such an alienation inviting it to forever remain outside the condition of engaging in the process of decreation. At issue, of course, is one of those governing passions where "one uproots supplementary energy from the self with a given result in mind and. . .one is from that point on attached to that result by vegetative energy" (2:320 = N 354). When the will or events eliminate that attachment coming "from outside" (2:320-21 = N 354), a partial or total death of the self follows. At first different sorts of motives coexist in our affection, but often attachment, becoming stronger, directs all our supplementary energy to the object of our love. Then vegetative energy leads to supplementary energy; when supplementary energy is fixed upon another object, that being becomes necessary to the preservation of our biological well-being or even of our life.[16] Even if these extreme cases are rather rare, everyday life frequently offers the spectacle of people who have undergone a partial loss of their ego because of an attachment. This occurs, for example, when human beings must confront the bitter truth that they have sacrificed their happiness and everything dear to them for no good reason. Weil considers the case of the husband who had prostituted his wife to Volpone and learns that he is not Volpone's heir. This man carried out actions that would have been impossible were it not for the good he had hoped to thereby obtain. The motive for his action has disappeared, but the impossible and yet completed action remains present. He appears to have committed the action without a motive: "The soul lives in the impossible without being able to leave, for it is impossibility achieved, past impossibility. . . . The soul commits the act again in thought, with the motive absent. Wishing his wife still had not been touched by another man . . . his thought goes back to the still recent time when this had been so. In order to rejoin the present, his thought must pass through that act. Now that act has lost the motive that alone made it possible. Thought falls endlessly into the past and can only rejoin the present by passing through the impossible."[17]

Still, there is no essential difference between a motive that has proved illusory and one that continues to nourish our supplementary energy; each motive being a function of the imagination, each one is changing and ephemeral. However, inside the Cave we cannot act without motives, even if our activity is morally correct and follows the direction of decreation. A correct action ought to be the fruit of a simple relationship the mind establishes between the general law and the concrete situation (cf. 2:22 = N 155–56). I ought to act thinking only of the relation of the moral law with the present situation, but a pure relation, a simple connection arises only from the domain of the intellect and cannot serve as a motive for the self. Pure intelligence, which grasps the relation of the particular goal to absolute good, can propose the course of action to us, but its power over the self is minuscule; only near the self can our energy renew its source. It is therefore

incumbent upon the self to provide supplementary energy with
motives that seem constant and solid to it. That is to say, we
need "relative goods thought of as goods beyond all relation"
(1:226 = N 145). The element "relation" (or "connection") is
intolerable to the self because it arises from pure intelligibility:
"What is needed therefore are motives escaping. . . *relation*, that
is, absolutes, idols."[18] Once more, the double inspiration of Plato
and Kant bears its fruit. Two parallel texts in the *Cahiers* relate
the theory of motives to the central allegory of the *Republic*:
"Idolatry. . . is a vital necessity in the Cave."[19] "*To think of relationships is to accept death. Center of Platonic thought.* [The goodness
of worthy people in the Cave is always limited by idolatry. . .the
forgetting of relationships. . .]."[20]

The goods of this world exist and are good only insofar
as they participate in ideas; their truth, their very reality is only
participation. But the self which places itself at the center of
the world cannot not take itself for an absolute, that is to say,
not consider its goods as absolute. Understanding that all that
is good in one's world is so only by virtue of its participation
in something transcendent implies the profoundest asceticism:
that of self-relativization, in its turn identical to full awareness,
that is, the acceptance of one's own mortality. Weil fully
understands that the theory of ideas, before being a metaphysical hypothesis, is an effort of religious and moral purification (cf. 3:118 = N 489–90); that is the reason she takes it
up again in the strictly ethical context of the Kantian doctrine
of motives. Idolatry, which is the forgetting of relationships,
is condemned in the developments of the *Foundations of the
Metaphysics of Morals*. Rejected is not merely the particular,
singular, ephemeral motive, but any action following a maxim
other than simple conformity to the moral law (cf. 2:322 = N
354–55). The real idols are moral values or commands prescribing a particular motive, even if it is quite generalized, as
an absolute and unalterable norm. Kant strongly insists on the
vicious and vitiated character of a maxim determined solely
by its content. Only the maxim's form can be a criterion of its
moral value, for the moral law to which it must conform is itself
only formal. In other words, the formal purity of the moral

law must have its subjective counterpart in the formal purity of the maxim.

It is here that Weil's analyses rejoin the famous analyses of Kant. As we know, motives fill the imagination and cause supplementary energy to flow. Idols, those motives solidified, give permanence and generality to our energy which, deprived of them, is suddenly unoriented; we are now forced to confront the void. There is void, or emptiness, in the general sense of the word, when the equilibrium of energy in a human being has been struck severely, in such a way that he or she must accomplish actions, endure privations, accept pain without being able to drink at the source of supplementary energy. Whether this be the result of a long process or a sudden blow, vegetative energy is exposed and used for ends other than the preservation of life. When motives are lacking, even a relatively easy physical effort taps into vegetative energy. If the activity of the concentration camp prisoner who must transport stones from A to B and from B to A all day long, unendingly, were accomplished as work with a view to an end, it would absorb and recreate supplementary energy without affecting vegetative energy. But in the case of moving stones, the prisoner has no goal except to avoid being killed; he has no objectives beyond monotonous acts he must accomplish solely because he has been ordered to. In this instance and generally as well, there is "[v]oid, when nothing external corresponds to an internal tension."[21] The absence of any motives translated into the void is a form of torture for the self and seems to correspond to the quarter-hour of eternity. There are three possible responses to the void: (*a*) one cannot tolerate it and tries to fill it with the imagination; (*b*) one does not manage to fill the void and consequently perishes, either dying or falling into a vegetative state [in these cases decreation does not occur but rather an externally caused destruction belonging to the phenomena of affliction (cf. Chapter 4)]; (*c*) the last possibility is, of course, decreation, accepting the void and still continuing to live and act. The void therefore takes the place of an ordeal; it entails either degradation or passage to the supernatural (cf. 1:226 = N 145).

When one tries to reorient "the energy freed by the disappearance of objects constituting motives," usually the motives one finds are baser (2:53 = N 175), owing to the phenomena of compensation set into motion by the "void-filling imagination."[22] This is not a mere psychological law, but a necessity of a metaphysical nature. All particular motives being errors, they are translated into evil actions, and thus through them one plunges into evil.[23] If one is not torn apart from the self in a decreative manner, one cannot fail to advance in evil. Evil, being autonomy itself, has a dynamic structure reinforced and developed with the appearance of each new motive. The world of the self is the totality of motives; as a note in the *Cahiers* states very explicitly, even "[w]hat one calls I, myself, is only a motive" (1:154 = N 97). Obviously the self is not a motive like the others; it is the formal element of all particular motives, that which carries out in them the refusal to conform to the moral law. Each motive is a function of the perspective one has adopted in the world, perspective itself being the very essence of the self. The void, that is to say, the end of the regime of motives, therefore appears as the state of being beyond perspective. Can one persist there? In what way? With these questions we are brought to the outermost limits of Weil's thought.

One might almost say that the whole problem of the evolution of her thought is summarized in her relation to Kant's philosophy. As a young teacher at the *lycée* in Roanne, she identifies the moral law and God's perspective without hesitation and as something that goes without saying,[24] just as four years before she had written on "the universe *in God*, or to speak quite differently, *in itself*."[25] In this context, to act without motive would mean to follow the moral law, and the question of the *possibility* of such conduct would be reduced to that of an a priori synthetic use of pure practical reason. At first glance, it is tempting to proceed to such a Kantian reading, even insofar as the metaphysics of decreation is concerned. As we know, Kant resolves the great paradox of practical reason by the intervention of *freedom*; through freedom man is enabled to adopt a maxim for which he feels no inclination. However, the third component of the being of man, the agent of decreation, is also called freedom by Weil. It is therefore through *freedom* that there is passage to God's perspective. Encouraged by this important parallel, one might be tempted to extend even further conjectures of possible analogies with critical idealism. The *Intuitions Pré-chrétiennes* attribute a creative power to the intellect in the realm of whole numbers (*IP* 154–55 = IC 187–88), and in this they echo the Kantian teaching that considers even mathematics as the realm of the a priori synthetic usage of *theoretical* reason. However, whereas Kant is content to justify the possibility of a priori synthetic judgments by a priori forms of sensibility, that is, by space and time, Weil appeals to free attention (*IP* 154 = IC 188); as a result, even a simple mathematical operation would be possible only thanks to *freedom*. This totally Fichtean "primacy of the practical" is, moreover, the basic meaning of the doctrine of attention. For Weil, the quality of the content received by the intelligence is dependent upon the quality of the exercise of attention, and the very idea of an empty attention implies that theoretical knowledge be preceded by a movement of the "practical faculty."

Such a conclusion is certainly well-founded, but its impact is singularly weakened for Weil's mature thought because of the slippery meaning of the notion of freedom. In fact, an intervening mutation of the basic elements of her metaphysics does occur; from this point on, the moral law is not compared to simple non-perspective, the latter distinguished from God's perspective, which transcends it. It now becomes clear that the structure of the decreative process can no longer be integrated into the problematic of the a priori synthetic use of practical reason, formulated by Kant with a view to explaining the possibility of an ever-renewed conformity to the moral law of the activity of a human being remaining subject to the attraction of motives. For Kant, the regime of division human beings are subject to tolerates no permanent cure; the struggle is always renewed, the effort is never "natural." For the mystic Weil became toward the end of her life, the goal is a radical mutation, the passage over a threshold (cf. 2:409 = N 413). Once this passage has been accomplished, one is established in the good; one's moral activity is henceforth explained from what might be called *analytical* judgments. In the end, therefore, Plato seems to prevail over the one who called him "the sublime philosopher" in the Transcendental Dialectic. Weil even dares to formulate several remarks on the proper action of the purified human being who has undergone death.

The only moment when the a priori synthetic use of practical reason seems to still retain its dramatic actuality is that of the passage from autonomy into decreated life. The ordeal of the quarter-hour seeming a whole eternity eloquently expresses the paradox that the obligation and the fact of following a non-temporal moral law represent for the human being subject to temporal motives. However, at this point even Kant is ultimately renounced; if the moral law of the *Foundations* is something neither in heaven nor on earth, one finally receives in the quarter-hour's ordeal "a vital inspiration directly from beyond the heavens" (*CS* 261 = F 294). This is *grace*, without which, according to Weil, one never passes from the Kantian synthetic condition to the analytic perfection of mystical Platonism. But the presence of grace demonstrates that not only Kant, but also Plato, are won over and integrated into Christian doctrine.[26] All this new synthesis, if it is a synthesis, in the end depends on the relation between grace and freedom; this is exactly the point where, as in any religious metaphysics, Weil's reaches its outer limits.[27] The contradiction, or rather the paradox, is inevitable wherever this question is posed. On the one hand, Weil insists on the fact that only grace can help us tolerate the void without deceptive compensation or abasement.[28] On the other hand, she says that supernatural aid comes only after one has endured the void, implying that one endures it by one's own natural means (2:23 = N 156). One can make an effort with a view to continuing to endure the ordeal only if one is fed by "supernatural bread" (1:226–27 = N 145), but receiving it depends on our desire.[29] The paradox is that "[g]race fills, but it can only enter where there is a void to receive it, and it is also grace that makes that void" (2:88 = N 198). To avoid any sterile speculation, let us say that the only correct "definition" of the relation of "nature" and grace is that they are inseparable; this is true to the extent that, if freedom is alienated, even grace cannot come to our aid.[30]

The void confronted each time motives disappear is of limited length and duration, and the quarter-hour is only its culmination. Quite often a long process is involved, and Weil identifies the void with the "dark night" of Saint John of the Cross (1:212 = N 135). In the dark night of the senses or of the spirit, the soul continues to believe and pray all the while exasperated by dryness and tortured doubt—that is, in a state without motives. It is a matter of using our faculties with a view to goals not natural to them, that is to say, in the void. The energy of the body must accept supravegetative goals, "sensible forms of the void": hunger, thirst, chastity (1:214 = N 37). Attention must tend toward the non-representable good (2:321 = N 354); desire is exercised without an object. In short, each one of our faculties must be considered "a demand exercised in the void" (*IP* 126 = IC 165).

But what does the void become once the ordeal has been victoriously endured? It continues to surround us all the while undergoing a transfiguration. If during the ordeal its aspect of psycho-physiological torment was dominant, in the decreated state it expresses the ontological mutation that has intervened in the human being. From this moment on one acts without motives[31] not because these are simply suspended, but because "the motive of motives," the self, is eliminated. It is not a neutral state, because—we repeat—one is not within non-perspective but within God's perspective. What is offered to us is a void fuller "than all fullnesses,"[32] and for this Weil returns to the use of the term "motive." She says that we must carry the motives for our actions beyond ourselves (1:96 = N 125), that is, have as our sole "motive" obedience to God which "carries action into eternity."[33] In this context, the very structure of the concept of motive is turned around; instead of being an aspiration toward the future, that is, toward a goal of the self, it contains a conformity to the "past," that is, to God's will. Determination by a supernatural mechanism takes the place of the deceptive teleology of the human condition.

Chapter 4

Suffering and Affliction

At the end of one of her letters to Father Perrin, Weil writes that each time she thinks of the crucifixion of Christ, she commits the sin of envy.[1] Indeed, suffering is in her view the privileged moment of the human condition, revealing its truth and making its cure possible.[2] Suffering is inseparably tied to the autonomous condition, located as an obstacle at the intersection of the two divine attributes, the good and necessity. Only through suffering can we eventually consent to the reunion of the divine persons, but through it also we run the risk of falling into the abyss where even our faculty of free consent will be lost for all time. Reflection on suffering, in the large sense of the term, is always the sign of a metaphysics of transcendence. It implies a break, a contradiction, the presence of something that ought not to be; at the same time, it brings grave threats against that very transcendence. In and through suffering we live our separation and difference from supernatural harmony and perfection; but, paradoxically, at the extreme moment when pain becomes our whole universe, we stop thinking of transcendence, being wholly absorbed in present agony. However, suffering rendered permanent and changed into wretchedness can ultimately break the individual, thereby entailing the end of transcendence, one of its poles being thus eliminated. This is obviously the central paradox of any ascetic doctrine which, through its desire to "purify" the body, must suppress the created. If, however, the paradox is truly conceived of as a paradox, that is to say, with full respect for the two factors constituting the irreducible contradiction

70

(cf. 2:368 = N 386), then, and only then, does the notion of asceticism emerge in all its metaphysical fecundity. The insistence on suffering as a privileged means of going deeper into transcendence, all the while subjecting the body to a terrible ordeal, confers eminent dignity upon it. Again we see how Weil's thought considers the earthly, the physical, the finite with utmost seriousness.[3]

The body has an immense decreative importance, for only in and through it can the self be destroyed. Hunger, thirst, and, in a way, sexual desire—all associated with the body—are neutral or even good, as long as they remain within the realm of biological life, confined to goals of vegetative energy. Once departing from the realm of the necessary, the desires of the body, now termed "carnal," cause supplementary energy to flow. The self can only be "uprooted" by pressure exerted upon carnal desires, fundamental motives of autonomy (cf. 3:154 = N 447). It can now be seen what the decreative function of the body in relation to the carnal consists of.[4] In the marvelous descriptions of the ordeal of the quarter-hour,[5] the body is described as "a lever by means of which the soul acts upon the soul" and by its discipline causes it to deplete "errant energy."[6] The body is a sword which cuts the soul in two (CS 177-78 = F 219-20), an instrument of torture that kills "everything mediocre in the soul" (CS 189 = F 230). It goes without saying that the famous Platonic metaphors of the body are enriched by the introduction of the opposition between the carnal and the body: "The body is a prison. The spiritual part of the soul must make use of it to close, wall up the carnal part. The body is a tomb. The spiritual part must make use of it to kill the carnal part."[7]

Through these images one perceives clearly the principal outline of Weil's ontology: the harmony of the good and necessity, which are in opposition to autonomy. In other words, the good is, in the final analysis, the superior unity embracing and unifying itself on the one hand and necessity as intelligibility—that is, pure obedience—on the other. There therefore exists an original alliance, beginning with God himself in us, between supernatural love and "physical and psychic matter."

It arises and is actualized in asceticism with a view to reducing the self from its vitiated condition of that-which-ought-not-to-be to pure non-being. Since it is only through a "breaking-in" by pain (1:201 = N 128) that the body is freed of the attachment of the self and becomes transparent (or as Weil says, following Hegel, "fluid") and obedient, physical suffering is the subject of a veritable ontological deduction.

This ontology justifying asceticism is probably of Platonic inspiration in a strictly metaphysical sense. The reunion of necessity as obedient intelligibility with the good is an interpretation of the doctrine of ideas. Each individual, obscuring element being exorcised from it, the participant, the body in this case, is revealed in the purity of its ideal structure and ultimately coincides with the idea in which it participates. If this interpretation is correct, then the metaphysics of the body at issue really is not one, because it values the body only insofar as it transcends itself. Physical necessity is integrated into the heart of the good, with the condition, however, of being idealized as a structure; and if the body must attain unity with the soul, it must first become essence.

However, there could be another reading of the theory of asceticism, even if it is doomed to remain in the state of a fragment or sketch: a metaphysics of the Incarnation which, in its turn, cannot not include a specific metaphysics of the earthly. It is not our intention to treat Weil's "Christology" but only to note that this immense insistence on the reality and dignity of suffering reveals an understanding of this world that the logic of this Platonism would admit with some difficulty were it not for the presence at its heart of belief in the Incarnation of the Word. One is quickly accused of dolorism if one insists at all forcefully on the great value of suffering, and yet the ascetic, or indeed any believer, has always sensed that something more complex and more profound than the mere exercise of a pedagogical method is involved in physical suffering. The Christian dogma of the Son of God incarnate to whom each of us is bound and related[8] enables religious intuition to structure asceticism on a metaphysics of corporeal reality. Only in the doctrine of the Incarnation is the integrity of the religious paradox—the irreducible and fruitful contradiction between the finite and the infinite—fully respected. It is true that Weil herself does not seem to have fully succeeded in defending the paradox. Even in decisive moments she yields to the profound temptation to condemn the finite. She believes that the Incarnation culminates in the death on the Cross and not in the Resurrection (*IP* 84 = IC 142–43), and she seems to impugn the idea of personal immortality.[9] Still, to the very extent that personal and psychic suffering is at the center of her thought, she leans toward the elaboration of a metaphysics of the paradox, that is to say, a concrete metaphysics. In the end, "the saving of phenomena" is what is at stake, and it is no accident that the only completed mature work is *L'Enracinement*.

If Weil does not manage to elaborate a complete and consistent doctrine of the concrete and of the body based on the Incarnation, the fact remains that for her the human being is integrated into the eternal movement the divine persons make between them through the Incarnation. The basic vision of her entire philosophy rests on a God suffering from being separated from himself by the obstacle of human autonomy. Decreation is the elimination of the obstacle; the human being is associated with the Passion of Christ and, rather than being a center of resistance upon the painful and separating distance, is from this point on part of the Cross reuniting God with God.[10]

The first movement in our participation comes from God. He traverses the infinity of space and time and touches our soul. We have the power to open or close ourselves before him. If we open ourselves, he deposits in us a particle of grace, and from that moment on, we have only to wait for it to mature, painfully; to wait for its moral and spiritual "force" to "grow."[11] Then the moment when the soul truly loves God arrives, and now it must pass through the universe to reach him: "Divine Love has crossed the infinity of space and time to go from God to us. But how can it make the trip going back when it departs from a finite creature? When the seed of divine love deposited in us grows and becomes a tree, how can we, we who bear it, bring it back to its origin, make, but in the opposite direction, the journey God made toward us, cross infinite distance?" (*AD* 96 = WG 134). The answer is that the tree growing in us was made in the image of the tree of redemption, the cross. Extreme suffering alone helps us to surmount the distance back to God. We are separated from him by the entire world of necessity. Through a hole pierced in it we can go toward God. When we drive in a nail with a hammer, the head of the nail receives the blow, but it is transmitted to the point. Extreme affliction, which is at once physical pain, spiritual distress, and social degradation, is that nail. The point of the nail is placed against the very center of the soul. The head of the nail is all necessity throughout the totality of time and space, piercing the soul in its center (*AD* 96–97 = WG 134–35). If even at this point the soul continues to direct its love toward God, then, in a mysterious dimension, the nail pierces a hole through creation, through the thick screen separating God from the soul; the soul can then attain God.[12] In this way decreation and its goals are achieved; when the soul reaches God, God can continue his eternal journey toward himself.

Suffering, obviously, is not always decreative. Quite to the contrary, it can be "useless and degrading" (2:124 = N 122), indeed, infernal, when it is only a purely external destruction of the I without the soul's consent and cooperation.[13] Decreative suffering, however, has two successive levels corresponding respectively to God's "journey" toward the soul and to the journey of the soul toward God: levels of expiation and redemption.[14] In the expiatory phase, suffering emerges as revealing, in the strongest sense of the word, the true structure of the human being. It is not a matter of merely drawing the curtain before a hidden reality that was previously constituted and only veiled; instead, it is "a violent operation" in which the screen hiding autonomy must be ripped from our flesh (cf. *AD* 95 = WG 133). Suffering "uncovers" the ontological truth of the human condition only by actualizing it; only physical suffering has the power to make us realize, by suspending or abolishing it, how much our autonomy is only a misleading outgrowth and that we are therefore entirely subject to "that necessity constituting the order of the world"

(*AD* 94 = WG 132). As a result, "[e]ach time we experience pain, we can truly say that the universe, the order of the world. . .the obedience of creation to God enter into our body."[15] In suffering and privation, supplementary energy disappears and vegetative energy is exposed; this is the void. But at bottom what is the void if not the realization that there is nothing resistant, substantial, "unbreakable" in us—that is to say, that we are vulnerable, fragile, destructible, *mortal*? In the void one meets death. The acceptance of the void implies the acceptance of death, that is, of a state without attachments, desires, and goals. Death is the at once theoretical and practical truth of our condition; I am already dead because my self is unreality, but in order to be able to *realize* that *I* am only a fiction, my self must reach "zero, its maximum" (cf. *CS* 327 = F 354). The self fights with all its might against even a merely theoretical realization of our mortality because it feels anguish before its own nothingness. Truth and death being on the same side,[16] "there is no love of truth without a total, unreserved consent to death."[17]

Obviously, "for an evil cause, if the stimulant is strong enough, the flesh will accept anything, knowing it can without dying. Even death undergone for an evil cause is not really death for the carnal part of the soul. What death is for the carnal part of the soul is seeing God face to face."[18] There is a mysterious relationship between seeing God and experiencing pain; in both cases one cannot avoid understanding that one is nothing. Each blow of suffering brings us this revelation, being "an injury brought by necessity making one experience that one is mortal" (1:98 = N 60). Weil likes to quote Aeschylus on "knowledge [gained] through suffering."[19] To see the truth of the world, one must be subject to necessity, undergo what one does not want to (cf. *PS* 119 = SN 191). The Cross of Christ is thus understood as "the only door to knowledge."[20] And since we have been created brothers and sisters of Christ, "[t]hose who have the immense privilege of participating with their whole being in the Cross of Christ go through the door, pass over to the side of God's own secrets" (*IP* 164 = IC 195–96).

However, nothing is more difficult than believing in our mortality, because that keeps us from forgetting our fundamental misfortune, the fact that we are not God.[21] That is the essential sadness of our condition, and the self spends its existence finding consolation. More generally: each time one encounters any pain or privation, the subtle mechanism of our autonomy starts to work to soften or hide it with a consolation. Even belief in the immortality of the soul can be only a sublime consolation[22] giving meaning to a phenomenon of which "the very essence...is absence of meaning."[23] By making of suffering an offering, one obtains a consolation that dilutes "its pure bitterness"; and instead of truly facing the void, one encourages the reappearance of supplementary energy[24] by supplying oneself with a new motive. Like attention and desire, suffering too is more fruitful when it is practiced in a void. One must not suffer for a particular end, but rather with a view to rejoining the state without ends; by suffering without being intent on a reward or ultimate goal, one in a way already lives in an eternal present. Weil expresses this simply in saying, "I must not love my suffering because it is useful to me, but because it *is*" (2:193 = N 266).

Let us stop at this brief definition. She does not say we must love suffering for itself, for its character as suffering; that would be, let us be reminded, attachment to a subjective psychological state which as such must be rejected (cf. *PS* 121–22 = SN 192–93). We must love suffering instead because it is reality itself. Suffering that no learned interpretation, no persuasive self-suggestion can erase is irreducible. What we must pursue and love in suffering is the reality of our very being: the irreducible reality our natural faculties come up against without being able to advance and to which they are endlessly forced to return (3:109 = N 483). Physical or psychical suffering is of such an irreducibility; it is contradiction in the full sense of the term.[25] The self wants to advance and prosper, and, being oriented toward life, it must necessarily choose the path leading toward its conversion and expansion.[26] Now, its advance is suddenly halted by suffering, the veritable negation of self-expansion, because it gives birth to the void.

Our condition is therefore contradiction; in that way, it participates in the structure of all reality.[27] We must renounce all pretension to a "natural" belonging to God because of the contradiction that appears in the form of suffering and the essence of which is death. Nevertheless, suffering and death give us the means to rejoin God through the imitation of the passion and death of Christ.[28]

Through contradiction we are separated from God, and through contradiction we will be reunited with him (cf. 2:368 = N 386). Is it therefore any surprise that our love for God must pass through suffering?[29] Indeed, even God's love for himself passes through suffering, because the contradiction between creator and creature covers an even deeper opposition: the one separating the divine persons. The creation shattered the unity between the Son and the Father, between the love and the might of God; this separation is the "divine pain"[30] cured only at the moment it reaches its paroxysm on the Cross.[31] Thus, even the unity within the Trinity must not remain simply "natural"; it will pass through the freely assumed ordeals of the Creation, the Incarnation, and the Passion. It might almost be said that God requires himself to surpass himself by making a gift through freedom of the harmony that would have in any case been his own by virtue of his essence. Even God seems to be obliged, or rather to want, to proceed to a second birth in which human suffering participates through imitation. According to the definition of the *Philebus* taken up again by Weil, pain is the separation of opposites,[32] the shattering of a state of our existence harmonious until then, where the peace of the body had been felt in the soul. What is important from now on is that, despite the disharmony reigning in the body, one can reconquer the lost harmony on a supernatural plane, which implies that "the loving soul is then constrained to make over again in itself the unity of opposites; inspired by the grace of God but cooperating with him, to do what God had done in the body entirely without it. . .it must. . .begin again and imitate the work of God. God redoes in it, with it what he had done without it."[33]

The state in which one participates in the Cross of Christ through redemptive suffering is called *affliction*. The description and analysis of this state are the subject of what is perhaps Weil's finest essay, "L'Amour de Dieu et le Malheur"[34] ("The Love of God and Affliction"), and the concept is found in many passages of the *Cahiers* and *La Connaissance Surnaturelle*, in the essay "La Personne et le Sacré" ("Human Personality"), in the magnificent third letter to Joë Bousquet, and elsewhere. Lived experience, metaphysics, and theology all converge in the most poignant and dramatic passages of her work.[35] Let us begin with her definition: "Affliction is an uprooting of life, a more or less attenuated equivalent of death made irresistibly present to the soul by the expectation or apprehension of physical pain."[36] Indeed, physical pain is an irreducible element of affliction without which any suffering is only imaginary.[37] But it is not equivalent to affliction; a toothache is a violent pain and yet it leaves no mark on the soul (*AD* 82 = WG 118). Pain must be accompanied by an interior suffering such as remorse, an acute sense of uselessness, anguish. Finally, "the uprooting of life is complemented by social degradation."[38] This degradation is felt particularly by beggars, prisoners, prostitutes, all kinds of human beings continually exposed to the mistrust and contempt of society. Whether these people have really committed crimes or not, they cannot escape the contempt and hatred of society. People are naturally inclined to make the wretched suffer by words or acts,[39] because "all the hatred our reason attaches to the crime, our sensibility attaches to affliction."[40] More terrible is that the afflicted come to hate themselves and vaguely feel they were created to undergo ill treatment.[41] They even become accomplices to their own wretchedness. This complicity puts a stop to any effort they might make to improve their situation; and sometimes it eliminates in them even the desire to be delivered from affliction, or else incites them, in spite of themselves, to flee from the means of their deliverance.[42] Complicity in one's own affliction does not exclude the search for compensations, although these are necessarily determined by the hopeless state of the one afflicted. A prisoner sentenced for life and a prostitute who knows herself definitively rejected by society are cut off from the past and have nothing to hope for from the future. How can they still lucidly confront the truth that the moment of their death is separated from the present only by a monotonous succession of identical moments of horror, disgust, emptiness, and pain? Thought is riven to the present[43] and tries to fill up the future with some sort of goal. The afflicted person tries to escape his or world by means of revery (2:324 = N 356), the most common form of which is debauchery, in which, for a few brief moments, one can forget one's wretchedness (cf. CS 262–63 = F 295).

Dream and debauchery are only privileged forms taken by the search for attachments in the human being deprived of a true end. Finding oneself in the void, one will use anything to fill it: "In affliction, the vital instinct survives uprooted attachments and blindly clings to anything that might serve as a support, in the way a plant's tendrils cling. . . .Gone is the supplementary quantity of energy supporting free will, through which one gains distance. Affliction in this form is hideous, as life exposed always is, like a stump, like the swarming of insects. Survival is the only attachment. It is at this point that extreme wretchedness begins, when all other attachments are replaced by the one of survival. Attachment is exposed. Without any object but itself. Hell."[44] Paradoxically, hell resembles paradise; the analogy between desire without any object and attachment without any object seems profound. In affliction one meets the two ultimate possibilities of our condition, and often even the afflicted individual does not possess the faculty to discern them. The difference is immense, however; in desire without any object we are reduced to pure receptivity, to pure opening, whereas in attachment without any object we become a kind of clinging, grasping, violent suction. When human beings have lost all attachments, without having renounced the faculty of attachment itself, they have not transcended their persons in a decreative way; they only sink beneath.[45] Expressed in terms of decreation: the self is destroyed from the outside with the cooperation and consent of the soul. This hellish depersonalization is due above all to *might*.

Might is that face of necessity contemplated by the non-decreated human being (cf. *IP* 47 = IC 182), and in the incomparable pages of her great essay "L'*Iliade* ou le Poème de la Force"[46] ("The *Iliad*, or the Poem of Might"), Weil analyzes it in its most horrible form: human violence. The true hero of the *Iliad* is the might that makes human beings into things.[47] Lycaon kneeling before Achilles and imploring him for his life is no longer living. One moment, he believes that perhaps Achilles will spare him, but he quickly understands there is no chance of this. He is then shattered, and his "knees and heart fail him."[48] Truly Lycaon was already dead when Achilles pierced him with his sword. Each time one is at the mercy of a man who incarnates might, one is only an inert object before him. When Priam begged him for the body of his son, Achilles pushed him away like an object; the old man no longer possessed that power of human presence that compels us to change our movements and gestures, that makes us behave differently than if we were alone (*OC* II.iii.230 = IC 28).

The power of might is immense and is exerted not only over the individual subjected to it. The person wielding it is subject to an intoxication preventing reflection (cf. 1:56 = N 32); he "is walking through a non-resistant environment, nothing in the human matter around him being of a nature to create between impulse and act that brief interval inhabited by thought."[49] Possessing might deprives us of the distance that is the source of knowledge; if it changes the vanquished into inert matter, it transforms the victor into a blind force consisting only of impulse.[50] But the impulse is hardly distinct from matter, and the question as to *why* a human being can consider another person as matter is answered by the fact that he or she has become matter. Nothing more. This is the reason why the power of might "is an authority as cold and unyielding as if it had been exerted by inert matter" (*OC* II.iii.233 = IC 31). This is why "[t]he power it possesses to transform people into things is double, exercised on both sides; it petrifies, in different but equal ways, the souls of those subjected to it and the souls of those who wield it."[51]

The victim of might, the wretched one, is no more subject to the sword of Damocles than the person wielding it, the warrior. The warrior's life is woven of the same unreality as that of the slave living at the mercy of the master. Danger seems abstract to him, the lives he destroys like children's toys.[52] But a day comes when the veil of reality is torn. Fear, defeat, the death of beloved companions make his soul bend under the weight of necessity. He understands that war is neither a game nor a dream but that it truly exists. However, it is an intolerable reality, because it includes death. All people must die, but for warriors the relation between death and the future is quite special: "For others death is a limit imposed in advance on the future; for them, it is the future itself, the future assigned to them by their profession" (*OC* II.iii.242 = IC 41). When the possibility of death is the constant companion of all the movements of the soul, one lives under a terrible tension; thought cannot journey to the next day without passing through the image of annihilation. The weight of this violence is too great for one to make an effort to get out from under it; the body continues to spread evil, and the soul remains in a sense impotent (*OC* II.iii.242 = IC 41–42), although continuing to long for its liberation. Again, the parallel with the victim of might, the wretched one, becomes evident. The afflicted person has an irresistible need to spread evil around him because he dimly senses that it is the only way to be rid of it.[53] The warrior has the same need, and that is the reason he seeks to destroy. He knows his future is death, but as long as he can assign death a "place" in someone else, it will not affect him. At the same time, and here all semblance of reasoning is abandoned, in killing another one takes vengeance on the fact that one is mortal oneself (2:216 = N 281). Lycaon implores Achilles, but the latter is implacable:

Come along, friend; you too shall die! Why so bitterly
    complain?
Patrocles too is dead, and he was far better than you.
And don't you see how fine and great I am?
I am of noble descent; a goddess is my mother.
But above me too are death and cruel destiny.
It will be dawn, or evening, or the middle of the day
When my life, too, will be taken by arms. . .[54]

Reflection on war is therefore very fruitful. In war, all that is forbidden is transgressed, all limits are surpassed; in war, human beings think themselves masters of the destinies of others and of their own. Nothing is farther from the truth, for at the supreme moment of bloodshed, the victorious warrior, turned into blind impulse, rejoins the vanquished in his depersonalization. In this state, one is matter, thus entirely subject to necessity. The exercise of might is an illusion: "No one possesses it; it is a mechanism."[55]

The identification of the highest degree of self-expansion with a mechanism reveals something of the very meaning of autonomy. The ontological status of the world of the self is that of the unreal manifested in a tangible way by criminals. They do not foresee the consequences of their acts; they do not realize the bounds of their existence and those of the existence of others (1:12 = N 3). In any autonomous activity whatsoever, an imaginary purposiveness masks a necessary causality to which alone it owes the power of making its imprint on the real. The strictly necessary structure of these acts is hidden by a vital autonomy inciting and motivating them, but in crime and in war where autonomy is perfected, an important transformation takes place. The simplicity of criminals (and soldiers) is in a striking way similar to the simplicity of freedom enabling us to execute the most impossible and absurd actions in dreams.[56] In dreams, the laws of time, space, and matter are under my domination, and yet I feel strangely paralyzed in the midst of my grandiose exploits. This mixture of license and constraint is found in war and crime where, by pushing the arbitrary to the limits, one comes eventually into contact with implacable necessity itself.

The reality of war, Weil says, is the most precious reality to know, because it is unreality itself.[57] The reality of war is the unreality of autonomy, in the sense of its final realization: in the domain of might, necessity pierces through the illusion of freedom. There is therefore no normative, ideal perfection for autonomy, because in its supreme manifestation it coincides with necessity. That does not, however, mean that autonomy, that is, the evil Weil identifies elsewhere with might (3:69 =

N 457), eventually dissolves into matter. Reaffirmed instead is the thesis that the third component is that-which-ought-not-to-exist, the essence of which is not inscribed in the two attributes of reality. An autonomous act can always be analyzed in terms of its physical or psychic structure, and in its pure state autonomy is free even from the appearance of independence in relation to the necessary. Nevertheless, evil is not "reduced" or "resolved"; only an ambiguity is resolved, that of its claimed belonging to the world of necessary being. The very purity of evil is compromised each time one tries to situate it in a phenomenal causality. Evil certainly possesses such a causality, but never *in its capacity as evil*. To protect irreducible reality from evil, it must be separated from its appearance in necessity. One might object that then "nothing" will remain of evil—indeed, "nothing" ought to remain—in the world of necessity, where all is explained by natural laws.[58]

Whether autonomy culminates in violence or is ultimately broken by it, the result is always depersonalization, "passage into anonymity." Affliction devours the personality; when one is face to face with affliction, one has the impression that it is not a particular human being, but affliction itself confronting one (2:172 = N 252-53). The one afflicted becomes so to speak opaque, distant, incomprehensible, finding no words to express what he or she feels. Affliction is mute.[59] Its muteness is nearly impenetrable to questions from others; for in order to ask questions, we must stop; and before stopping in front of an afflicted person, we must direct our gaze upon him or her. Now, this is impossible for those who are non-decreated; attention violently turns away from wretchedness because it reveals our own nothingness in the fragility and vulnerability of another human being. If I wanted to contemplate and understand affliction, I would need to say: "A play of circumstances I do not control can take anything whatsoever away from me at any instant whatever, including all those things that are so much mine that I consider them as being myself. There is nothing in me that I cannot lose. A chance event can at any time abolish what I am and put any vile, contemptible thing whatsoever in its place" (*EL* 35 = SE 27).

To think this with all our soul implies the acceptance of death. This is the reason the soul shrinks back at the sight of affliction, just as the flesh shrinks back in the proximity of death.[60] Trying in this way to escape the reality of our condition (cf. PS 124 = SN 194) makes our ears deaf in the presence of the afflicted. Affliction is thus unknowable; those who have not experienced it cannot turn their gaze toward it, and those who are at its center prefer to close their eyes.[61] The instinct of self-preservation surviving in those who are afflicted compel them not to know their situation through either apathy or untruth.[62] Therefore, there is no natural compassion[63] toward the afflicted, because such compassion implies renunciation of the self. The true intersubjectivity perfected in compassion toward the afflicted is supernatural. One must be transported into the perspective of God to be able to offer oneself as ransom for another; it is precisely this that compassion demands. Afflicted ones are by fate deprived of the humanity the attentive and loving gaze of the compassionate person gives back to them, reproducing in their "behalf the original generosity of the creator."[64]

The price of this re-creation is high. Affliction is a reality that does not dissolve under the compassionate gaze so as to liberate the afflicted person; affliction must be taken upon oneself. What is the concrete meaning of this sacrifice? First, one must be able to contemplate affliction in others, and this is possible only for those who have contemplated it in themselves, who have lived it themselves. To fix one's gaze upon one's own affliction instead of turning it away is to accept one's own nothingness.[65] Once more, we return to the ordeal of the quarter-hour; during the time one forces oneself to contemplate the hideous truth of one's condition, vegetative energy is tapped and is finally uprooted from the self. And this uprooting is its liberation; the close dependence it had in relation to a particular self now being eliminated, vegetative energy is opened to the supernatural.[66] A "real transformation" takes place "at the very root of the sensibility, in the immediate manner of receiving sensible...and psychological impressions" (AD 118 = WG 159), and it makes the soul "vulnerable to the wounds of *all flesh"* as to its own.[67] Here, therefore, is the necessary physiological basis thanks to which it can be affirmed in a not merely symbolic sense that true compassion implies the acceptance and the taking upon oneself of the suffering of others (cf. 2:216 = N 281). It manifests the advent of a new ontological order in which, the troubling intermediary of autonomy set aside, necessity is docilely subject to the good.

Supernatural compassion redeems the afflicted, but can there not be a moment when it arrives "too late"? Is it possible for degradation to go so far that nothing can save the soul from destruction? Weil does not manage to answer these questions unambiguously. On the one hand, she is unwilling to admit that the supernatural point in the soul is subject to the vicissitudes of matter or the schemes of autonomy; on the other, she is firmly convinced of the absolute might, the destructive might of affliction (*CS* 89 = F 139). Affliction always falls on an individual through the blows of blind and brutal necessity.[68] It is therefore natural that everything subject to necessity, all physical and psychic matter, be entirely subject to affliction. If there is a secret point excepted,[69] it must perhaps remain inaccessible to consciousness, the fine tip of necessity. But the real question is whether the depth of our soul is really exempt from destruction or eternal punishment. In the final analysis, Weil, who believes in Hell, answers with an obscure no (cf. *AD* 175 = WG 225-226): "A blind mechanism taking no account of the degree of spiritual perfection constantly tosses people about and throws some at the foot of the Cross itself. It is up to them only whether to keep their eyes turned toward God through the upheaval" (*AD* 88 = WG 124–25).

The two central ideas of this classic passage concern the power of chance and the freedom of our consent. Each human being has his or her own system of relations between vegetative energy and supplementary energy, that is, a subjective limit of affliction (*AD* 83 = WG 119), the transgression of which precipitates the self into a process of destruction (2:299 = N 339). However, chance, which is at the very center of affliction, is unaware of these differences.[70] For some the limit is reached sooner, for others later; all the same, each person has "in a period of his or her life the possibility to take up root in God,"[71] to ensure that his or her energy may be uprooted from the service of autonomy. One can obviously benefit from this possibility to different degrees. Most often, the destruction of the "I" has begun before affliction sweeps down upon the person, still far from perfection. Such a soul cooperates in the process, but part of the destruction is accomplished from the outside. In this way the soul loses the energy that ought to have been transformed into supernatural energy, and will never gain it back.[72] When the destruction of the I occurs entirely from the outside, the soul is annihilated (2:296 = N 337). If, however, before disappearing, the I has the time, out of rebellion, to hate the good, that is the existence of hell (2:305 = N 343). It is therefore possible to distinguish between the destiny of those who have not taken up root in love, who have not sufficiently paid attention to God, succumbing to affliction and becoming annihilated, and the destiny of those others who choose hell out of hatred for God. But this distinction goes against the logic of Weil's thought; she herself criticizes it for not being precise or intelligible (ibid.). On the one hand, the annihilation of the I ought not to be able to engulf the supernatural foundation of our being. On the other, the neglect of "taking root in love" and the positive act of rebellion against it are both manifestations of the same sinful attitude of inattentiveness; theirs is a difference not of kind, but of degree. Involved in both cases is a wrong use of freedom, which always leads to hell and never just to annihilation. If Weil hesitates to adopt this route, it is owing to her profound inclination to identify freedom for the good with freedom itself, in this way preventing any effort to ontologically ground the mystery of damnation. Consent makes the decisive choice in the ordeal of affliction. But it is identified with the good, and one cannot see how the good could refuse consent to paradise and choose hell.[73] We are therefore brought back to the fundamental difficulty of the metaphysics of man. If the unity of the person precedes good and evil in making the choice between them, then the noumenal becomes neutral. If, on the contrary, there is an irreducible duality in man between good and evil, then all fundamental unity is made unthinkable. In leaning toward the second option, the philosophy of decreation is far from having resolved the antinomy of all speculative anthropology.

The best use of a faculty is when it is exercised in a void, and the supernatural faculty is no exception to this law. However, its "object" being God and not an earthly good, physical suffering and privation do not entail for it a true ordeal through which affliction can be perfected into redemptive suffering.[74] The plenitude of affliction is to continue loving God when he is absent: "Only one who like Job in the depths of affliction still tries to love God feels in its fullness and at the very center of his soul all the bitterness of affliction. If he renounces loving God, he would not suffer in this way.... In this state the soul is torn, nailed to the two poles of creation, inert matter and God. This rent is the reproduction in a finite soul of the creative act of God."[75] It is the moment when the supreme finality of affliction emerges. The "function" of a human being is to consent to the existence of the world and, through the world, to the existence of his or her creator. To consent to the existence of something means to love it. Like a beggar, God waits for the alms of our love. But will he receive them? Under good conditions, in good health and confident, we believe, or at least we dimly sense, that our will is sovereign in this world.[76] But under the blows of affliction, this illusion disappears. If, however, we continue to praise God's creation, if we consent to it, we then give the sole irrefutable proof that we truly love God: "In this way affliction is the surest sign that God wants to be loved by us; it is the most precious witness of his tenderness. It is a completely different thing from paternal punishment. It would be more accurate to compare it to the tender quarrels through which a young engaged couple assure each other of the depth of their love."[77]

If one only confronted in affliction the crushing weight of necessity, it might be said that only processes internal to an ontological economy of salvation are involved. If love for God only had to pass through the ordeal of physical suffering, one would never go beyond the confines of the real, one attribute of which, necessity, would be slowly sublimated into the other, the good. However, through redemptive suffering an encounter with evil itself is effected. Since they most often appear in an indissociable mixture, only through suffering can action over sin be exerted.[78] The possibility of such action still remains incomprehensible; how can compassion toward sin be explained? And yet it is precisely because compassion must be exerted upon evil in redemptive suffering that it is supernatural.[79] Whether they "deserve" compassion or not, sinners suffer from the greatest affliction in the world, the refusal they make to God. Decreated beings can take upon themselves the sin of others in the form of affliction, but how shall they successfully manage its transformation into suffering? This metaphysical mutation[80] remains a mystery only truly illuminated in the context of the doctrine of the Incarnation as a dogma of positive theology.[81]

Chapter 5

The Experience of the Beautiful

Gustave Thibon recounts that he once gave Weil a book by a well-known contemporary philosopher. She read a few pages and then exclaimed with disdain: "Admit it is impossible to have a beautiful soul and write so poorly."[1] After reading this exclamation, one will not be surprised by the importance attributed to the beautiful in the process of decreation.[2] Weil herself was gifted with a very fine artistic sensibility, and even during the years of her last mystical period, she continued to discern in the beautiful a kind of sacred function. Her preferences in art always go toward the great manifestations of genius depicting the tragedy of human life and the search for God with an impersonal tone and absolute majesty, simplicity, and bareness. The *Iliad*, the Book of Job, the *Bhagavad Gita*, Aeschylus and Sophocles, the Song of St. Francis, *King Lear*, and Racine's *Phèdre* alone receive her unreserved admiration.[3] Ancient Greek and Roman sculptures, Romanesque architecture, Giotto, and Velasquez[4] appear to have the same virtue in her eyes; and in music, in addition to Gregorian chant, Monteverdi, Bach, and Mozart radiate "purity and grandeur."[5] These few names give an idea of the range of Weil's interests and knowledge in the artistic domain; they leave no doubt that she was resolutely opposed to any kind of estheticism.[6] In fact, her reflections far surpassed the sphere of art, and she came to connect artistic beauty so closely with being (and to a lesser extent with the good) that the beautiful itself is often presented as a veritable tautology of the real, that is to say, of the intelligible.

The beautiful is that which we are capable of contemplating, a statue or a painting we can watch for long moments, something we can pay attention to (1:129 = N 81). But attention can be exercised only upon what is real, what is. The identification of the beautiful and the real follows from this.[7] Obviously this identity does not mean that the beautiful is something of the order of substance, hypostatized; the real, as we know, is only the network of necessity limiting and organizing the material world. The presence of necessity in the universe is essentially a harmony Weil liked to designate with the Stoic term "order of the world." Necessity, an eternal disposition of God (CS 307 = F 336), demonstrates the obedience of the cosmos to the Lord, an obedience the radiance of which is beauty.[8] Everything that is, is beautiful, since all is in harmony with the will of God, therefore obedient.[9] The total unity of this obedience is the order of the world; and since the Logos is the "organizer" of the world, Weil does not hesitate to identify the beautiful with the Incarnation.[10]

This identification is a striking formulation of the role of mediation assigned to the good, but the interpretation one adopts can determine one's reading of Weil's metaphysics. The mediating role of beauty means that this material world is not entirely abandoned to the indifference of necessity, but that it is radiant with a supernatural presence distinctive to it.[11] This is not a contingent or transcendent presence, but a marvelous immanence. Whether that immanence is understood, as Kant would have it, in a "regulative" or "constitutive" sense is the first question that must be asked. Indeed, there is no other key notion in Weil's thought that better reveals a dual Platonic and Kantian heredity than her notion of the beautiful. From her earliest works, her treatment of the beautiful is strongly penetrated by strictly ethical elements, but it is only in the mature period that the influence of Platonism seems to win out. At this time esthetic reflection appears in a characteristically ontological language; however, we believe that a "critical" interpretation still remains possible and is even necessary if one would defend the coherence of Weil's thought when she speaks of the two fundamental attributes of God.

In spite of the brief formulas so categorically expressing the good in ontological terms, Weil's central preoccupation remains explaining the mediating role of the beautiful in relation to the human soul engaged in decreation—or rather, describing how universal obedience, apparent as the world's order, relates to the human being in the form of the awareness of the beautiful. Required of us is a loving consent to necessity, the divine order of the world; but for the material beings that we are, this is not possible without the cooperation of the senses. Neither the abstract conviction of the intellect nor love hesitant before God is enough to engage our entire being in the difficult path leading to the loving acceptance of the weight of necessity. Necessity can only be loved because it appears as beauty to the sensible part of our being and arouses its complicity.[12] Only in this way can the sensibility experience the real presence of order and eternity in matter.[13] Contemplation of the material world gives birth to awareness of beauty and cannot fail to be loved: "When we are alone in the midst of nature and disposed to attention, something brings us to love what is around us and yet which is only made of brute, inert, mute, and deaf matter. And beauty touches us more vividly the more manifest necessity appears, for example, in the folds gravity impresses into mountains or the waves of the sea, in the trajectory of the stars. In pure mathematics also, necessity is resplendent with beauty."[14]

The essence of the awareness of beauty—Kant would have spoken of the sublime—arising from contemplation of the world is the profound intuition that this necessity, one aspect of which is made of brutal coercion, has another one: obedience to God.[15] And "[b]y the effect of providential mercy, this truth is made sensible to the carnal part of our soul and even in some way to our body" (*IP* 158 = IC 191). Because it appears beautiful to us, we can feel all the sweetness of obedience through the iron links of necessity. Each one of us is in this way as though predisposed, in accordance with a natural complicity, to love necessity; that is why, among "the implicit forms of love for God," love of the beautiful is the easiest, most common, and most natural. Even if mutilated or deformed, a certain sense of beauty is rooted as a powerful motive in the human heart. This innate inclination to love beauty is the *snare* God most frequently uses to "vanquish" the soul and open it to his grace. The idea of a "snare of God" originates in a Homeric hymn. Persephone, daughter of Demeter, was playing in a very beautiful field. The skies above her were smiling at the scent of narcissi; the whole earth and the wide ocean were smiling, too. Hardly had the young girl stretched out her hand to pick an enticing flower than she fell into Hades' trap; she fell into the hands of a god. When she escaped, she had eaten seeds of the pomegranate binding her forever; she became the god's spouse.[16] Persephone is the symbol of the soul caught by the beauty of the world. The somber underground world to which she was taken is "expiatory suffering," the "Night of the Senses." The pomegranate seed is the seed of grace placed in the soul.[17]

God's snares are hidden everywhere in the world; everything around us reveals obedience to necessity and thus can appear with the radiance of the beautiful.[18] Obviously, the only perfect beauty is that of the universe, and all partial, secondary beauty has value only as an opening to the universal beauty emanating from the world's order (*AD* 123 = WG 165). Carnal love, too, in the end comes back to love for the order of the world. Every human being feels a vague love at the sight of the sky and mountain, toward the silence of nature and the warmth of the sun; but that love is incomplete and unhappy, because it is directed toward that which is incapable of responding: matter. We then wish to turn that same love toward a being who can respond, answer yes, give himself or herself over. That is why, when awareness of beauty is associated with a human being, we think the transfer of love is possible; but in reality desire continues to be directed toward universal beauty as an ultimate goal.[19] The beauty of another human being becomes the equivalent, in the imagination, of the order of the world.[20] And since the order of the world is the presence of God, "[t]he desire to love the beauty of the world in a human being is essentially desire for the Incarnation."[21] Once more, the dogma of the Incarnation seems to open up into a metaphysics of the concrete. We have already seen that the eminent value of suffering can be understood only by taking as a point of departure a reflection in which the human compound truly participates in that real unity of the finite and the infinite, the supreme manifestation of which is the Word Incarnate. The same relation is found in, and alone can legitimate, each human desire turned toward a concrete object. Each concrete being belongs to the network of necessity, and this very belonging, as participation in the world's order, is the presence in it of the good.[22] This presence is felt by the desiring soul as the beautiful, enabling it to indirectly turn the body toward the supernatural. Each concrete desire is justified because of the radiance that the good, through the beautiful, exercises over sensibility.

But—and here we return to the original question—what is the ontological status of that which is radiating in this way? Paradoxically, the many peremptory affirmations on what the beautiful "is" only state tautologies drawing attention to the validity of our conviction that the beautiful is not a properly ontological level. On the one hand, a certain number of texts squarely identify the beautiful with God or the good.[23] On the other, in the great majority of cases, the good is defined as a relationship or a harmony, as a structure or network of relations. If we set aside the first group of texts as the evident exaggerations of mystical rhetoric, the beautiful is confined to the world of *order*. Of course, it is not order itself, and in the only completed work where she expressly treats the good (*AD* 117–37 = WG 158–81), Weil is careful to specify that "[t]he world's beauty is not an attribute of matter in itself. It is a relation of the world to our sensibility."[24] The beautiful is therefore, as we have said, the sensible experience of the order of the world. It is not an objective and ontological category, but a reaction of our sensibility with respect to the order of the world.

If we now have established that the beautiful has only a "regulative" status in Weil's esthetics, her esthetics still remains non-Kantian. The order that, as beauty, fascinates and stirs the sensibility is the order of necessity, an intellectual and intelligible order. Rather than being confined to the domain of formal and non-conceptual relations, beauty is above all mathematical. In the final analysis, the beautiful coincides with the intelligible, whose radiance it is. Such ultimate conclusions bear witness to, beyond an "intellectualistic" esthetics, a latent monism found in all metaphysics, even in Kant. The conviction that all that is formal and ordered, even mathematics, is beautiful demands to be put alongside the doctrine of attention, where every action of the soul, even a simple mathematical operation, is a work of freedom. There is nothing contingent in these vast identifications; they derive from the basic ambiguity of the ontology of the two attributes of the real. Weil aspires to find a true distinction between the might and the love of God, but once might has been exposed in terms of necessity, the distinction is blurred and fades. A vertical continuity, and not a horizontal parallelism, is developed between the good and that which is bound to it by its order, necessity. This unification of the good and the intelligible can be traced back to the relation between the good and ideas shown in the *Republic* and that even Kant seems to admit when he subsumes into the noumenal category the in-itself of things and the in-itself of the human soul. The question still bears upon the bringing into relationship of the two causalities, and, by trying to give as answer the intervention of the beautiful conceived as the Incarnation, Weil shows that she is not unaware that the beautiful must be present in this world only through its own free and loving will.

There are two essential attitudes we as human beings can adopt in relation to the world surrounding us: we can seize and appropriate it to ourselves, or we can contemplate and respect it. A famous verse from the *Upanishads* helps Weil to formulate this truth in touching poetic form: "Two birds, inseparably united companions, are in the same tree. One eats the fruit of the tree, the other watches without eating."[25] The unknown author of the *Mundaka Upanishad* wanted to symbolize by the two birds the two eternally contradictory parts of the human soul: "The great human sorrow, beginning in childhood and continuing until death, is that watching and eating are two different operations."[26] Their separation is the work of original sin,[27] and in the present human condition one almost inevitably opts for eating. However, salvation is possible only for those who prefer watching to appropriation; that is to say, for those "in whom awareness of the beautiful has placed contemplation" (*CS* 251 = F 286). Distance is an essential element of contemplation,[28] and through it one can understand the propedeutical role played by beauty in asceticism leading to holiness (*S* 133 = SN 11–12). In the vitiated intersubjectivity of autonomy, the other is never an end, but always a means used without hesitation if our interests appear to require it. The other is only an element in the world of the self and thus is not separated from it by any line of demarcation. One keeps a distance with respect to the beautiful object that pleases us "without interest," having no intention or impulse to appropriate it. Approaching, touching, eating are improper actions entailing "stain" and destruction,[29] whereas awareness of beauty implies a certain renunciation of possession.[30] It is only when established in the supernatural that the soul can be satisfied without appropriation,[31] but the contemplation of beauty already realizes an image of a like perfection in this world.[32] "Watching and waiting—this is the attitude that corresponds to the beautiful" (2:413 = N 415), to the beautiful giving no hold to the imagination through which the self hides the reality of an external thing, tries to modify it, refuses to acknowledge it, all of this with a view to filling up its own emptiness.[33] There is an intimate link between the state of emptiness and that of contemplating the beautiful, with the difference that through the beautiful our sensibility, all the while motionless, receives satisfaction. That the beautiful may be the object of a pure desire is the supreme mystery of this world: "It is a radiance that calls to the attention but gives it no motivation to stay. Beauty always promises, and it never gives anything; it incites a hunger, but it has no nourishment for the part of the soul that looks in this world to be satisfied. It has nourishment only for the part of the soul that watches. It incites desire, and it makes one feel clearly that there is nothing in it to be desired;

for above all else one wants nothing in it to change" (*EL* 37 = SE 29). But when one does not want to change the object of one's desire, one desires simply that it be (2:293 = N 335). And such precisely is perfect desire: desiring what is and desiring only that it be (3:210 = N 550).

Of course, desire for the beautiful does not yet mean one is firmly established in the perspective of God, but in her moving descriptions, Weil is often forgetful of the difference.[34] The role of perfecting she attributes in her maturity to the experience of the beautiful is powerfully anticipated in her earliest writings. I see a temple, she writes in the fine paper "Le Beau et le Bien,"[35] and the first effect of this sight is to make me stop. The name of the god and the artist hardly interest me; my mind is filled with the temple alone. The temple I admire is "an order of stone," an order that is not only mechanical, but that also implies a finality. However, that finality is "without an end"; "the order of stone" is sufficient unto itself. It points to no other far-off ends: "It is there; that is all I can say about it. It is the object."[36] The beautiful temple is the object, and strictly speaking, "the beautiful is the object par excellence."[37] The beautiful is the object, and all that is objective is like an object, that is, contains in a certain way the order and harmony characteristic of the beautiful. People have the habit of saying that the virtuous act is beautiful; its beauty comes from the fact that it expresses the application of an eternal law and that it is blessed with that austerity lacking in the actions of those who follow their subjective interests and inclinations.[38] By refusing to follow our inclinations, that is to say, in wrenching ourselves from ourselves, our actions become good.[39] Such a universalizing depersonalization is at the root of the contemplation of beauty, the state of watchfulness and freedom par excellence: "When we sleep we are mingled with the thing, and each of our desires changes the thing...to wake up is precisely to refuse to lend life to the dead thing.... Being a slave to things is agreeing to change them; freeing oneself from them is to want to change only oneself. Now, no one wants to change the temple.... The same movement by which we free ourselves from the object makes us acknowledge the object as beautiful."[40] To say that I am not the temple comes down to placing it outside myself, as an object, that is to say, as something beautiful. This renunciation can teach us also to refuse what the self gives birth to and maintains in us: our passions and our feelings. In this way we become free. Keeping ourselves separate from the object, which is the attitude proper to the contemplation of the beautiful, is the apprenticeship founding our freedom, that supreme good. It therefore follows that there is a close relation between the beautiful and the good:[41] "it is by the same movement that we detach ourselves from the thing and that we make an object of it, that is, the beautiful."[42] "Apart from this action establishing the unity of the good and the beautiful by wishing it, all is sleep."[43]

Detachment from the objects of this world, which alone nourishes contemplation of beauty, is the model for all detachment. When we desire the object, all the while being detached from it, we desire simply that it exist.[44] But how is it possible to desire something that already is, that one already has, since, in contemplating a beautiful object, one is already in the state of possession corresponding to beauty? Weil answers that question through a reinterpretation of the Kantian theory of "purposiveness without a purpose." We attribute purposiveness to an object, *The Critique of Judgment* tells us, simply because we can only conceive its possibility in supposing a causality according to purposes, that is to say, a will that would have organized it according to a certain rule. Purposiveness itself can be taken for an end when we do not put the causes of the form (of the object) we conceive into a will, even if insofar as its possibility is concerned it cannot be conceptualized otherwise than if it had been deduced from a will.

Therefore we can observe a formal purposiveness without an actual purpose. All goals, when we represent them as causes of pleasure (*Wohlgefallen*), imply an interest on the part of the one they please. Only the simple form of purposiveness, purposiveness without a purpose, implies no interest, and it is for Kant the specific cause of the pleasure of beauty which consists in a certain harmony and a certain regularity.[45]

In Weil these sober and meticulous developments burst into striking formulas in which the critique of esthetic judgment becomes a foundation course in the metaphysics of asceticism. The essential moral neutrality of esthetic pleasure is abandoned for the mysticism of the *Phaedrus*, in which the chaste love of beauty indicates spiritual perfection. In this context of purification, "the hunger for purposiveness"[46] undergoes a universalizing formalization. A purpose is the natural goal of a desire; the tragic paradox of the human condition is that the non-decreated human being cannot live without goals, when in fact there are no genuine goals in this world. Usually it is thought that the goals of a person are particular objectives that only enrich, and hide, the principal goal, life itself, or rather its preservation. For Weil this view is absurd. Existence is a goal only for vegetative energy, a purpose only when one is facing the firing squad (3:126 = N 495). The supplementary energy nourishing the daily life of the self aims toward exterior goals (3:213 = N 546). The miser is so obsessed with his riches that he strives to exist through them, the riches having become the condition of his existence. He does not desire simply to exist, existence not being a good; he wants the riches, but they are inseparable from existence itself. Thus purposiveness moves endlessly back and forth between the riches and the miser.[47] This infernal circle is the distinctive quality of great human passions when a person, a group, or an object, being chosen as an absolute purpose, becomes the condition of my existence; through them and beyond, my real purpose is again existence—which cannot be a purpose for a human being. Therefore, neither the particular object nor existence itself can be purposes. Obviously, the miser (or opium addict or nationalist) is an extreme case, and "reasonably" selfish human beings have many goals and purposes that are not conditions of their existence. When they realize that one of their goals can put them in danger, they abandon it, even if this requires some wrenching. However, the fact remains that, even though we change them, we continue to depend on goals in general. The condition of human existence is the totality of its purposes; it is therefore existence that is aimed for through and beyond these purposes. But the totality of purposes is not a totality, because existence is not one.[48]

That neither particular objectives nor existence as such can be true purposes is explained by the fact that in this world there is but one purpose: the will of God, the occurrences of which are only means (3:321 = N 626). This world is devoid of all purposiveness implying a particular purpose.[49] Decreation itself can also be defined as the disappearance of the illusion of purposiveness that hides the truth of necessity: "If we take ourselves for purpose in the world, the world is chaotic and without purposiveness. If we set ourselves aside, the purposiveness of the world is manifest; but there is no purpose. God is the sole purpose. Yet he is not in any way a purpose, since he does not depend on any means. Everything that has God for a purpose is purposiveness without a purpose. Everything that has a purpose is deprived of purposiveness."[50] Therefore, as long as one desires something as a purpose, it is, by that very fact, deprived of its innate purposiveness: being a link of necessity in perfect conformity with the will of God: "That is why we must transform purposiveness into necessity. It is what one achieves through the notion of obedience. Suffering joined to necessity leads us to purposiveness without a purpose."[51] To conceive of necessity as a purposiveness without a purpose means our having understood it as obedience to God. At the first stage where one learns that always in this world there are only causes and never purposes (*AD* 133 = WG 176–77), one abandons the personal point of view of purposes for the universal perspective of purposiveness without a purpose. At the second stage, the one of loving consent through suffering, purposiveness without a purpose must become a general source of desires without objects. The "mechanism" of such a decreated state where desire is exercised without natural objectives is analogous to the esthetic pleasure incited by the awareness of purposiveness without a purpose in the perception of an object. To the questions how can one desire what one already has, how can one desire something without wanting to appropriate it, we can answer with Kant that the pleasure one feels in contemplation of the beautiful "reinforces and reproduces itself of itself."

The continuation of the pleasure of contemplation has its source in contemplation itself.[52] There are no "practical" reasons for this pleasure; a beautiful thing does not imply any good except itself, such as it appears to us. We are drawn to it without knowing what to ask of it. We desire only its existence; we possess it, and yet we still desire something (*AD* 124 = WG 165–66). Everything is a means in this existence; only beauty cannot be used as a means toward something. It is good in itself, but without our finding a particular good or an advantage in it. The aspiration to beauty is the goal hidden behind all earthly pursuits; beauty confers a touch of purposiveness upon things. Otherwise, there would be no desire, that is, no energy, to pursue them.[53] But beauty is also the purposiveness that excludes purposes. If, while reading a poem, we can explain why a given word is in a given place—for example, to make an idea distinctive, or for an alliterative effect—the poem is not really beautiful. A striving after effect entered into its composition; therefore, according to Weil, no genuine inspiration occurred.[54] The desire for the good does not aim for the realization of any particular goal; it is desire for what does not change, for what is not in the process of becoming.[55] The ends of purposiveness in general (not purposiveness without a purpose) are revealed by their manifestations: anticipations, plans, hopes, all categories of the future, of becoming. But purposiveness without a purpose, the purposiveness belonging to the beautiful, appears detached from the future and focused on what *is* (3:309 = N 618). That is why the desire for the beautiful is the only desire the object of which has nothing to do with becoming.[56]

The immense importance of the experience of beauty resides in this: through it we serve our apprenticeship in detachment. More than any other thing, the beautiful has the power to make us live for a certain length of time in the universal perspective where desire is freed of all particular inclination. This is possible only through a transformation at the very heart of the sensibility, placing energy at the service of a decreative goal: "In a general way, everything that is desired is a source of energy, and energy is on the same level as desire.

Beauty as such is the source of an energy at the level of spiritual life, and this because the contemplation of beauty implies detachment. A thing perceived as beautiful is something we do not touch. . . . To transmute the energy furnished by other objects of desire into spiritually useable energy, an act of detachment, of refusal is necessary. . .the attraction of beauty in itself implies a refusal. . . . The beautiful is thus a machine for transforming lower energy into higher energy" (*SG* 120 = SN 124). Even if the beautiful is only "the copy of the good" (2:189 = N 264), it represents a disinterested objective the pursuit of which requires an uprooting. This has repercussions in the sensibility and entails suffering described by Plato in the *Phaedrus* as the taming of the unruly horse, the carnal part of the soul.[57] When the soul sees a beautiful being who becomes the object of its love, the sinful part draws it violently toward the beloved. But once in its presence, the soul is suddenly reminded of heavenly beauty. It reveres this beauty in the loved one, draws back, and forces the rushing horse to stop with such violence that it falls on its side: "When the unruly horse undergoes this treatment frequently, it is humiliated and obeys the will of the coach driver; and when it sees the beautiful thing, it dies of fright."[58] The death of the self is sought in the experience of the beautiful;[59] even if isolated acts of contemplation do not complete the process of decreation, repeated encounters with beautiful things will nevertheless unfailingly wear the self out. There is a certain bitterness inseparable from the beautiful (2:228 = N 288), originating in the forgetfulness, abandonment, and self-renunciation carried out in contemplation. At this point we begin to distinguish a profound convergence of the awareness of beauty and the awareness of suffering. Still, their relationship is to be sought not in the psychological states they produce but in the attitude they make us adopt toward the real. At first sight, this seems contradictory; in the experience of the beautiful, we are detached from the real we are contemplating, and in suffering we are attached to the real that is tormenting us. The problem of this opposition can be solved only by the notion of compassion.

Weil notes in the *Cahiers* that there is a mysterious relation between feeling with compassion the universal misery of the human condition and experiencing the beautiful (2:215 = N 281). Two short notes will help us understand this secret relation: "Beauty. A fruit one looks upon without reaching for it. Also a misfortune one looks upon without drawing back" (2:218 = N 283). "Contemplating what cannot be contemplated (the affliction of others), without fleeing, and the desirable without approaching: this is the beautiful."[60] Contemplation of the affliction of others is supernatural compassion; contemplation of the desirable is renunciation, the model for which is contemplation of the beautiful. In both cases, one must keep a distance. Not fleeing and not approaching prove acknowledgment and acceptance of reality. Beauty is the manifest presence of the eternal order of reality, whereas affliction is the most eloquent witness of the essence of our condition. We acknowledge that these exist and that they must be accepted because they exist.[61]

That many works of art, works of genius, can represent the most dreadful human sufferings without diminishing their horror, and yet translate them into pure beauty seems to prove that compassion, the contemplation of affliction, is intimately connected to beauty. Homer, the author of the Book of Job, and Shakespeare in *King Lear*[62] all fixed their attention on horror, and their gaze uncovered the beauty hidden in it, which is none other than the reality of that horror expressing the human condition.[63] When an artist fixes attention on the horrible thing being represented, this is another form of the same attention the Good Samaritan gives to the wretched man lying half-dead by the side of the road. In general, all forms of artistic creation are acts of self-renunciation; the person of the artist effaces itself completely before reality (cf. *EL* 16–17 = *SE* 13–16) made to appear beautiful. The Samaritan makes the unconscious victim of bandits exist through similar creative attention; therefore, "[c]harity toward one's neighbor, being composed of creative attention, is analogous to genius."[64]

Nearly forgotten in this specifically ethical interpretation of distance in the beautiful is its distant Kantian origin in "pleasure without interest." Instead of guaranteeing complete neutrality, distance becomes the very basis of participation.[65]

The poet of the *Iliad* was capable of translating the tragic truth of the human condition into the matchless songs of his great poem, for, in detaching himself from his ego, he placed himself in a universal perspective from which he could feel the sufferings of others as his own. It was only through the direct understanding of the human condition revealed in the tortured existence of those whose lives and acts he portrayed that Homer could accede to perfection. The poet does not rebel, does not turn away from misery; he contemplates that which is horrible, suffers, feels an irreducible bitterness, and continues to love God.[66] Brought to its highest point in the work of genius where it surpasses itself, the beautiful achieves decreation. This is the culmination of the mediating function of the beautiful; through the distance it adopts toward itself, creative genius becomes sensitive to the sufferings of others. Representing them in its works, it gives consent to suffering that is from now on its own, all the while offering contemporaries and posterity the possibility of a decreative experience. Homer, Sophocles, and Shakespeare offer no misleading consolation; they represent horror as it is and in this way make acceptance of universal necessity possible for the reader or spectator (cf. *S* 142–44 = SN 18–20). Beauty, like affliction, confronts humanity with something irreducible: "In the beautiful—for example, the sea, the sky—there is something *irreducible*. Like physical pain. The same irreducibility. Impenetrable to the intellect. Existence of something other than myself" (2:257 = N 308).

Once more, we encounter the key notion of contradiction, which, being the manifestation and essence of the real, lies at the source of beauty and of pain. Physical suffering arrests the functioning of the intellect; our natural faculties no longer being of use to us, we stop, watch, and wait (2:413 = N 415). We are face to face with something we cannot change, an irreducible object in front of us. In the realm of knowledge, that which beings encounter as an obstacle is a contradiction. Weil thinks that precisely it is contradiction that is beautiful in the purest form of knowledge, mathematics. The beautiful is the manifest presence, the brilliance of reality. One is certain of reality when one meets something one could not have invented oneself, necessarily originating externally (2:369–71 = N 387–88). The "circle" is certainly my creation; it exists only by virtue of my intellect in action; but I discover it as the site of a certain triangle, and that it *is* so is certainly not my invention. The young Weil, inspired by Kant, thinks that the beauty of geometry resides in such unforeseen correspondences,[67] but later she insists on another aspect of this same fact. She says that beauty in mathematics resides in the contradiction manifested by the presence of an eternal law independent of all I have been able to create (2:371 = N 388).

What is the feeling experienced in the face of that presence? It is the characteristic of beauty to cause pleasure; thus the contradiction that usually incites bitterness and anger seems here to create a joyful state. The paradox is intended and is taken up by Weil, whose ambition is to prove that, in spite of the fact that they are opposite states of mind, joy and suffering have a common essence, one of revealing reality. Awareness of the beautiful, that pure pleasure "without attraction" spoken of in *The Critique of Judgment*, is joy; one might even say that in general, "pure joy is nothing other than the awareness of beauty."[68] Since beauty is manifest appearance, the striking sign of reality, joy can be only a feeling, an awareness of reality. Weil expresses the identity of joy with the awareness of reality in many texts,[69] but this plenitude of the awareness of the real[70] has nothing to do with a vitalist or existential self-expansion. One can experience "objective" joy without any particular motive. I am joyful because the objects of my joy exist and, by the mere fact of existing, they accomplish the will of God. The object of my joy is thus the object par excellence: that which is independent of me and which I try neither to touch, nor to appropriate, nor to devour: "I experience joy because of sunshine, or the moon above the sea, or a beautiful city, or an admirable human being," but I do not formulate any demand in relation to them; indeed, my self is absent from that joy (2:231 = N 291). In other words: "Perfect joy excludes the very feeling of joy, because in the soul filled by the object there is no corner free to say 'I' " (2:58 = N 179). Joy in which all association with the self and sensibility is put aside, that "transcendental joy" (2:231 = N 291), is awareness of the real, essential to the process of decreation.

While joy is analyzed in terms of its kinship with suffering, it is shown as violently opposed to sadness. Weil describes sadness as a loss of contact with reality, that is, as evil.[71] She plainly condemns it as "a wrong de-creation, at the level of the imagination."[72] In keeping with the Christian mystical and ascetic tradition, she considers sadness as an end in itself as something sterile and even ungodly. Being a loss of contact with reality, sadness goes hand in hand with illusion. Through sadness we cannot fulfill our natural vocation, which is to understand the misery of our condition and be reduced to what we really are: nothing. Sadness does not achieve decreation, does not make us capable of abandoning our perspective. On the contrary, it is a sign of pride; I am certain of not being able to wait for any aid outside myself; I know I am alone and without any hope. Hope would be a sign of humility and openness toward some external, unknown thing from which I might receive help. When in a state of profound despair one contemplates death as the irrevocable conclusion of existence, something that must be seen as an absolutely unique fact, the meaninglessness of one's existence, death is not considered as the essence of the human condition and true image of decreation; it is identified with one's own death, and its "right use" is mistaken.[73] Fascinated by the idea of our own death, we put ourselves again at the center of the world and are drawn to idolatry. Whether we hold our lives dear or, caught in fascination, incline toward death, we remain idols unto ourselves. It might be noted that holding life dear is an even better form of autonomy than idolizing death, because living only with the perspective of its own death closes off the soul and makes it impenetrable, whereas the frenzy of goals, desires, and motives at least puts one in contact with others. In the final analysis, sadness is the gravest of sins because it has as its basis the total incapacity or refusal to understand the obedience of creation to God. In the despair of sadness one comes to deny the power of God itself, and this is a form of atheism.

In sadness one is unaware of the almighty power of God, implying refusal, and this same practical dimension of the theoretical faculty is found even more forcefully in its positive use. For Weil, knowledge of God means loving consent to his existence. The privileged role joy and suffering have in decreation originates in the fact that they are the most powerful instruments of the faculty of knowing. Through this faculty we learn that God is and that we ourselves are not. But a wrenching apart is required to make this knowledge attain practical fullness. A purely theoretical knowledge of these truths is possible for the intellect; it can extend for some time to our whole being when we are fascinated and nourished by the joy of the beautiful. However, in awareness of the beautiful the self is only forgotten and suspended, whereas in suffering it is tormented until death.[74] It therefore appears that suffering has preeminence over joy (cf. 2:124 = N 222). This corresponds to Weil's profound spiritual aspirations, but the internal logic of her thought forces her to admit an equivalence between joy and suffering, helping and completing each other as possible paths in the search for God.[75] The memory of the revelation of reality through joy keeps us from plunging into despair, and the joy felt in the knowledge of our nothingness can be inscribed in our sensibility only by suffering. "Joy and pain are equally precious gifts, both of which must be savored fully, and each in its purity. . . ." The reason for this is that "through joy, the world's beauty penetrates into our soul. Through pain it enters into the body. With joy alone, we could no more become friends of God than one can become a sea captain by only studying books on navigation. At the level of physical awareness, pain alone is a contact with that necessity constituting the order of the world; for pleasure does not include the impression of a necessity. A more elevated part of awareness is capable of feeling necessity in joy, and that only through the intermediary of the awareness of the beautiful" (AD 94 = WG 132).

The central task of the process of decreation is our coming to feel and understand in all things the obedience of the universe to God. It is an apprenticeship requiring time and effort. Those who have reached its end realize that the differences between events in this world, whether they be cause for suffering or not, are no more important than those recognized by someone able to read a single sentence reproduced several times in red or blue ink and printed in different characters: "Whoever does not know how to read sees only differences. For someone who knows how to read, all that is equivalent, since the sentence is the same. For one who has completed the apprenticeship, things and events, everywhere, always, are the vibration of the same infinitely sweet divine word. This does not mean that one does not suffer. Pain is the coloration of certain events. Before a sentence written in red ink, the person who knows how to read and the person who does not see the red in a similar way; but the red coloration does not have the same importance for the one as for the other" (*AD* 93–94 = WG 131). The main thing is that, in joy and in suffering, we are in contact with reality and feel the universe through each sensation.[76] These are only two different modes of contact with God, and the contact itself alone counts. That with which the contact takes place is "something that no longer is affliction and is not joy, and is the central, essential, pure, intangible essence common to joy and suffering, and is the love of God itself."[77]

That suffering and joy have a common essence, all the while necessarily remaining different, for the duration of the process of decreation is a fact that eloquently bears witness to the fundamental monist tendency in the hidden structures of Weil's thought. Through suffering we participate in God's sacrifice; we are "bound" to the divine attribute of love, whereas through the awareness of beauty, we take on the order of the world, we are united to the attribute "necessity." Once decreation has been achieved, we see the unity of the two attributes of God and then experience "the love of God," the common source of joy and suffering. Weil's hesitation over the respective value of suffering and joy and her natural preference for the latter, which is "the way of Christ" (cf. *IP* 168 = IC 199), express the central difficulty of her entire ontology. On the one hand, she radically separates the Sovereign Good from necessary being; on the other, she firmly believes that even the latter is inseparable from God. Only the Good is good;

but God is also necessity, and therefore necessity, too, is good. Thus, as we have already said, the good is the unity of oneself and necessity, which means that wanting to defend the omnipresence of God in his two radically different attributes, one ultimately abolishes their essential distinction. All that is noumenal having become good by virtue of common origin in God, it is understandable that instead of being able to preserve a coherent autonomy for the beautiful, one practically merges it with the intelligible which, in its turn, assumes continuity with the good. Weil's Christian insight prevents her from drawing these conclusions following from her rationalist metaphysics, but they are all the same expressed in those texts on the beautiful where esthetics, which "is the key to supernatural truths" (3:323 = N 627), is assimilated into mysticism. That the tenderness of Christ appears equally in affliction and in beauty[78] correctly expresses the ultimate consequence of her thought, even if Weil endeavors to present the experience of the beautiful as a simple foundation course for decreation.

Chapter 6

Time and the Self

Long before she outlined the foundations for her metaphysical and religious anthropology, Weil was already haunted by the idea that time is the determining component of the human condition. In a long paper written in 1926, she explains that time is the form of an existence whose principal characteristic is that of being mediated,[1] and it is precisely time that forms the mediated character of existence. Nothing is immediately given to us in this life. When I desire and want to attain something, I can satisfy my desire, attain my goal only through the mediation of time. Time separates what I have from what I am going to have, what I am from what I am going to be. I feel that time weighs upon all my acts because nothing is immediate for me; nothing can be accomplished outside of time. I exist, that is to say, I act; I want, that is to say I am not sufficient unto myself since everything I do passes through the mediation of time. The law of my existence is that all of these instants are separated and reunited by time. I live so to speak outside myself in time which is not myself and which, however, is present everywhere in my life.[2]

Time expresses my radical powerlessness to act without an intermediary.[3] This iron law of mediation actualized in the indispensable role of time is the central enslavement of human life. It truly is the source of all human subjection:[4] "[W]e have no power over the present because it exists," quotes one of Weil's pupils; "we have no power over the past because it exists no longer; we have no power over the future because it does not exist yet."[5]

We have been determined as subject to time. We cannot change the fact that time "passes," but we have a certain power over "how" it passes. This "how" is the special, personal characteristic of our consciousness of time. We "feel" time; we are aware of it according to the way we fill "our" time and according to what we fill it with. We are surely slaves to time, but a pact exists between slave and master. By virtue of that pact, we have some mastery over our time in many moments of our lives (cf. *En* 255–56 = *NR* 301). Still, time is a difficult partner, and we must always renew our efforts to retain control over it. While working in factories, Weil experienced how time becomes intolerable when the activity one carries out is deprived of rationality, that is, a certain understanding of the connected movements and the immediate and future goals of these movements. If we have this understanding, we are then able to mentally survey a greater unit of time than the brief moments of the gestures of working. But thought can not sink into a series of endlessly repeated moments. It needs something reasonably varied, a certain diversity of movements, in order to have a vivid mental image of the completed action. In Chapter 7, we will make a more detailed analysis of the special problems of time in work, but for the moment it seems sufficient to insist on the fact that the lack of initiative and monotony engendered primarily by assembly-line work are only striking manifestations of the ever present, although often unnecessary, subjection to time. What is important in a human life, we read in the *Journal d'usine*, is "the way one minute is linked to the next, and what this costs a person in his or her body, heart, soul—and above all in the exercise of the faculty of attention—to effect that linking minute by minute" (*OC* II.ii.267).

If the linking of successive moments is a free, rational act, that is, originating in personal deliberation and foresight of the unfolding of the action in question, then we control the time in which the action is accomplished.[6] But when we do not foresee the next minute because they are all alike, when we are forced to repeat the same movement in the minutes that follow, we no longer have power over the future; we are reduced to the present.[7] In this case, a human being, like a material thing, simply endures the passage of time and lives, so to speak, in the naked present.[8] Living in the present moment and being forced to make the same movements all day, all year, all one's life creates monotony. But monotony can appear under two totally different forms: "Monotony is what is most beautiful or dreadful in the world. Most beautiful if it is a reflection of eternity. Gregorian chant. Most dreadful otherwise. The circle is the model for the beautiful kind of monotony, the oscillation of a pendulum for the atrocious kind."[9]

Nothing great exists in this world without some monotony, and as Weil notes, there is more monotony in a Bach concerto or Gregorian chant than in an operetta. Monotony is simply a sign of our life in time: "we have been thrown out of eternity, and we must really go through time painfully, minute by minute" (*OC* II.ii.304 = SWR 69).

We must necessarily share in this monotony, but we can give it a different content according to the way in which we reconcile it to the vocation of the human spirit to rule over time. Time for the peasant and time for the worker are illustrations of this difference: "The absolutely uniform, and at the same time varied, and continually surprising succession of the days, months, seasons, and years is exactly suited to our misery and to our greatness. . . . The work of the peasant obeys this rhythm of the world out of necessity. . .the sun and the stars fill time beforehand with a limited variety of structures given order by regular returns, structures intended to house an infinite variety of absolutely unforeseeable events partially deprived of order" (*OC* II.ii.304 = SWR 69).

This is why the "model for the beautiful kind of monotony" is the cyclical character of the succession of events, where the human spirit retains the possibility to survey and foresee, without, however, any power to alter what it surveys and foresees. In an opposite way, the time of the worker is the illustration of "horrible monotony":[10] "Uniformity and variety are mixed there also, but this mixture is the opposite of that procured by the sun and stars. . .the future of someone working in a factory is empty because of the impossibility to foresee, and more dead than the past, because of the identicalness of instants following each other like the tick-tock of a clock. A uniformity imitating the movements of clocks and not of constellations, a variety excluding all rule and consequently all foresight makes time unlivable, unbreathable for human beings."[11]

The horrible monotony in which human life is suspended in the naked present is opposed to the "beautiful monotony" or at least the approximation of it, where the human spirit can grasp what it is subject to. "Beautiful monotony" is all the more precious if it is confronted in the ever-changing world of becoming, or even in the world of reasonable goals, where our hunger for purposiveness is appeased by the healthy nourishment of limited goals, those practical havens for our ever insatiable hopes, desires, and plans. The world of becoming where goals are pursued is the world of the self, whereas subrational monotony is the dominant trait of vegetative life, *beneath* the self. This monotony corresponds to a kind of energy that is, so to speak, *beneath time*, whereas the world of ends and aspirations raises supplementary energy "to the level of time."[12] But there is an eternal and hidden part of the soul to which there is a corresponding energy "beyond time." The ultimate goal of a human being is to destroy the intermediate sphere of the self and render vegetative energy subject to the supernatural in such a way that, already in this world, one can live "beyond time" (*CS* 182 = F 224). This means changing one's relation to events occurring in time, and the gradual change of this relation is identical to the progress of the decreative process. Finally, living beyond time is shown to be the characteristic of the decreated state since decreation means "the end of time."[13]

In a note in the *Cahiers*, Weil states that time is the Cave.[14] Time is the self's environment where it pursues its goals of self-expansion. The darkness of the Cave is a component of human illusions and ignorance, in the same way time belongs to the fabric of which life and death are woven. The illusion that the self rules over the future as its particular fiefdom determines the whole system of its finality and gives it the deceptive feeling of an effective and deserved continuity. However, time is not only the essential element of personal existence; it can also serve as a chosen instrument for transcending it. Time is also the Cross,[15] the weight of necessity making the soul feel how vulnerable and profoundly subject it is to the mediation of time. The time shown to be the instrument of expiation (cf. 2:196 = N 268) is the consequence of original sin; by his disobedience to the will of God, Adam was excluded from eternity and imprisoned in time.[16]

Time is therefore the consequence of, and punishment for, sin (*CS* 153 = F 198). But its meaning goes far beyond humanity, however much it is linked to it. Time is not only the human cross, but is also, and above all, God's cross.[17] It is the sign of God's renunciation in the act of creation, for "God himself cannot make what has existed not to have existed" (*CS* 90 = F 140). Time is the abdication of God. This means that his act of creation and original sin are only different "effects" of his renunciation, of which time is the manifestation.[18] Time is the consequence of the fall (cf. 2:348 = N 373). The originally Kantian sense of the subjectivity of time receives a new meaning. Time is the form of "representations" human beings alone can conceive, but it is precisely the supremely personal act of original sin that "causes" time "to be born." Without humanity, there would be no time; time is the limit God imposes on himself through human existence. He is not in time, but his patience, waiting for us to consent to his love, "binds" God to time (cf. *CS* 91 = F 141).

Time is the enslavement God imposes on himself; it is the infinite distance between God and God all through which divine love circulates.[19] A sensation of dread and feeling of absurdity accompany the realization that for Weil God himself "owes" his supreme reconciliation to time, to the fruit of sin. According to the dialectics of decreation, the Fall is a *felix culpa* not for humanity only, and evil is an essential element not in the economy of human salvation only, but also in God's. Obviously God has freely chosen to submit to an ontological system in which good is not perfected without evil and the real achieves full reality only after going through the unreal. But this choice has been made, and now all is paradox. In the present context, this can be summed up by saying that the eternal is reconciled with itself only by time that eliminates itself.

The self-elimination of time signifies that it is the active milieu of its own surpassing. God created in order to be loved, but he was not able to create someone or something that would be God, and he cannot really be loved by someone other than God—thus, a contradiction. In other words, the contact of the creature with God and of God with a certain point of the creation are two contradictory facts. The contradiction must be resolved by "becoming," by the appearance of time within which the process of decreation unfolds.[20] The seed of love at the origins of the process bears fruit in its time, the void it creates "grows through the simple flow of time. . .if the length of life were indefinite and not limited by death, this growth. . .of the void in which God lives would continue until the achievement on this earth of the state of perfection."[21]

The seed of eternity bears fruit in time, according to the "progress," "the flow" of time. The earth in which this seed is planted is the uncreated part of the soul, but the rain and warmth that make it grow are time. Time is therefore in some way a party to eternity.

"The state of perfection," according to some of Weil's texts, can be reached already in this life; we can accomplish a complete change in our system of temporality, still remaining subject to time as the formal and universal condition of all our representations. We are created in such a way that our lives cannot stay devoid of purposiveness, even for an instant (3:217 = N 555). All purposes being in the future, the search for purposiveness projects the self in its direction. Purposes are like reassuring fires in the dark future we are anxious to reach, and we are anxious too to be the ones who light them. Thus even the past also is the realm of purposiveness, for victories, successes, pleasures are to be found there—compensations for our efforts and pains (2:159 = N 244).

The future is the true dimension of personal existence, the essence of which is "directed effort."[22] We cannot live without the illusion of mastery over the future; even the most elementary needs of the body, like hunger or thirst, "cry out" for future satisfaction. They are reflected in the "carnal part" of the soul in the form of the claim to govern the future: "The arrogance of the flesh consists in believing it has a hold over the future, that hunger gives it the right to eat, thirst to drink imminently. Privation disabuses it of its illusions and makes it feel in anguish the uncertainty of the future, the absence of influence, the total powerlessness of human beings over even the immediate future" (CS 47 = F 101). The entire life of the self is directed toward the future (CS 43 = F 97–98), because its substratum is supplementary energy, "produced" only by motives whose ends are in the future (or in the past) (2:67 = N 184). Supplementary energy belongs to particular desires, and the only way to destroy it is to see to it that these desires are no longer directed within time (2:170 = N 251). This comes down to breaking the ties of the present with the future and the past.

We think that the energy we have spent in the past constitutes an investment, and we hope it will bring in interest. Also in recalling pleasures and honors we have acquired, or good deeds we have done, we can feel a kind of contentment, a deep satisfaction, or pride. All these feelings seem in some way to give new life to energy. For a miser, the thought or sight of his riches is a source of energy. His riches are the materialization of all his past labors, of the energy spent over long years. When his treasures are stolen, something of his "frozen past" is taken away from him (2:64 = N 183). It is the same with jealousy. The infidelity of a loved one makes us lose our past; jealousy is the awareness of the fragility of the person: my past is at the other person's disposal. We experience the same loss of the past when someone dear to us has died.[23] In mourning the loss of others, we are really mourning our past and our future, both escaping from us.

Breaking ties with the past is the only way to escape from enslavement, but that implies also breaking ties with the future.

One must renounce one's own past, which entails the renunciation of future compensation for past acts, ordeals, and sufferings.[24] This renunciation is the true essence of all renunciation (cf. 2:64 = N 183). To renounce the past and the future is to stop in the present; this means the knowledge and acceptance of our nothingness. We are only a point in time (CS 47 = F 102). Being reduced to the present moment also implies a sinless state, since sin is essentially a claim to mastery over the future, the refusal of future love or suffering. It is also revolt against past suffering, or the refusal to repent of an evil act committed in the past: "If we contemplate ourselves at a specific moment—the present moment, cut off from past and future— we are innocent.... Isolating a moment in this way implies forgiveness. But this isolation is detachment."[25]

In the short essay on the "Our Father," Weil best explains the implications of renunciation of the past and future, the tearing away from becoming (3:210 = N 550–51). She made the "discovery of the Pater" during her stay at Gustave Thibon's farm in the Ardèche valley (AD 40 = WG 71). The daily recitation of this prayer with "absolute attention" was the basis of her deepest spiritual experiences (AD 40–41 = WG 70–71); and it was at the end of her stay, or just after her departure, that she wrote a spiritual and metaphysical commentary on the Lord's Prayer (AD 167–76 = WG 216–27). This meditation is her only mature writing almost completely devoted to the moral implications of the human being's relationship to time and to its influence on the life of prayer.

From this essay and a passage in the Cahiers that is its outline (2:258–60 = N 309–10), we learn that human beings are capable of conceiving of the totality of time under the three aspects of the past, present, and future, and even that we need to conceive of it under these three aspects because they are the form of our awareness of time in the process of decreation. When we think of events taking place in the totality of time as constituting God's will, we consider that totality as the past, as if everything had been determined once and for all.[26] Finding the will of God in all things that happen and as a result wanting these to happen is the "perfect request" that "tears us away from the imaginary within the real, from time within eternity, and out of the prison of self" (*AD* 168 = WG 217). In perpetuated desire, we consider the entire universe as something absolutely determined once and for all by the eternal act of the creator, something essentially "in the past," although it must continue into the future.[27] But the Lord's Prayer is also a call to turn toward our own past. It asks us to give back to our debtors "all we think our due. . .all the rights we think the past gives us over the future."[28] We must "[a]ccept that the future still be unsullied and intact, strictly bound to the past by ties we do not know, but completely free of ties our imagination believes it imposes. Accept the possibility that anything, and anything to us in particular, can happen, and that the day tomorrow can make of our entire past life a vain and sterile thing" (*AD* 173 = WG 223).

We must believe that the ties between past and future events have no relation to our wishes, desires, or needs. This amounts to our realizing that we have absolutely no power over the future, not even over our own future. We must understand the falseness of our principal demand on the universe, that of the permanence and continuation of our personality. Such understanding implies renunciation of the future.[29]

To think of the totality of time under the aspect of the future is to consider it as the location of events filling us with hope or fear.[30] Such feelings must not take the place of our obligation to desire and love all that happens because everything takes place in conformity with the will of God. The immense difficulty hidden in this demand is that we cannot think of the future without anguish: I myself who must love and desire future events, I myself can be destroyed in the next instant. We must not even have recourse to the sublime consolation that only the self, that "fleeting and automatic product of external circumstances" (*PS* 115 = SN 188), is subject to destruction. We must not believe that the uncreated part of the soul, the supernatural in us, is not subject "to time and the vicissitudes of change," because then we do not really accept our own nothingness (cf. *AD* 175 = WG 225–26). True humility, an essential part of the procession of virtues accompanying the decreated soul, is waiting, and waiting serenely, for what time will bring, even if change or destruction must strike at the heart of our being.[31]

Acceptance of waiting, a certain immobility, is essentially an attitude of the present. For the self, the essence of time is the future, the link between the past and the future and between the present and the future. Time becomes the location of decreation only at the moment when, ceasing to be an arrow pointed toward what is to come, it is changed into a needle moving in a circle that is always the same. Tearing the future away from time is an operation similar to emptying desire of its objects and purposiveness of its purposes; all of these involve emptying a human being of the self. Strangely enough, being emptied of one's self is the only state in which we need no intermediaries to put us back together. The self once forgotten or having forever disappeared, we live without past or future and in the present moment. In this state of detachment time is only an image, a "moving image" of eternity, being simply the framework within which the necessary events of this world unfold.[32] Nevertheless, it is not natural for human beings to be satisfied with such a system of temporality (cf. 1:27 = N 12); we desire the infinite power of eternity, and our time becomes a dangerous "substitute" for it (2:159 = N 244). Nothing is more difficult than renouncing power over the future, for our efforts need to be directed (2:110 = N 213) and are not when we live only in the present. Moreover, we are anchored in the future because it is the site of all progress, and the desire for progress is inseparably linked to the instinct for expansion. The sight of a road inspires the desire to walk,[33] because the road appears as the very image of time; it implies progress, passage directed from the past toward the future.[34] The road one is going to walk on implies a certain feeling of possession, of mastery. But a road in the form of a circle would not contain the same motivating character. Walking in order to return to the same point gives the impression of having made no progress and exercises no appeal. A similar psychological mechanism is found in the miser's passion for the succession of numbers (2:47 = N 171). This progress has extraordinary power over human beings; it can be measured, and at the same time it has no limits; it goes straight toward infinity. This indicates that we have precise and clear points of reference in life; we can measure riches, count the fruits of our labor, and at the same time be intoxicated by the infinite perspectives open before us.

It is always the future that fascinates and attracts us, and the particular ends it puts forth are pretexts to pursue it. The condition of my existence is the totality of my goals, but the essential element of my purposes does not reside in the particular and limited pleasures and benefits they bring to me. Pleasures and benefits influence the self to choose one purpose over another, but the underlying reason for its choice is that the self needs purposes as such. People and things motivate the actions of a human being, but that they motivate the self is explained by the need for expansion that is the very essence of the self (cf. *IP* 138 = IC 175). All expansion is necessarily future; one therefore does not aspire toward the future because it is the "frame" for pleasures and profits, but because it is the "frame" for self-expansion.[35] One comes to desire the future without necessarily wanting to attain a concrete goal. It seems that future events are not desired because they are motives for the self, but, on the contrary, they are motives for the self because they are in the future.[36] Still, one might note that if particular ends serve only as pretexts, the search for the future itself only disguises escape from God. To live oriented toward the future is to have confidence in the illusory power of mastery over events to come, in the continuity of personal existence— in short, in our own infinity. Striving toward the future is therefore shown to be the principle of autonomy, because it is, in the end, the principle of the unity of the self.

Again Kantian theory has undergone a profound meta- morphosis. Weil insists on the non-existence of time,[37] which is only the a priori formal condition of our representations. However, the awareness of time is an irreducible fact supposed by the transcendental deduction: without awareness of time, we would be only this Humean bundle of perceptions, the "dust of self." In Weil, this guaranteeing role of time becomes exclusive, even if the unity itself remains functional. The unity of the self is not due to a substantial center, because the self has no center separate from its periphery. The self has no being; it has only having.[38] It consists of this: having, possessing, appropriating. The self is not; it extends and attaches itself; it is the function of maintaining the dynamic network of its possessions. Besides, even this description is not really correct because it continues to represent the self in terms of space, in terms of its incapacity to keep a distance from the object of its desire. Space symbolizes exteriority; through it the self appears as a relation between itself and its goals, whereas in reality there is only a purely interior relation, one between two of its different moments. All this is no way contradicts the reflection on the fact that existence in its nakedness cannot be an end for the self and that in reality the sole end of the self is itself. This is because it is *to have* that the striving for the preservation of the self in a vacuum requires goals at each instant, and they will accomplish the mediation between the self now and the self later. As a result, self-expansion, through and beyond the particular objects in which it is embodied, is the striving of the self oriented in time toward its own continuity. The self is therefore a striving oriented in time, and this definition perfectly suits its ontological status. At issue is an interior and subjective "event," and the separation with the world of objective necessity thus is respected and the self can claim to occupy a sphere of its own. However, all form of real existence being denied to this striving, its identification with the self confirms the basic unreality of our autonomy.

The structure of the self can now be understood as a pure striving toward the future, and this somewhat dramatic expression shows the modification undergone by the notion of the awareness of time in relation to its origins in *The Transcendental Aesthetic*. It is true that the fact of adopting a subjective maxim as the motive for actions implies governing activity not by an unchanging, and thus eternally present, law, but according to a future goal; still, as for the genesis of theoretical knowledge, time does not ever seem to infringe upon the indispensable but neutral role critical idealism bestows upon it. The ties between the solely phenomenal knowledge of things and our subjection to the laws of time are direct and irreducible, but there is no reason to suppose a moral or metaphysical fall at their origin. It is otherwise in Weil, who believes in the solidarity of time and original sin. Without her having elaborated a doctrine on the corruption undergone by theoretical reason in the Fall, "the primacy of the practical," through the intervention of the doctrine on perspective, is fully apparent in her view on time. The pure temporal ambition that constitutes the self is never abstract and neutral, revealing the essential fact that the functional unity of the self is always practical. Obviously, the wrong kind of practical unity is auto-nomy, which vitiates even our theoretical operations or rather makes it impossible to adopt a truly theoretical—that is, respectful and non-prejudicial—attitude toward the real. It follows paradoxically that the primacy of the practical is expressed here by the requirement to transform that which must be into being, and will into knowledge. This means that "perfection," in the practical order, is precisely the renunciation of a practical position. Time must become again what it is, the simple frame for representations following universal neces-sity, that is, the will of God. One is then reduced to the present.

Considering the totality of time under the aspect of the present has two meanings. The first is to reveal eternity and its radiance, beauty, in all the events occurring in the universe.[39] The second meaning of our reduction to the present is expressed in the sentence of the Our Father that Weil translates in this way: "Our bread, the supernatural bread, give us this day" (*AD* 170 = WG 220). The supernatural bread is divine grace in the form "of transcendental energy" that carries out actions by means of our soul and body without nourishing the self.[40] Emphasized is the adjective "daily," for we cannot ask for grace once and for all; we cannot accumulate a supply of grace. We cannot bind our will today for tomorrow; we cannot conclude a pact with God to have his grace tomorrow, even in spite of ourselves. Requesting his presence is the equivalent of consenting to that presence: "Consent is an act;

it can only be actual. We have not been given a will that can be applied toward the future. Everything that is not effective in our will is imaginary. The effective part of the will is effective immediately; its effectiveness is not distinct from itself. The effective part of the will is not effort directed toward the future. It is consent, the yes of marriage" (*AD* 171 = WG 220).

The way of "learning" ever-renewed consent passes through beauty or suffering. When we contemplate beauty, we give our consent at each moment that it continue, that it not change. Thought does not venture into the future, nor does it evoke the past; it is in a sense outside time. We are so filled with joy that we are not aware of time passing; we forget the self for a certain length of time. The contemplation of beauty uproots us for brief moments from the natural orientation in time in order to bring us into eternity.[41] More important, the contemplation of beauty teaches us a new relation to time in general. The two horses of the *Phaedrus* are like symbols of our consciousness of time. The unruly horse wants to rush headlong into the future, while the obedient horse stops and waits in the present. The contemplation of beauty is one of the best possible forms of the "education" of our consciousness of time. It teaches us to forget the self and, in a way, contributes to its destruction; but without suffering, this destruction will not be accomplished. Suffering carries out the destruction of the self by destroying its particular consciousness of time. Physical pain alone can put human thought in chains,[42] because when we suffer, we can think of nothing other than our suffering. Joy and pain both can turn our orientation away from time (2:111 = N 213), but in different ways. Joy raises us up into eternity, pain plunges us into time (*CS* 154 = F 199). While contemplating beauty, we are not aware that time passes; while feeling pain, we find time intolerably long. To decreate our sinful relation to time, to transcend it, we must escape it as well as plunge into it; this is what occurs in affliction. In affliction, one is as it were crushed by time, for our natural capacity to govern it is weakened. One has no power over the future and no more comforting memory of the past; one lives in the present, the realm of humiliation and pain where even false consolations become impossible. This state is equivalent to the imminent approach of death, the horror of which is due principally to the fact that it forces us to realize that now we can no longer expect any compensations.[43] Thus not to ask for future compensations for a past expenditure of energy is to accept death (2:107 = N 211), a state with neither past nor future. By our consent, the horror of being without an orientation in time can be transformed into pure suffering; we accept that our being is reduced to the present, to a momentary state. As a result, death is a momentary state, and since we are without sin when we live in the moment (2:65 = N 183), death is the state of innocence par excellence (cf. *CS* 47 = F 102).

Decreation is the process of transforming our relationship to time, but time itself, in its "objective" reality as necessary condition for our representations, plays a highly important role in this transformation. The death of the self must necessarily take place in time, that is, before physical death. What is required is a radical transformation of our awareness of time, the precondition of which is our remaining in time. The mistaken attitude toward the directed continuity of time is exorcised only by the passage of time, whose assumed weight amounts to the acceptance of necessity. Time is not a simple neutral frame in which decreation is carried out; it is its active environment, because only through it do we separate reality from dream. Our goal as human beings is eternity, but we can only reach it through time, by feeling the painful and heavy pressure exerted on our being by the passing of each moment. "Time leads out of time" (2:211 = N 278); indeed, it leads toward eternity. Obviously, this does not mean that we can ever have actual and total awareness of all that was, is, or will be, this being characteristic of an eternal subject, which a human being is certainly not. But we can have an attitude of eternity toward all we grasp, because we live in the present, that reflection of eternity in our consciousness of time (cf. *IP* 33 = IC 98). We have said that God is bound to time inasmuch as he is bound to humanity, but it can also be said that humanity is linked to eternity inasmuch as it is linked to God. A human being becomes linked to God and achieves that attitude of eternity when "crossing" the whole of time, that is, when destroying the capacity to be oriented in it. Our resolution not to refuse our consent to suffering, to its lasting hours, weeks, or a whole lifetime, is what "transports us to the end of time, into eternity."[44]

It is not difficult to understand that once again it is a matter of the ordeal of the quarter-hour, this time revealed on its own terms; in terms of time. During the quarter-hour, decreation is completed: "In any degree of pain whatsoever, when practically the whole soul cries inwardly, 'Let it be over, I can endure no more,' let one part of the soul, even if it were to be infinitesimal, say: 'I consent that this last throughout the perpetuity of time, if it suits the divine wisdom that this be so' " (CS 176 = F 219). The soul plunged into the abyss of time gives its consent to stay there and even to be more deeply sunk into it; it is deprived of power over the future and consents to it. The soul makes a choice between refusal and acceptance, but the choice is made, or at least carried out, in time. The quarter-hour is the duration of that consent, and its indispensable character is an eloquent proof of the role of time as a component of decreation.

The preliminary condition of consent is the annihilation of that part of the soul existing at the level of time through the destruction of supplementary energy.[45] When this energy is destroyed, vegetative energy is exposed and must sustain the acceptance of pain. However, vegetative energy is beneath time, serving only to maintain physiological mechanisms having nothing to do with the future designs of the self. As a result, a form of energy without connection to time must sustain pain during a certain time; it must become the channel of a will that at each instant accepts pain the next instant.[46] This quarter-hour of suffering is the equivalent of a perpetual duration for the soul; it will "cross the indefinite length of time" during the ordeal and pass over to the other side, into eternity.[47]

The meaning of this test lies in its being an ordeal. The passage of time destroys the object of all our attachments and enables the self to discriminate between what is essential to it and what is not. Milarepa, the great Tibetan saint, abandoned all his earthly possessions, keeping only a bowl for food. One day the bowl broke, and he suddenly realized that he had not understood that the bowl was perishable and, like the bowl, so were all other things on this earth.[48] For Weil, the meaning of this anecdote is to reveal the perishable and unessential character of our attachments through the universal fragility of their objects. The passage of time breaks the objects of our passions, breaks all that is corruptible in them, and, as a result, it "tears seeming apart from being, and being apart from seeming, with violence" (2:137 = N 230).

An analogy with the role of space represents another aspect of the discrimination between the illusory and the real exercised by time: "In sensible perception, if one is not sure of what one sees, one changes one's position while observing. . .and the real emerges. In the inner life, time takes the place of space. With time one is changed, and if through the changes one keeps one's gaze directed upon a certain thing, in the end the illusion disappears and the real appears. The condition is that attention be a gaze and not an attachment."[49] The duration of time is a component of the act of attention perceiving reality; this is true for both the esthetic and ethical domains. When one contemplates a painting by a master for three hours, over the course of those three hours contemplation changes in nature; from a superficial and fleeting pleasure, it ripens into a joyful participation that suspends self-expansion. With respect to the contemplation of the possibility of an evil action, ultimately the temptation is in a sense exhausted, and one can no longer act on it. However, if a human being, motionless and waiting, fixes attention upon the possibility of a good act, he or she will necessarily accomplish it. Always at work is a transformation of energy following upon a change in perspective.[50] Acceptance of the passing of time makes it possible to maintain a distance from what we are in the process of observing; we achieve a more faithful reading of the relations of the external world because we ourselves have consented to bear the weight of the real. Only by means of the duration of time can the abstract faculty of pure intelligence be realized as practical attention consenting to the external good, even if that entails a wrenching apart and renunciation for the self.

It is therefore not only in ascetic detachment that the irreducible reality of time plays an important role; it is indispensable also in active charity toward one's neighbor. Indeed, the reality of time is the basis of this obligation, consisting in keeping a human being with all our might from being snatched up by suffering or death, although suffering and death belong to the divine order of the earth willed by God. It cannot be denied that there is a "contradiction between accepting all possible things, without exception, in advance, in the event they were to occur, and, at a specific moment, in a specific situation, going almost beyond the limit of what one can do to prevent a certain thing from happening." If there is a solution for this contradiction, it is to be sought in becoming, in time. "The duration that separates an event to come from the present is real. One prepares oneself to accept someday a possible given misfortune in the future when it is over, but one does not confuse it with the past" (1:79 = N 47–48). I must be ready to accept the death of a dear one when his or her death has already taken place, when it has become part of the order of the world; but if there is a moment when that person is in mortal danger and I have the power to save him or her by reaching out my hand, I must do it. In doing this I am not rebelling against the order of he world. At the moment of danger itself, that person's life, and not his or her death, is a fact; that life, and not that death, is a part of the order of the world. In the same way, the power to save that person, which belongs to me, is part of reality, of physical necessity, since it originates in the spatial position of my body and the "mechanical energy" it contains (1:79–80 = N 47–48). I am not rebelling against the order of the world when I do everything in my power to save a human being, on condition that I am ready to accept his or her death when it comes.

These two attitudes—a supreme effort to save someone and perfect acceptance of that person's death—are both required for the consent I owe to the order of the world. I exert myself to save someone because his or her life is a present fact, and

I accept his or her impending death because, at the moment it occurs, it will be a present fact. But as long as it is not a present fact, as long as I am separated from it by duration, I have the right (and the duty) to fight against it. Owing to the reality of duration these two attitudes are radically different from each other and at the same time wholly justified.

Acceptance of the reality of time always underlies the correct attitude and just action; it is only through time, the structure of human subjectivity, that we understand and assume the reality of our condition. Time carries a human being toward death, toward "that which we cannot bear and yet which will come. 'Let this cup be taken away from me.' "[51] Indeed, the only violence we undergo is the violence entailed by the passing of time,[52] but we must not ask that it stop. That would be a form of revolt against the order of the world of which "my" time is an integral part. Wanting to "escape from time" (1:51 = N 28) is a sin, and at heart, "[a]ll sins are attempts to flee from time" (CS 47 = F 102). We must accept time, the fact that it leads me to suffering and death, and, inseparable from it, the end of all dominion over time. Diving into the abyss, which is complete subjection to time, is identical to renunciation as such (2:122 = N 221): it forces God to send us eternity (CS 57 = F 111). In this way, "[v]irtue is to undergo time, to press time against one's heart until the heart is crushed. Then one is within the eternal" (CS 47= F 102). When one accepts everything that can happen as the unfolding in time of the eternal decisions of the divine wisdom (CS 333 = F 360), one is brought into the perspective of God himself, into eternity (CS 92 = F 141–42). Eternity is the time-consciousness of the decreated state; one continues to live in time, but it has become neutral and indifferent, and one imitates from this moment on "the abandonment of inert things to time."[53] This is neither immobility nor inaction, but the accomplishment in an eternal present of the actions prescribed by the will of God.

Chapter 7

Non-Acting Action

Up to this point we have addressed what might be called the "passive" human response to God's call. The notions of obedience, attention, void, suffering, contemplation of beauty, and renunciation of power over time speak especially of things humanity is confronted with and must endure, accept, or abandon. Nothing has yet been said about the activities that must accompany "the ripening of the seed." The achievement of decreation does not signify the end of life, since one "accepts from God a new creation,"[1] where energy "at a new level"[2] "nourishes" desire without object. The human being, who then lives in "eternity" (cf. CS 178 = F 220), carries out actions that are signs of perfect obedience. Obviously, the decreated state must not be considered something completely static, as a perfection that, once attained, could no longer be changed, even in the sense of a more profound union with God. However, it has now been shown that, after the ordeal of the quarter-hour when the soul is united with God, a moment must come when one is as it were established in the decreated state, having received from God a new existence and continuing to act only for "the salvation of others."[3]

There is no absolute distinction between decreative and decreated activities. Even if decreative activity precedes decreated activity in time, it is comprehensible only because of the latter.[4] Most human beings are capable for a few moments in their lives of suspending autonomous activities, whether they are absorbed in purely intellectual work or guided by highly altruistic motives; in a way, they anticipate the decreated state. The immense majority of people do not have the vocation to transform these fleeting glimmers into uninterrupted light; instead, they must exercise a patient and incessant effort in order to make their daily activity conform more and more to the action belonging to the new creation.

The distinctive trait of the decreated state is a "passive activity" (*AD* 149 = *WG* 194) that Weil calls "non-acting action." The origin of this notion is to be sought in the *Bhagavad Gita*;[5] and indeed in the margins of Weil's copy of this great poem she copied out several lines of major importance for her theory of non-acting action: "Those who can see inaction in action and action in inaction are wise among human beings; they are balanced when effecting action"; "As busy as they might be, in reality they do not act, accomplishing action only with the body, contracting no stain"; "becoming impassioned only for the good of all beings."[6]

Non-acting action is a concept akin to desire without an object and attention in the void. It implies a certain "formalization" of the concept of action emptied of its "personal" elements, and it denotes only a certain succession of physical movements that must be accomplished out of obedience to some sort of necessity. At heart, it is a compromise between moral and metaphysical immobility, fitting to the decreated state, and movement, necessary for all physical action. What can be deplored in an action is not the fact that it implies movement, but rather that this movement aims toward a particular end. The ideal is to reach a stage where "movements are no more action than is immobility."[7] In a physical action expressing and embodying a just intention, the conflict between necessity and the good gives way to their reconciliation. This reconciliation is above all the work of consent, of the good, eliminating autonomy; but it must be manifested also at the level of necessity. This means that if the physical movement is not in itself vitiated, some movements express and favor more than others the submission of necessity to the good. Among all sorts of movements, circular movement is the most perfect, because it is the spatial image of the motiveless state. Again, the direct influence of Plato is strong; the teaching of the

Timaeus (taken up again in the *Laws*)[8] affirms that circular movement is like divine intelligence, whose movements and "revolutions" always occur in the same place. The movements of our intellect are naturally, though imperfectly, circular; but the study of moments of the divine intellect, that is, of the "revolutions" of spheres and stars, corrects this imperfection and enables us to imitate the divine circular movement.[9] This movement is "divine" in itself,[10] being the least evil corruption of immobility, the least perverted manifestation of becoming. If already there must be movement in the world, it must at least be the nearest possible thing to repose.[11] This is the case with circular movement, at the end of which one is precisely at the point of departure; it has no goal, unlike rectilinear movement that only exists with a view to its goal. Movement in a straight line is an image and expression of self-expansion, whereas an action closing back upon itself represents contemplation, which does not touch its object (3:17 = N 423). Nevertheless, it is not only the spatial symbol of motiveless human action; being a movement that changes nothing and circles back upon itself, it is also the "perfect image of the eternal and blessed act that is the life of the Trinity."[12] This is why the circular movements of humanity are in a way an imitation of God that is the very essence of decreation.[13]

Without being a circular movement in the spatial sense of the term, dance contains its characteristic virtues. It goes nowhere; it has no goal; and it is subject to strict rules representing necessity (cf. 2:402 = N 408). There is no perfection in dance if it is not purified of all "external" motives. Excitement of the senses, for example, will certainly break its rhythm and balance. Dance is an imitation of the progress of human beings before the Fall who, as is said in the *Symposium*, moved by a rotating motion,[14] whereas the straight motion characteristic of humanity suffering the consequences of the Fall is the principle of sin and error. Directed toward a goal, it is at the service of self-expansion.[15] Seen from another angle, it is the sign of the consciousness of time, whereas activities analogous to circular movement imply the right awareness of time: non-dominance over time, non-orientation in time, reduction to the present. Celestial bodies in circular movement "measure" time (cf. *Timaeus* 38b–c), symbolizing that neither time nor what takes place in it must have any goal or end. We can understand that there is no finality in the world, and consequently in human life, by contemplation of the "circular movement of the sky around us," which is "the unfolding itself of the time in our life" (2:395 = N 403–4). Such contemplation puts us in an eternal present: "That insatiable desire in us that is always turned outward and has an imaginary future as its domain is something we must force to circle back upon itself and direct its point toward the present. The movements of celestial bodies that divide our life into days, months, and years are our model in that regard, because returns are so regular that for the stars the future does not differ in any way from the past. If we contemplate in them this equivalence of future and past, we pierce through time into eternity, and, being delivered from desire turned toward the future, we are delivered also from the imagination that accompanies it and is the sole source of error and untruth."[16]

There is besides circular movement another example of movement that is an image of immobility, rhythmic movement. It is an image of immobility because it contains stoppings occurring according to a certain order. Rhythm is defined by these stoppings and not by mere regularity, because, although regular, the tick-tock of a clock in itself has no rhythm (1:169 = N 107). Therefore, the element of "movement" is determined in relation to stopping, that is, in relation to immobility (cf. 1:154–55 = N 97–98). It is a particular case of purposiveness without a purpose; this is the secret of the universally recognized beauty of rhythmical movements. They depart from a stop and die with a stop. They come back again to the same position they had before their departure; as a consequence, they can be considered from a certain angle as being without a goal, without ends. However, the beauty of circular movement is due to the fact that is directed toward nothing (2:399 = N 406). These two types of beauty are present when a good runner ends a successful run. His head and body are motionless, while his arms execute a cyclical movement. Between the two cycles, there is always a stop.[17] However, rhythmic stoppings make the runner's movement not only more beautiful, but also more effective,[18] because they are analogous to intellectual activity when the moments of emptiness filled by attention make subsequent thought more pertinent and more noble.[19] The excellence inherent in rhythmic motions is defined in this way in one of the articles in *La Condition Ouvrière*: "All series of movements that participate in the beautiful and are performed without degrading contain brief stoppings, quick as lightning, that constitute the secret of rhythm and give the observer the impression of slowness even in extreme rapidity" (*OC* II.ii.296 = SWR 61). And Weil adds: "It is natural and it is fitting for us to stop when we are doing something, even for the space of a split second, to become conscious of it, like God in the Book of Genesis."[20]

Circular movements and rhythmic movements express obedience to a center or to stoppings, that is, to something motionless representing the necessary structure of physical reality. But one goes beyond a mere image of non-acting action and attains an approximation of it only in labor. Labor as rational action expresses the position of non-perspective in which non-decreated human beings can situate themselves by the use of intellectual faculties; taken up as a void, it is an apprenticeship and even a fragmentary presence of non-acting action in autonomy. Labor is the notion unquestionably dominating Weil's early thought, and it retains an immense importance even in her mature writings.[21] There being many studies of her ideas on the spirituality of labor, we will consider it here only in its relation to decreation. Her personal experience of life in the factories and fields greatly helped her thought to evolve, but long before those long, difficult months, she was haunted by the problems of labor. Like all of her circle at the Ecole Normale Supérieure, Weil was fascinated by the views on labor and laborers of the utopian socialists of the nineteenth century, and she gained from these the firm conviction of the necessity of manual labor for the intellectual, surpassed in importance perhaps only by the need of the manual laborer to share in the highest accomplishments of human thought.[22] It is with a tone of impassioned rhetoric that her first published writing praises this privileged means for the human being to meet and take up the necessity that is labor. In labor one becomes detached from wishes, emotions, and goals, and acts according to objective laws. "Labor, as opposed. . .to persuasion, to magic. . .is a series of actions having no direct relation either to emotion or to the goal pursued." Whatever its wish, I meet the external world through and in my labor, and I obey its laws: "the changes produced by me are without affinity for my desires and my plans; they do not bear the stamp of my will and are made as they would be made if they were produced by another cause."[23] Labor occurs in space and in this way makes me realize the subjection of my body to necessity. But by virtue of the fact of being bound to time, it proves to me also that I am subject to necessity in what is deepest in me: the sense of my continuity. Contrary to instinctive, capricious, or impassioned action, in work there is no place for the immediate; there is an object to attain, implying a series of acts to accomplish in duration. All activity strictly speaking implies a like succession of moments, gathered into a plan by a firm intention; activity is always labor. Moreover, this active unity is the form of my continuity; I exist only while laboring, because otherwise there is no other link between the successive moments of my self. It is because "instant travels" in time and space are forbidden to me that I am condemned to labor, implying a mediated character and acknowledgment of distance. But this acknowledgment changes into something real that is self-sufficient.[24] Already these early writings explain labor as organically linked to two essential elements of decreation: objectivizing distance, that precondition of non-perspective, and self-abnegation.

But the young woman who wrote on the rationality, nobility, and dignity of labor was to encounter it at its worst, or, if one prefers, in all its truth. She thought that the factory was a place where "harshly, painfully, but all the same joyfully one comes up against real life" (*CO* 19 = *SL* 20). Instead of this, she found a "dismal place where one does nothing but obey, shatter all that is human in oneself under constraint, bow down, let oneself be brought down beneath the level of a machine."[25] The pitiful, subservient, confused situation of the factory worker greatly contributed to the development of her concept of affliction,[26] but basically her denunciations are aimed less at the lamentable human relations produced by factory life than at the conditions and organization of industrial labor. The critique of labor, the human activity par excellence, takes on the proportions of a critique of daily existence, deprived of its true moral dignity because of the lack of rationality in human action. Weil seems to owe a debt to Marx for the description of the alienation of labor, but it is also certain that she pushed it further than the author of *Das Capital*.[27] We shall see that the Hegelian foundations of the theory of alienation[28] are eclipsed by a Cartesian reading of the metaphysical and moral criteria of good and correct human activity.

Weil's first and weightiest accusation against modern labor is that it reduces the worker to playing the role of a tool. A medieval artisan and a specialized worker of our time are masters of their work; their mind controls their movements, since they must anticipate all the activity to be accomplished. They must continually discover concrete applications of general methods, and while they work they must concentrate on their movements and at the same time think of future movements. The complicated nature of their work does not permit them to sink into an automatic attitude. People working on an assembly line, however, have nothing to create. Their role is very simple: to repeat the same movement or sequence of movements. Awareness of the present movement is not accompanied by the representation of past movements, of the whole series of past movements as conditions of the present movement (*OC* II.ii.298 = SWR 63). However, all this applies, although to a lesser extent, to any activity that is not completely primitive. Human beings must almost always understand and learn an action before carrying it out with their hands; but when they realize it, the realization is no more than the more or less exteriorized and objectivized result of the activity of thinking and is not accompanied by the process of thinking (cf. *OC* II.ii.78–79 = OL 91–92). In modern labor, even this realization is not the fruit of the workers' own thought; they must understand it only to the extent required for the skillful and rapid execution of their acts. All labor lacks rationality because there is a break between thought and action; the execution of a plan is not effectively overseen by the mind, and thus the methodical character of labor is definitively compromised. For Weil, labor is methodical only when "thought is in action," which is obviously not the case when there is a break between thought and action. Naturally, that does not mean there is no method in the labor; what Weil tries to show is that there is a real distinction between "methodical" and "what is in accordance with the method." It is certain that the movements of the assembly-line worker are in conformity with a method, but there is no method in the mind of the worker, because his or her hands execute automatic gestures: "there is method in the movements of work, but not in the thought of the worker. One would almost think that method transferred its center from mind into matter. . .one finds oneself before the strange spectacle of machines in which method is so perfectly crystallized in metal that it seems that it is they who think and the people attached to their service who are reduced to the state of automatons."[29]

Insistence on method calls to mind the Cartesian origins of Weil's reflection, and she is even led to identify methodical action with freedom (*OC* II.ii.81 = OL 95), which is essentially constant mental supervision of all our activities.[30] This continuity is broken when the worker, instead of contemplating the intelligible relations prescribing such and such an action, only follows a routine. Such a person does not fully exercise the faculty of attention but sees only substantified fragments in which the totality of the relation is parceled out. Such fragmentation, reducing the intelligible structure of the real to a dust of frozen atoms, is the favorite process of the human intellect when it has to confront the harsh demand of paying attention to a complicated network of invisible relationships. No one was more afflicted than Descartes by that original weightiness in the operations of the mind, and the doctrine of the *Regulae* on a universal mathematics has as its goal to liberate the understanding from the slavery of different figures and qualities by reducing the multiplicity of forms into pure relations of a mathematical nature. The ambition of Descartes is not to "quantify" the world but to describe the real in the most generally intelligible terms, which are, in his view, of a mathematical character.[31] We are free only if our action exercises perfect control over matter, and that is achieved only to the extent to which it is assimilated into it. As long as "the essence of the circle is circular" (cf. *S* 25 = FW 40), that is, figurative, it continues to show a heteronomy in relation to the understanding that conceives it. Reason realizes its own essence, which is pure relation, only there where it coincides with its operation; but this is not possible when this operation, instead of conceiving a relationship, is content to note a figure. One understands why Weil compares Descartes with Marx (*S* 107 = SN 72); what the communist thinker deplores in the separation of intellectual and manual labor and in any kind of "specialization" is that they force human beings, instead of aspiring to total mastery over the mechanism of their action, to settle for a mixture in which formulas prevail over reflection. The routine of the alienated worker is incompatible with attention to relationships, and it deprives human beings of the correct, theoretical attitude toward necessity.

Labor is the anticipation of non-acting action, because it is rational; neither caprice nor passion orients our action; that is the reading of objective necessity. Labor is always the correct solution of a certain problem posed to humanity, and as such it requires non-perspective in the use of our intellectual faculties. It must not only be a solution that is correct, but the best solution, and there is only one best solution to a given problem. In this way labor is analogous to just action in general, and there is a passage from the theoretical realization of objective laws to total conformity with necessity.

There is no choice in a non-acting action because it must follow from a given situation (cf. 1:93 = N 57) and express a recognized necessity. It is acting proceeding from a certain situation, establishing and expressing the unique equilibrium corresponding to it.[32] Being an expression of necessity, this action is beautiful, and as in a correct addition, the personality must not have any part in it. The role of the individual is rather passive; one has only to let necessity act within.[33] One's only "obligation" is to fix our attention on the possibilities offered to us, to consider them with a purity and an integrity such that the possibilities arising from either the deceiving imagination or the instinct for self-expansion must disappear one after the other;[34] one will act in a certain way because one cannot do otherwise.[35] The model for such an activity is that of the obedient slave (cf. 1:195 = N 124), and it is all too obvious that obedience and non-acting action are not different concepts (2:67 = N 184). The essential attitude of obedience is waiting, and when an individual who is waiting receives an order, he or she carries it out without its involving any personal goal; the person has only to make no effort to act because prescribed acts flow almost automatically from a soul in the state of waiting.[36] The act is not carried out because it is the fruit of a subjective emotion or internal debate but because it is in conformity with the laws of necessity that obedience impresses upon our soul. True obedience is possible only when, the self having been decreated, one has become "transparent" (2:290 = N 330). Rather than being an obstacle before the will of God, one is from now on a penetrable milieu that becomes its channel. One must be an instrument of contact between God and one's neighbor (2:329 = N 360). One must "[b]e pushed by God toward one's neighbor as the pencil is pressed down by me on the paper."[37] Indeed, this fundamental passivity is the only correct form of charity toward one's neighbor. It is often repeated that one must help one's neighbor "for God" and that one must always see God present in those one is going to help; but all this is, in a certain sense, false because: "The true goal is not for us to see God in all things, but to allow God to see through us the things that we see. God must be on the side of the subject and not the object in all the intervals of time when, leaving contemplation of the light behind, we imitate the descending movement of God to turn toward the world."[38]

Decreated human beings therefore act only as slaves. Each time they carry out an act, they do it to help their neighbor, and they are sent by their master. The help they give the neighbor comes from the master; they themselves have no part in it.[39] What Weil means by "acting as a slave" is wonderfully described in her meditation on the parable of the Prodigal Son. The Prodigal Son is definitively reconciled with his father after having exhausted his supplementary energy. After the reconciliation, the father often sends his son to the city where he knows the places of debauchery and the taverns. But he does not stop there; he goes straight to the shops where he buys what his father, and not he himself, needs: "When, after the reconciliation of the Prodigal Son, he goes into town with money, it is not as a son who takes away his share of the inheritance, but as a slave given responsibility by the master to make purchases none of which will come back to him and for which no one will thank him. Walking to town, running from shop to shop, making the required purchases until the money given him is spent, coming back carrying heavy loads, or else going penniless into the fields and spending the day laboring—it is all the same to a slave. If the slave has faithfully spent the money for the prescribed purchases, he is neither thanked nor rewarded. He might be reproached for not having sought out the cheapest stores. If he has taken a penny to put it aside or spend it on himself, he is beaten."[40]

A slave is pure passivity but works all day; he or she works for the master but has no share in the harvest. In the same way, the decreated human being must not renounce action in itself but simply be detached from its fruits.[41] In a splendid image, Weil relates action with no anticipation of fruit to the sacrifice of Christ, and action that does anticipate fruit with the sin of Adam: "The tree of sin was a real tree; the tree of life was a beam. Something not giving fruit, but only vertical movement" (3:160 = N 517). This vertical movement designates the journey toward God, the most universal form of which is labor.

If the lack of foresight and the incapacity to continually supervise activities crush in human beings what is most precious in the self, its active continuity,[42] the non-domination of time in labor, accepted and assumed, has decreative value.

To labor, if one is exhausted, is to be subject to time in the same way as is matter (1:126–27 = N 79). One no longer governs moments to come, one goes through time from one moment to the next, passively, like a tool: "To labor is to put one's own being, body and soul, in the world of inert mater, to make one's being an intermediary between one state and another of a fragment of matter, to make it an instrument. Laborers make of their bodies and souls an appendage of the tool they are wielding. The movements of the body and the attention of the spirit are functions of the requirements of the tool, which is itself adapted to the matter of the labor."[43] This assimilating continuity accomplished between human beings and matter in labor by its action will lead us to conform to the true relations of things (2:44 = N 170). A violent and constant effort of apprenticeship is necessary in order that the body become "fluid" and learn the required movements; otherwise, one remains in the imaginary without being able to put oneself in an attitude of obedience toward the external laws that follow from necessity.[44] This heroic but docile confrontation with reality is made permanent only by the acquisition of a "habit" of labor,[45] which, as subordination to understood necessity, makes one win "possession of the world":[46] "For only they possess nature and earth whose bodies these have entered into through the daily suffering of limbs broken by fatigue. The days, the months, the seasons, the heavenly vault endlessly turning above us all belong to those who must cross the expanse of time separating dawn from sunset each day by going painfully from tiredness to tiredness. They accompany the firmament in its rotation, they live out each day, they are not dreaming."[47] Obviously, the possession in question has nothing to do with self-expansion; if the self is present in labor, it is only through suffering and as something to be sacrificed daily (cf. 2:44–45 = N 170).

The decreative dimension of labor is now apparent. By the rational acknowledgment of the necessary relations our body must obey, labor implies the suspension of personal perspective. Paradoxically, when that submission to rational relationships becomes permanent, this entails, through the wearing down by fatigue, loss of the ability to contemplate them. The analysis of labor seems to support the view according to which non-perspective is the "point of view" of the intellect which, by its nature, cannot be made permanent. A universal perspective toward the real can be adopted by the intellect, but the intellect is not able to help us to remain in that perspective. Being established in a universal perspective is possible only through consent; non-perspective made permanent is therefore not really different from what Weil calls the perspective of God.[48] One must have died before attaining the perspective of God, and one quickly finds death at the heart of labor. According to the Book of Genesis, death and labor are the wages of sin, but they are also the means of our reintegration into obedience to God.[49] What is death if not the transformation of a being made of quivering flesh and thought into a small pile of inert matter (*En* 255 = NR 300), and labor implies a similar transformation; through it one decomposes "one's own living substance into inorganic matter."[50] It is a matter of a partial death that can be likened to the Passion of Christ, that archetype of all decreative activity.[51] Those who labor sacrifice themselves daily for others. Therefore, through labor we come in a way to participate in the Redemption (1:126 = N 78). The essence of the redemptive suffering of Christ was not simply consent through obedience to suffering, but also death. The supreme act of obedience for a human being is thus to consent to one's own death: "Consent to death, when death is present and seen in all its nakedness, is a supreme, instantaneous wrenching apart from what each person calls *I*. Consent to labor is less violent. But where it is complete, it is renewed each morning the whole length of a human lifetime.... Immediately after consent to death, consent to the law that makes labor indispensable for the preservation of life is the most perfect act of obedience given us to make" (*En* 256 = NR 301–2).

Obviously, if labor subjects us to obedience, suffering, and a "partial death" (2:40 = N 167), much more is needed to make what is in this way imposed externally be accepted and taken up by the freedom of consent. The fact of being deprived of the disposal of our time has a paralyzing power over us, and it might be asked whether one runs the risk of confusing the obedience of a person highly advanced in decreation with the torpor of an individual sunk into a vegetative state.[52] Weil is quite aware of the fact that nearly always the possibilities for decreation contained in work are left unfulfilled, and that submission to the external, instead of purifying, is degrading. The immense mass of non-decreated beings is not capable of non-acting action because they cannot act without motives. All reflection on the "spirituality of labor" aims only toward the question of knowing how to fill the void created by the absence of motives without being forced to introduce base and entirely selfish motives.[53] It is by reading the supernatural symbolism in the movements and matter of labor that Weil believes it possible to find the means to spiritualize labor, but what concerns us here is the absence of motives, which is the secret itself of non-acting action.

Non-acting action, the renunciation of the fruits of one's actions, is equivalent to the absence of motives. But how can one act without motives? "One says: if I have no more motives, how will I act? Why will I act? But that is the miracle of the supernatural. Silence within yourself all motives, all motivation, and still you will act, moved by a source of energy other than motives and motivations" (2:164 = N 247). In other words: "When one has silenced all motives and motivations, energy remains, clinging to God. And it acts, because it is action. It acts in the particular, because it is physical (one can also say physiological) energy" (2:234–35 = N 293). In the non-decreated state, only contemplation of the beautiful expresses purposiveness without a purpose, enables us to understand the mystery of non-acting action. The mystery is that we execute actions for the good of other human beings, make "useful" things, make efforts to obtain these earthly things without being attached to them. Since non-acting action is without motives and expects no fruits, it originates in detachment.[54] As long as we are attached to things, what we see is not their own reality, but the "reality" of the self transferred into them.[55] Only the death of the self will give their reality back to the things we are in contact with, since we will stop considering them as simple projections of our self. Thus "perfect detachment alone allows things to be seen naked."[56]

All the preceding developments converge to present the essence of detachment at the instantaneous state of death where alone one sees the truth, one is the truth. Truth is *relationship* in all the domains of reality, and the misfortune of humanity is that we are incapable of contemplating it in this way. One should think keeping before one's eyes both the general rule underlying a concrete operation and its relation to the givens of the problem. This is always the same incessant need of substantiation that afflicts and debases our activity; in the Cave of personal existence we cannot act without motives, without fixed relations converted into absolutes, idols. In the same way, our theoretical activity needs signs, symbols, images established into rules or unalterable in essence.[57] "Idolatry" in practice (2:13 = N 150) and "superstition" in theory (*S* 25 = FW 40) are the forms the inventing imagination takes on in its fierce struggle against love and reason. Moral and religious idols and intellectual superstitions in the form of images and symbols are a screen in front of the pure relationships that constitute the intelligible structure of universal necessity of which a complete reading, implying consent, is the basis of our true freedom. All these fixed fragments in which the imagination parcels out reality will have to be fused together by non-acting action, which is at all levels permanent submission—submission that is essential, not merely contingent and arbitrary—to relation.

For the young Weil, the supreme manifestation of that submission was methodical thought. Later, she believed it to be found in the supernatural charity of the saint. How organic the evolution of her thought was, all appearances to the contrary, is shown by the formulation of her views on the influence inner perfection can exercise over physical movements. The Hegelian notion of the "fluidity" labor creates in the entire being of the slave, related to habit developed in the body by the apprenticeship of labor, is a constant companion of Weil's meditation. Nevertheless, labor is only one particular manner of "teaching" the body submission to necessity, and the general principle of giving an interior level expression at a physiological level seems to undergo change during the last years of her thought. As a student, she spoke of "the severity and rigor" characteristic of the movements of the virtuous individual,[58] and fifteen years later, in an astonishing passage of the *Cahiers*, she went so far as to declare that "a saint does not have the same movements as a crook when they are both walking down the street."[59] For Alain's pupil, the supreme ideal to be attained in human life was control of oneself and control of the world by methodical thought; the rigidity of the movements of the good individual is explained by the fact that even "[t]he body yields before a methodical thought."[60] When the rational perfection of the lucid submission to necessity is integrated and even subordinated to love for God, when Weil comments on the myth of the *Phaedrus* as "an attempt at a psychological and physiological theory of the phenomena accompanying grace" (*SG* 119–20 = *SN* 123–24), then she is almost necessarily led to the idea that mystical states can have their physical counterparts, that grace penetrates even life and the sensibility.[61] The passage from methodical thought to grace expresses the progression of the ideas of non-perspective to the perspective of God. One is always guided by the relation found at the center of the three dimensions of non-acting action: in the view of moral relationships, in methodical thought, and in the body's fluidity in rigorous movements. The continuity of the different spheres of human action (cf. *S* 252 = *SL* 126–27) answers the requirement of a metaphysics whose secret dream is to "save" all the levels of the real until they come together in an immaculate and perfect unity.

The non-acting action through which the decreated human being enters into relationship with his or her neighbor does not always avoid causing suffering; and being detached from the fruits of one's acts does not only mean renouncing personal gains but also, in a sense, being detached from the suffering one causes. There are cases where one can, indeed, must, impose suffering or even death, and Weil attempts to outline a theory of punishment and war[62] in a decreative context. Her favorite theme for meditation is the dilemma of Arjuna in the

Bhagavad Gita. The holy king Arjuna must confront his relatives on the battlefield, with "uncles and grandfathers, preceptors... sons, grandsons, and comrades too" (*Bhagavad Gita* 1:26). The sight of all these dear ones who are now to become victims to his sword makes him sad, and pity sweeps over him (1:28 sq.). His cause is just; however, he would rather withdraw and not put the life of his kin in danger. But Krishna, the god incarnate, exhorts him to enter into battle, since it must take place and he must conquer. Arjuna cannot draw back because the law of "dharma," which Weil identifies with necessity,[63] destines him to fight. However, Arjuna, who will not fight for personal goals, is only the instrument of the Lord[64] who tells him: "It is the action that is your concern, never its fruits; let the fruit of the action never be your motive" (2:47). Whatever he obtains, he must become detached from it (2:48) and feel neither joy nor pain; he must act only for the sake of service to the world. If all these conditions are fulfilled, his action will be of greater value than meditation (2:37), and it will be one of the paths for reaching the Brahman. Arjuna is a "kshatriya," someone whose "nature" and vocation require him to fight, and if he meets this obligation, it will lead him toward perfection. As one of the great commentators on the *Bhagavad Gita* says: "The pursuit of a war (according to law) preceded by knowledge of the *atman*, but carried out with no interest in the result, constitutes in itself a means of self-realization."[65] At the moment when Arjuna was hesitant and full of pity, he almost did not recognize necessity and almost did not act in keeping with it. It was quite natural that he felt pity, but he ought not to have been tempted to let pity rule him: "Arjuna's fault was to have said that he would not fight instead of imploring Krishna, not at that moment but long before, to prescribe to him what he had to do."[66] Arjuna had no choice at the moment of his inner torment, since in reality the choice had been made long before the moment of deliberation.

According to the original meaning of the law of Karma, the actions one must carry out in present existence are determined by the good and evil accomplished during previous existences, whereas for Weil this law means that the present actions of a human being follow necessarily from his or her past moral decisions. One is free to choose, but not at a given moment, because a moral choice cannot show a significant discrepancy in relation to the degree of ethical perfection of the whole person. Even the good does not do without the help of duration; it is only slowly, patiently that we modify and really acquire our moral habits. This does not mean that we are not responsible for our action at the moment when we have no more choice; beforehand, we did have choice, and we have made the commitments that brought us to our current state on the path of decreation, expressed in concrete form by our acts only.[67] Because of his own Karma and that of his opponents, Arjuna found himself in a situation such that, no longer really having a choice between battle and retreat, he had to engage in battle. There remained only one thing for him to do: "by remaining in a state of contemplation throughout his action, questioning it, staying outside it, striving toward the non-represented best, to prepare himself to do better later on."[68]

Arjuna no longer had any choice between battle and retreat, but many people think they are forced to choose between violence and passivity. But does one know whether one must fight, whether one must inflict suffering or death in a given situation? How can one know that one is required to use force? These questions are crucial; non-acting action can well be the action of the person who has gone back into the Cave, but the non-decreated person also must try to accomplish it.[69]

It is hypocritical to say that "force does no harm."[70] All one can try to do is to intend to cause the least amount possible. When one knows one cannot avoid the harm of violent action, "except in performing an even greater one, then it is not I who perform it, it is necessity itself."[71] Although one knows this, one does not feel any less all the horror of the misfortune that occurs: "When one understands what affliction is...one understands that it is for God to inflict it through his own instruments. Namely, matter, water in floods, fire, and human beings whose souls are not open to the light, the social beast. One does not have the choice whether to impose affliction.... When one knows what affliction is, it is easier to die than to inflict it.... But as there are circumstances when dying is necessary, even though the soul rebels, as did Christ, there are circumstances when it is necessary to impose affliction. These are circumstances when one is bound to the social beast by strict obligation."[72]

This magnificent passage of extraordinary depth refers to the Hindu king Rama who, after having freed his wife Sita from Ravan, her abductor, rejects the queen before his entire army, saying that she has been defiled. However, when the God Agni saves Sita from the flames of the funeral pyre she had chosen and proves to Rama that the queen has remained pure, the king declares that he never doubted her innocence, but that he considered this test necessary to demonstrate her purity before the assembly of the people.[73] Rama had to repudiate Sita because the wife of the king must be above all reproach and suspicion. Otherwise, the balance and moral order of the society of which he is the center and the pillar would have been compromised. Still, is there an infallible way of discerning whether this order one comes into conformity with is the divine order of the world, or a totalitarian regime secreted by the social beast?[74]

In spite of its inherent dangers and weaknesses, the idea of non-acting action expressed in a violent act can lead to the most profound religious and metaphysical speculations. It can imply redemptive suffering, the essence of which is to continue loving God, absent when one is victim to affliction. When the individual who is decreated or on the verge of achieving decreation inflicts suffering upon others, by virtue of "universal compassion," that person also suffers from the pain he or she causes. This is the case when the king Rama repudiates his wife, since his act is imposed on him by the laws charged with maintaining social equilibrium, which, being an imitation of the order of the world, expresses the will of God. The king himself is a decreated man, and he is the first to suffer from the harm he inflicts, but his pain is the absence of God.

Despite the fact that the self of an individual is not there when he or she inflicts suffering (more precisely, the person no longer has any self), Weil thinks that God is absent from him or her at the moment of the violent act: "Contact with might, from whatever side one makes contact (handle or tip of the sword), deprives us for a moment of God."[75] These moments are in a way equivalent to the test of the quarter-hour. We are called to suffer the absence of God and the suffering we are in the process of inflicting; at the same time, we must carry out the action continuing to deprive us of God and make us suffer. The definition of redemptive suffering under the form of violent non-acting action is this: "The perfectly pure being, if forced by the obligation of his or her state to cause evil, passively endures this constraint; he or she is only the site through which the evil coming from without passes through; and even there, passing through, evil is transformed into pure pain" (3:146). The redemptive character of the act is completed when God is made present in evil, his presence being an absence that is felt. While carrying out a violent action, we are deprived of God and overwhelmed by the evil we are creating, but the fact of feeling the absence of God in evil makes God present in evil, which will be changed into pure suffering.[76]

When natural pity makes redemptive violence repellent to us, we proceed to a false imitation of decreation (2:231 = N 290), because instead of obeying God, we follow a subjective inclination. Killing someone is, in general, an expansion of self; but for Arjuna, it would be a supreme act of renunciation in relation to those around him. His pity has personal motives, and yet non-acting action must always be an imitation of the creation which is, because of God's withdrawal, the supreme form of decreation. There are no motives in the eternal act God accomplishes for an infinite "end": the completion of union with himself. Non-acting action is participation in the supreme decreation of God for an infinite end, for God himself (cf. 2:180 = N 258). All the while based in a speculative theology, the idea of non-acting action has its very natural "verification." A passion is a state in which we suffer from the limits imposed on us by a capacity to act other than our own, whereas in an action we suffer from the contradiction our being is subject to because of the effort made to accomplish something in this world. Creating a work of art or giving birth to a human being are the highest forms of action, and at the same time it is in them that tension, pain, and agony are most completely present. The supreme form of abnegation is creation, because one causes something else to exist from which one is absolutely absent; and, whether one inflicts harm or offers help, non-acting action can only be creative. One might even say that true action is always creation and that there is only non-acting action, because wherever there remains a residue of the self in the work, the individual has not succeeded in making his or her intentions wholly pass into reality.

Perfect non-acting action is the expression of a correct reading of necessity from which the self is absent, and we have seen that, in certain cases, necessity can require us to cause harm. It remains to be seen why we must help others, this help being the reason for which one accepts being "recreated" after the test of the quarter-hour (cf. CS 182 = F 224). If Weil was thinking only of the spiritual assistance given others to help them perfect their decreation, that would seem to harmonize better with her doctrine that nothing is of any importance except the individual's relationship with God. But she insists that it is necessary to assist non-decreated individuals even with their material needs (cf. CS 170 = F 213). Given the reality of time that separates two moments of the order of the world, I can accept any suffering that can happen to others, all the while doing my best to help them avoid it. However, it remains to be shown why I *must* do all this if only spiritual values are important. Obviously, the simple fact of suffering, having no relation with the supernatural, is so horrible that it must be relieved (2:226 = N 288). Yet the heart of the problem is not here. Others must be helped in their material needs because if they are not protected from suffering coming from the outside, suffering that has not been accepted, they might sink into a state preventing them from entering into the process of decreation (cf. 2:186 = N 262). Weil expresses this position most explicitly in one of her writings from London. She states that there is a "connection established within human nature between the expectation of good, which is the very essence of humanity, and the sensibility. . . . Through it, when, on account of the acts or omissions of others, the life of a human being is destroyed or mutilated by an injury or a privation of body or soul, it is not only the sensibility in him or her that suffers the blow, but also the aspiration to the good. There has then occurred a sacrilege against what is sacred in that person."[77] However, if our only reason to help the other is a simple natural inclination, it must be followed only if, after attentive scrutiny of the situation, one sees no possible objection to it.[78]

Our self must be absent from the charitable act insofar as possible, but that does not mean that the individual toward whom the act is directed is a mere object. Even if the laws of decreation require the abolition of the personality, this process can occur only by a consent working through the personality. I can only be a mere instrument of God, but I must love the individual I am helping as a person: "God is not present, even if he is invoked, wherever afflicted persons are merely an occasion to do good, even if they are loved as such. For then they are in their natural role, their role as matter, things. They are loved impersonally. And we must bring them, in their inert and anonymous state, a love that is personal."[79]

There is a natural human inclination to feed the hungry in which the act of giving food itself is only an external sign showing true recognition of the person of the other (2:237 = N 295). However, the way in which charity is given is not indifferent; it can be thrown toward the sufferer with indifference or contempt, and it can also be given with respect and love. Two persons are face to face, one weak and one strong; and the strong one has the almost irresistible temptation to treat the weak one, on account of his or her weakness, as a thing, an object. If the strong one resists this temptation and treats the other as an equal, he or she can save the other from affliction, showing in this way supernatural generosity and compassion. If the weak one knows his or her own weakness and recognizes that the other has the power to treat him or her as a thing, then supernatural gratitude answers supernatural generosity (*AD* 104 sq. = WG 143–44). In such cases, sufferers are saved from their affliction and are "recreated" in the same way as the person who has endured and triumphed over the test of the quarter-hour: "Whoever being reduced by affliction to the state of an inert and passive thing returns at least for a time to a human state through the generosity of others—such persons, if they know how to welcome and feel the true essence of that generosity, receive at that very instant a soul born exclusively of charity. They are created from on high of water and the spirit.... Treating one's suffering neighbors with love is something akin to baptizing them."[80]

In general, a charitable act does not only have the negative role of preserving human aspirations toward the good. It can also have a positive use in decreation, because "[t]hose whose inner gaze is not directed toward the source of grace in such a way as to receive light can still have real contact with God if, by a wonderful encounter, they are the object of an action performed by a creature who has become a mere intermediary through perfect obedience" (2:237 = N 364).

When supernatural gratitude responds to supernatural generosity, a kind of equality is established between non-equals, and this is friendship. In any "natural" affection, on a greater or lesser scale, one human being pursues the other with affection because he or she needs the other or believes to have found in the other "the good." But affection is pure only when we do not simply seek a good in a being, but when we wish good for him or her (AD 154–55 = WG 200–201). Because it implies the power to renounce the self, the greatest good is to freely dispose of oneself;[81] therefore, pure affection, which is friendship, consists in respecting and desiring the preservation of the power of free consent in others as well as in oneself: "In perfect friendship... [t]he two friends completely accept being two and not one; they respect the distance the fact of being two distinct creatures puts between them. It is only with God that a human being has the right to desire being directly united."[82] Although friendship is a bond between two persons, being an anticipation of decreated intersubjectivity, it must necessarily contain something of the impersonal.[83] It is the manifestation of a universal feeling centered on a particular human being only on account of our innate limitations.

The ideal of friendship is an affection toward a human being that can be expressed not in spite of the universal character it shows in its purest form, but precisely because of this universal character: "Friendship has something universal in it. It consists of loving a human being as one would like to be able to love individually each of those who make up the human race. As a geometer looks at a particular figure in order to deduce the universal properties of a triangle, so one who knows how to love directs toward a particular human being a universal love. Consent to the preservation of autonomy in oneself and in others is by its essence something universal. Once one desires this preservation in more than one being only, one desires it in all beings, for one stops placing the order of the world in a circle around a center in this world. One transports the center beyond the heavens."[84]

Necessity is present in every bond between people, but in friendship its weight is not felt. Among all possible compensations, that of attachment and affection brought by another is the compensation most to be desired in this existence, but a friend renounces it out of love, freely. The necessity underlying all earthly situations in this way submits itself to freedom; this is the meaning of the Pythagorean expression that "[f]riendship is an equality made of harmony." There is harmony because there is supernatural friendship and reconciliation of two opposites, necessity and freedom (*AD* 157–58 = WG 204), and this is conceivable only as an imitation of the life of God. If there is perfect, supernatural friendship, it can only be the share of two decreated beings. In this world the purity of friendship is measured by the transformation of the tie that binds the friends into a relationship, and, in the Cave of personal existence, one can never attain a total transformation. Pure intersubjectivity exists only where the attachments of the self do not make human relationships into idols; indeed, one can speak of genuine relationship only in detachment. Once delivered from the superstition of figures in knowledge and from the idolatry of relative goods raised to absolutes in love, our thought and our power to act are purified into relation; in friendship, our being itself is established in relation. If in autonomy our whole life depends on the recognition the imagination of others bestows on us, in detachment too our existence is a function of the existence of others. Intersubjectivity still exists, but its content is radically changed; instead of being one among the millions of isolated centers that try to devour each other, one takes one's place in a transcendent network no beam of which hides an opaque and closed nucleus. To be truly in relation means being only relation, never being oneself. Only in this way does one imitate the perfect relation that is the very essence of divinity: "Pure friendship is an image of the original and perfect friendship that is the friendship of the Trinity and the very essence of God. It is impossible for two human beings to be one and still scrupulously respect the distance separating them if God is not present in each of them. The point where the parallels meet goes on to infinity."[85]

One might be tempted to observe that friendship must be the rarest and most difficult form of the imitation of God because, through obedience and suffering in the process of decreation, we only imitate God's pilgrimage toward himself, whereas in perfect intersubjectivity one participates in the reunion of divine persons. However, such a reflection is only a consequence of the limited perspective imposed on our thought by the law of temporal succession. In God, pilgrimage and encounter, separation and reunion are simultaneous, and it is perhaps as a function of that divine simultaneity that we must reconcile the final alternative of the metaphysics of decreation, the alternative between an endless process of decreation and a decreated state in which one is forever established.

Conclusion

Weil surely occupies a special place in the history of French thought, where religious reflection has always shown great restraint in matters of speculation. Mystics, protected by the solid walls of theology and scholastic philosophy, devoted their writings to the "practical" problems of prayer, contemplation, and moral conduct; philosophers interested in religious questions wrote armed with the conceptual instruments of metaphysics and epistemology, or were content to meditate on God and humanity without claiming to construct a system. Weil's way of thinking, in which metaphysics and mysticism support each other and merge, that penetrating gaze before which moral actions and religious acts are transposed into ontological perspectives, is not a familiar one in the French tradition. And yet despite a basic affinity, the abyss separating it from Gnostic speculation and German idealism is quite perceptible. Greece and Germany certainly exercised a powerful influence on the formation of her thought, but instead of Plotinus, Hegel, or Schelling, we find Plato and Kant at the source of her inspiration. She has in common with these two great philosophers a certain prudence which consisted in not following the speculative perspective suggested by a beautiful idea through to the very end and in being humbly content with the unfinished and incomplete. Not to exhaust the whole scale of its possibilities by choosing only one of these is perhaps the secret of the strength and fecundity of any thought, and Weil shares with Kant and Plato the sober humility that compels such restraint. This reticence before drawing final conclusions offered by the rational structure of the idea one has conceived may be explained by the fidelity Weil wishes to maintain to her own religious experience and to what is taught by the Revelation and the writings of the "authentic friends of God" (cf. *AD* 47 = WG 79). In Weil, the word is not detached from reality, of which it ought to be the humble and groping expression; it is not alienated in complicated and prideful dialectics, but intends to be faithful to the Word.

This same impassioned fidelity to spiritual experience leads Weil toward a radical reinterpretation of the ideas of her mentors. The vicissitudes of the notion of the good and of the notion it implies, purposiveness without a purpose, exemplify the tautological passion of mysticism grappling with different aspects of human experience she wants to reshape with a view to the single end, love for God. Weil has a penchant for terms like "purposiveness without a purpose," "desire without an object," "attention in a void," but these expressions approaching a Kantian "formalization" more than anything reveal the agony of a soul who loves God and neighbor confronting the impossibility of earthly existence. If one nonetheless tries to find the basic motivation making her avoid and reject the human condition in favor of a purifying reduction, one must confront what we would fearfully call "resentment against being." As we have said before, having no ambition to psychology, we have no wish to address a supposed masochistic passion alleged to push Weil toward the desire for self-destruction and make her long at the same time for the end of this world.[1] We too wish to remain faithful to the word, to Weil's word, and it is with her word that we hope to understand the different levels where her negation of being takes shape.

It might be said that two major ideas are expressed all through her work: the first, which she attempts to control and qualify from its inception, being itself is evil, and the second, which she develops in an outline of anthropology: only a certain level of our being, a certain mode of our existence, is evil. Coming from a Heidegger, the question, "Why does anything exist? Why isn't there nothing?" would cause astonishment. In Weil, without its being stated, this question resonates with bitterness throughout the entire work. We have seen that she easily "abandons" being to God, because being is not identical with the good, and it is the good that matters. Being is not only something too opaque, too definite, and too finite; one also has the irresistible impression that it is superfluous, that one can do without it—indeed, that one must do without it, because there is something corrupt in it. It always implies action and tension, and this defiles the purity of the good. Being is never without might, and the Good is pure weakness; all that is might can undergo the destructive influence of might, but weakness, pure non-being, cannot be destroyed; it alone is incorruptible (*IP* 57–58 = IC 120). It is through non-being that we "participate" in the good, not through being (3:193 = N 539) which harms the good and which, it seems, ought to be eliminated in some way; thus the law of this universe is the necessity that "all things indiscriminately fall" (2:185 = N 261). However, observations so negative implying the identity of being and evil are relatively rare; one of Weil's major preoccupations is to qualify her rejection of existence by restricting condemnation to one of its particular levels, the self. If she does not manage to give a clear and coherent definition of evil, she nevertheless outlines the bases for an anthropology opening new perspectives before a less "accidental" explanation of humanity as a "divided kingdom." We have seen that the traditional dichotomy of spirit and matter, of soul and body, yields to a tripartite division, and sin is detached from matter and the body to be fully integrated into the self-expansion of the individual, identified with original sin.[2] Matter is neutral and has nothing to do with the moral; our body is not a principle of sin. It serves only as a pretext to the soul for "not seeing God"; it is a veil and a shield behind which the terrified soul hides. Seeing God implies that one turns away from the self and gives attention to an external reality; that is exactly what the self wants to keep us from doing, because, let us recall: "There is something in our soul that is repelled by genuine attention much more violently than the flesh is repelled by fatigue. That something is much closer to evil than is the flesh" (*AD* 76 = WG 111).

Obviously, this enemy of attention is our instinct for self-expansion, and it is this instinct we destroy by giving attention to reality. But in this instance, evil and sin are contained in the very center of the individual being of each human being, not only in the mere material part of the human mixture. "Situating" evil in this way does not show the corruptness of human acts as contingent to humanity; it shows humanity as fully responsible. Such a view of sin poses the moral question as inherently connected to the question of being, thus providing new and profound bases for ethics. However, these bases contain a mortal threat to the meaning of the struggle in the human being seemingly obscured by Weil's absolute requirement of eliminating the self and, in the final analysis, any individual center of existence.

The accomplishment of decreation implies the elimination of the self, but what, one might ask, remains after this elimination? Weil speaks of "matter as if it were conscious" or "of a soul replaced by the Son of God," and some of her texts almost go so far as to say that this elimination of the self only reveals "a fragment of God," the divine spark that is the foundation of our being.[3] However, all these metaphorical formulas do not manage to erase the simple truth that if the "content" of the individual can be changed, a basic continuity must remain between decreated human beings and their previous non-decreated personalities, because they owe their second birth solely to efforts exerted during non-decreated life and to consent, the faculty of which was always in them.

Thus one might say, when Weil speaks of death as the truth of the human condition (cf. CS 25 = F 285), that, perhaps, she is not thinking only of the death of the autonomous self, but of the death of the entire human being. Surely the way in which Weil centers life around death is much purer than Heidegger's free project and free assumption. In *Being and Time*, stress is placed on *my* death. I do not become detached from myself; only my attachment is moved toward my death as toward that which alone can give its meaning to my existence. In Heidegger, "assuming one's death" consecrates the authenticity of the person; in Weil, *accepting* a death common to every human being liberates me from the dream of being a person, and, in a certain way, means reduction to the species, to essence, to use Schelling's terminology.[4] Thus salvation is found in liberation from the accident of existence because, for Weil, unlike Sartre, existence is the sickness of essence and not of being. Death is therefore really an "essentification," one with two different dimensions. On the one hand, one can say that the essence common to every human being is composed of what remains after decreation of the self: free consent and matter. On the other, the pure, genuine, incorruptible essence of humanity, its "ideal," can emerge like the nothingness produced by death. Her efforts undoubtedly strove to establish a theory of death based on the first dimension, in order not to identify everything in humanity with evil, with that-which-ought-not-to-be; and thus she proposed the distinction between the "created" and the "uncreated." But from time to time, her strong resentment against being shatters this classification, and through the gap the cold winds of death and nothingness chill us. And she will ultimately condemn human existence as such: "Adam before sin is not conceivable; one can only conceive a causal, not a temporal, anteriority between his creation, his sin, and his punishment. The whole of humanity sinned, outside time, in having its own will" (2:196 = N 268).

This passage clearly implies that the fact of having committed original sin belongs to the essence of humanity, and humanity did not really have a choice; it was forced to "choose" sin. If this is the case, then Weil seems completely logical in saying that God's crime was to have created us as finite beings and that we must forgive him for having made us exist.[5] But it is not only human existence (cf. 3:230 = N 564), it is even being as such that to her seems to contain something cruel and tragic; the desire to explain the fact that being exists leads her to establish a division within divinity between a mighty and impersonal God and a powerless God who is love.[6] For Weil, this division appears as a rending within God, and she tries to describe its cure. As we know, she conceives of this cure according to one of the most audacious soteriological theories in history. Redemptive suffering implies the redemption of humanity, the redemption of evil, and the redemption of God; feeling the absence of God while being overwhelmed by evil makes God present in evil. Evil will be transubstantiated into "pure suffering," and in this way the final obstacle before the encounter of God with himself will disappear. Here is Weil, the implacable critic of human baseness and nothingness, representing humanity as armed with the most precious power: that of being the indispensable collaborator in the restoration of harmony within God! What a strange route this thought has taken: the sight of fallen human existence makes her sense the corruption at the very heart of being itself; to exonerate God of all complicity in being, she divides him in two; and finally, to cure the division, she appeals to humanity.

The idea that human beings are indispensable to the happiness of God is an old religious intuition of an Eckhart or Angelus Silesius, and contemplated from within the world of the mystic, this thought which is at first shocking slowly becomes the source of deep spiritual inspiration and affection. But when it is about to serve as the basis for a theory of the nature of humanity, it leads to the absurd and even to sacrilege, because it seems to imply that the world of humanity is necessary in some way to the perfection of God. Obviously Weil takes care not to describe history as the return of the Spirit to itself, as a maturation, a becoming aware of God. For her, each time a human being is decreated, and this without the least connection to history, God is healed; thus the Lord is not at the mercy of a group, but of a weak person, something perhaps much more beautiful. The fact remains, however, that as long as a human being exists in this world, the freedom of God is not complete. The reconciliation of divine freedom with the fact of the Incarnation and the death on the Cross is one of the principal goals of the Christology of the Fathers and of Scholasticism, but it does not appear to be at the center of Weil's preoccupations. The attempt of any speculative Christology is to allow itself to sink into a pantheistic continuity in order to be able to proceed to the desired synthesis between the cosmic Christ and the historical Christ. But the fundamental attitude of her thought that, by rejecting earthly existence, aspires only to the supernatural seems to have preserved Weil from the pantheistic error which, moreover, she resolutely denounces.[7]

But it is precisely the exclusivity with which she opts for the transcendent that exposes her to a pitfall perhaps as serious as that of pantheism. In order to retain the absolute purity of the good, the finite undergoes a reinterpretation which, at the cost of the deifying ransom of its intelligible structure, reduces it to nothing. It is by this monism of essence that classical metaphysics remains irreducibly opposed to the freedom of the biblical God in the creation; and if Weil understands that the world must come from God out of love and not necessity (cf. *IP* 128 = IC 166), the philosophical foundations of her thought condemn her to remain with the Greeks.[8] It is this Hellenic turn of her mind that keeps her from grasping the historical character of the Incarnation; for her, as we know, "[t]he crucifixion of Christ is an eternal thing" (3:230 = N 564). The closed attitude toward the historicity of the Incarnation only illustrates her total lack of a sense of history in general. Indeed, nothing repelled her more than the idea of progress, of the perfection of humanity through history, of a historic people privileged by the Revelation. At the bottom of her violent rejection of the election of Israel can be found the anger of the intellect scandalized by the "confusion" of the contingent with the Absolute. Weil was too much a Platonist to be able to attribute true intelligibility to anything other than essence, and when the contingent manifests itself through the life of a human group based on blood relations, she does not forget that "[b]lood is. . .carnal life, principle of all defilement."[9]

However, the misunderstanding of the historical and the condemnation of contingency coexist with attempts to outline a concrete metaphysics based on the Incarnation, as shown especially in her view on suffering. But in the latter domain, she is inspired less by the metaphysical principles governing her Christology than by a properly religious experience and interpretation of the life and suffering of Jesus Christ. In the final analysis, one is driven back to the often debated question: to what extent was Weil Christian and Catholic? Probably, as she expressly says, in many areas her ideas do not coincide with those of Catholic theology. To take an inventory of her "deviations" or to try to interpret her most daring formulas with ecumenical magnanimity is not our intention. But if one speaks of the "project" at the origin of her world of thought, nourishing and maintaining it, we state without the shadow of a doubt that it is Christian. However, Christianity came relatively late to open and develop her conception of the world, and the Christian theology she knew only very superficially influenced her far less than her own experiences of Christ and her reading of the Gospels and some of the mystics. The central dogmas of the Church become key notions in her thought, but the speculative formulation she gives them cannot be genetically traced back to Christian philosophical and theological systems. Indeed, she knew very little of Christian philosophy of the Middle Ages,[10] and if a number of her formulas recall the Fathers of the Church or even Thomas Aquinas, this similarity is due above all to common sources.

No thinker of this century was more influenced by Plato than Weil, and almost all the fundamental questions of Christian Platonism are debated in her work, the sole example of Christian and Platonic mystical speculation in our century. That this work is incomplete and problematic, abounding in paradoxes, lacunae, and contradictions is undebatable. Some like to repeat that, if she had lived longer, she would certainly have systematized and organized her thought. It is more than probable that she would have written many other wonderful studies and essays like "The Love of God and Affliction," "Human Personality," and "The *Iliad* or the Poem of Might," but we are convinced that Weil's thought is constitutionally, and not just accidentally, incomplete and paradoxical. And perhaps that is one of the reasons that makes it so fascinating. One feels that her ideas are put on paper at the very moment of their birth, and also that they emerge, like Pallas Athena, in full armor. Her paradoxes provoke violent reactions and her lacunae can be exasperating, but what Péguy said of Descartes also holds true for Weil: "A great philosophy is not one against which there is nothing to say. It is one that says something.

It is not one that has no holes. It is one that has fullnesses."[11] It is nevertheless a fact that these "fullnesses" will never be the foundation for a school of thought; the "phenomenon" of Simone Weil is unique and inimitable. In the era of existentialism, of dialectical theology and Biblical renewal, her speculative mysticism bears witness in a solitary way to the greatness and the shortcomings of Christian Platonism.

Notes

Introduction

1. Weil herself wrote to Father Perrin: "If no one is willing to pay attention to the thoughts that, how I do not know, have come to settle in such an inadequate being as myself, they will be buried with me. If, as I believe, they contain truth, that will be a pity. . . . I want you to direct the charity you have showered upon me away from my person and toward what I carry within me—which, I like to think, is worth much more than I am" (*AD* 68 = WG 100).

2. A chronological table to help the reader situate Weil's writings in relation to the events of her life is presented at the end of the present work.

3. For example: "A propos de la doctrine pythagoricienne" ("The Pythagorean Doctrine") (*IP* 108–71 = IC 151–201) in *CS* 29–36 = FLN 85–91; the beginning of *Intuitions Pré-Chrétiennes* (*Intimations of Christianity among the Ancient Greeks*) (9–21 = IC 1–10) in 3:225 = N 560; "A propos du Pater" ("Concerning the 'Our Father'") (*AD* 167–76 = WG 216–27) in 2:256–60 = N 309–11; an extremely important part of the essay "L'Amour de Dieu et le Malheur" ("The Love of God and Affliction") (*AD* 87–98 = WG 123–26) in 3:25–26 = N 428–29; "Conditions Premières d'un Travail Non-Servile" ("Prerequisites to the Dignity of Labor") (*CO* 261–73 = SWA 264–76) in 3:276–79 = N 595–98.

4. The only writing that can be considered a systematic work of philosophy is "Réflexions sur les Causes de la Liberté et de l'Oppression sociale" (*OC* II.ii.27–109 = OL 37–124). Among the last writings, two are very complete essays of philosophical and religious problems on a rather large scale: "Formes de l'Amour implicite de Dieu" ("Forms of the Implicit Love of God") (*AD* 99–166 = WG 137–215) and "La Personne et le Sacré" ("Human Personality") (*EL* 11–44 = SE 9–34). The study "A propos de la doctrine pythagoricienne" (*IP* 108–71 = IC 151–201) is the most important exposition of the foundations of her religious metaphysics.

5. In an unpublished text, Weil mentions Plato as the best example of a "true philosopher." Also "true" philosophers for her are Kant, Descartes, Lagneau, Alain, and Husserl ("Réflexions autour de la notion de valeur," ms., 1939–42).

6. *En* 218 = NR 257. And, thanks to the first note, written in London, of *La Connaissance Surnaturelle,* one can gather what she understood by a "true" philosophy: "The proper method of philosophy consists in clearly conceiving insoluble problems in their insolubility, then in contemplating them with the help of nothing more, fixedly, untiringly over a period of years, without any hope, waiting" (*CS* 305, cf. *CS* 335 = F 335, cf. F 362). On the difference between religion and philosophy, cf. *PS* 65; SL 130.

7. "Reason must exercise its function of demonstration only in order to manage to confront the true mysteries, the true undemonstrables, which are the real. The non-understood hides the incomprehensible and on these grounds should be eliminated" (3:308 = N 617).

8. *CS* 163 = F 207; cf. *AD* 46–47 and 54–55 = WG 77–70 and 85–86.

9. *CS* 79–80 = F 131, cf. 2:204 = N 273. Cf.: "The intellect cannot control mystery itself, but it is in perfect possession of the controlling power over the paths that lead to mystery, that climb up to it, and over the paths that lead back down. It thus remains absolutely faithful to itself in recognizing the existence in the soul of a faculty superior to itself that leads thought beyond it. This faculty is supernatural love." *CS* 80 = F 131; cf. *LR* 54 = GTG 131.

10. Cf. 3:65 = N 454. Cf. her invectives against the prevailing notion of Providence: for example, *LR* 54 = GTG 127–28.

11. See especially IP 108 sq. = IC 151ff.

12. A text probably written in New York conveys this tendency of her speculative thought: "The story of Christ is a symbol, a metaphor. But it was formerly believed that metaphors occur as events in the world. God is the supreme poet" (*CS* 149–50, cf. *CS* 163 = F 194, cf. F 207). See also *PS* 24.

13. *CS* 99–100, 176–83, and 186–93 = F 148–49, 219–25, and 230–34.

14. 3:298 = N 611. Cf. "After all, there is perhaps but one person saved in a generation" (*CS* 183 = F 224). And a very typical passage in the *Cahiers* says that "the vocation proper to humanity is to walk on water" (2:60 = N 180).

15. "De la Perception ou l'Aventure de Protée" and "Du Temps," *OC* I.121–58.

16. See her analysis in Chapter 5 below.

17. *OC* II.i.288–89; *OC* II.iii.49–66; *OC* II.iii.99–116 = *Politics* 2 (1945): 51–56; SE 154–76, 177–94.

18. *OC* II.ii.27–109; OL 37–124.

19. Letter from Alain to Simone Weil (1935) in the introduction to *OL*, p. 8.

20. Cf. *AD* 36–38 = WG 66–69, *PS* 81 = SL 140. Cf. also "Prologue" (published in *CS* 9–10 and at the end of *Cahiers* 3, no page number = F 65–66), which seems related to an experience of Weil's dating probably from the beginning of the year 1939, the date put forward by her mother in a short written statement she gave me about thirty years ago.

21. During the years 1925–31, Weil speaks rather frequently on religious subjects in her essays and notes; for example, she left a fragment on "le dogme de la Présence réelle" (*OC* I.92–93); she writes on the Christian martyrs (*OC* I.434); here and there she cites the Gospels (*OC* I.91, 92, 268, 388, 389, 394); and she writes sentences such as: "We are always going toward God refusing and leaving behind us matter shaped by us in that movement of refusal" ("Le Beau et le Bien," *OC* I.72). But this does not mean that she was truly interested in religious problems (see also *AD* 32 = WG 62), and she spoke with contempt of "so many senseless superstitions" professed by religions (*S* 12 sq. = FW 31–32). However, it must be acknowledged that as early as these years she possessed some ideas on the philosophical and moral implications of religion as such and of Christianity in particular, all betraying Alain's influence especially; and, as Simone Pétrement's excellent article shows ("Sur la religion d'Alain avec quelques remarques concernant celle de Simone Weil," *Revue de la Métaphysique et de la Morale* 3 [1955]: 306–30), this influence left its mark even on her mature thought. The key to this concept, which can only really be understood in the light of the first chapter of the present work, is the following sentence: "The real God is not powerful as he is seen in the Christian religion" ("L'Habitude," *OC* I.275). The period 1935–39 produced very few texts with any relation to religious subjects. One of her notes declares that Christianity is "a slave's religion" ("Philosophie, Enseignement," Bourges-Saint-Quentin, ms. f. 78, 1935–38?). This phrase was written *after* her experience in the fishing village in Portugal of which she was to write later: "There I suddenly had the certainty that Christianity is above all the religion of slaves, that slaves cannot not adhere to it, and myself among the rest" (*AD* 37 = WG 67). Another note contains a short reflection on affliction, the will of God, and spiritual life

(*OC* I.402). It is very interesting to read in a letter to Mounier that "Christian morality is morality pure and simple" (ms., 1936–38). Cf. also *CO* 125 = SL 23, *AD* 32 = WG 62. Her daily attendance at Mass and her desire to obtain a missal during a stay in Rome around Pentecost in 1937 seem to have been motivated by her interest in Gregorian chant (letter to her mother, Tuesday after Pentecost, ms., 1937. Translated in R. Rees, *Simone Weil: Seventy Letters*, pp. 81–81). However, even at this time she was comparing Jesus to Epictetus (*EHP* 245 = FW 253). In another letter she said that in the spring "she never forgets that Christ is resurrected." Finally, there exists an older and rather curious passage from which we dare not draw any conclusions: "As for the 'need to resemble God' arising, it seems, from a liver ailment, a certain Plato, whose works might well be, even now, more useful than all the books on psychology to anyone who wishes to understand human nature, once wrote that everything of value in human action or thought consists of 'a certain imitation of God' " (*OC* II.ii.354).

22. *OC* II.iii.227–53. "Quelques Réflexions sur les Origines de l'Hitlérisme" ("The Great Beast") (*OC* II.iii.168–219 = SE 88–140) can be considered as providing the transition between the two periods.

23. It appears that the last pages of *CS* were written a few days before her death.

24. "Cinque lettere a uno studente," *Nuovi Argomenti* 20 (1953): 80–103.

25. For example, Albertine Thévenon in the introduction to *CO* (12–13). This continuity is magnificently illustrated by comparison of the two following passages. Weil writes in a student paper: "Every saint has refused any happiness that would separate him from the suffering of humanity" (*OC* I.71). Sixteen years later, struggling against her desire to request baptism, she writes to Father Perrin: "when I imagine concretely and as an imminent thing the action by which I would enter the Church, no thought gives me greater pain than that of separating myself from the immense and wretched mass of unbelievers" (*AD* 17 = WG 48).

26. Cf. the idea of purposiveness without purpose, Chapter 6.

1. The Notion of Decreation

1. "Note conjointe sur M. Descartes et la Philosophie Cartésienne," in *Oeuvres en prose* (Paris: Pléiade, 1961), 1385, 1405.

2. Decreation: 2:206, 239, 242; 3:201; CS 16 = N 275, 290, 298, 545, F 71. De-creation: 2:180, 192, 208, 230, 231, 257, 260, 290, 303, 306, 314; 3:91 = N 258, 261, 262, 266, 276, 290, 309, 311, 331, 342, 344, 349, 471.

3. On the importance of this notion for the philosophy of religion, see Henri Duméry, *Philosophie de la religion* (Paris: Presses Universitaires de France, 1957), I:295ff.

4. *CS* 67, 83, 264 = F 120, 136 297; *AD* 105 = WG 144; 2:75 = N 190; *AD* 106 = WG 145; *IP* 148 = IC 183; 2:80 = N 193.

5. *CS* 68 = F 120; 3:225 = N 560; and especially *PS* 35–36 = GTG 80; cf. *EL* 48 = *Philosophical Investigations* 3; *CS* 262, 394 = F 296; 2:392 = N 401-2, 403; *CS* 49 = F 103.

6. Revelation 13:8, quoted in *AD* 106 = WG 145; *CS* 14 = F 70; 3:230 = N 564, etc.

7. 3:230 = N 564. Another representation of the separation of God from himself is the myth of Prometheus: *IP* 99 sq., 56 = IC 65, 119; *EN* 251= NR 296.

8. We take the liberty of noting the strange similarity of these views with the Kabbalist notion of Tzimtzum, that withdrawal and self-limitation of God in the creation. Moreover, in its original form in Isaac Luria, the Tzimtzum is a sort of necessary crisis in the life of God (G. Scholem, *Les Grands Courants de la Mystique Juive* [Paris: Payot, 1960], 277–81) = *Major Trends in Jewish Mysticism* (3rd rev. ed., New York: Schocken Books, 1954). It is only with his disciple Chaim Vital's interpretation of this withdrawal as a free act of love on God's part that the relation to Simone Weil becomes evident (G. Scholem, *Zur Kabbala und ihrer Symbolik* [Zurich, 1960], 149 = *On the Kabbalah and Its Symbolism* [London: Routledge and Kegan Paul, 1965]). Without wanting to multiply the parallels one could mention that similar concepts are found in the works of Schelling (*Werke* VII [Stuttgart, 1860], 429) or Hamann (*Sammtliche Werke* II [Vienna, 1950], p. 171).

9. *AD* 89–90 = WG 126–27, *CS* 27 = F 83, *IP* 166 = F 197. Cf. Perrin and Thibon, *Simone Weil telle que nous l'avons connue*, p. 41 = English pp. 33–34.

10. Cf. *CS* 48 = F 102, *IP* 157 = IC 189-90.

11. *En* 247 = NR 293; cf. 3:107, 126 = N 482, 496; *SG* 168 = IC 199; *EL* 77 = SE 221; *OL* 233 = OL 177-78; *OC* I.289-91, etc.

12. Cf. 2:337; 1:156, = N 365, 98 etc.

13. 2:331, cf. 3:104 = N 361, cf. 480.

14. Perrin and Thibon, p. 41 = 33–34.

15. 3:62 = N 452. It is a question of necessity in the *Psalms*. God imposed a limit on the waters: "Thou hast set a bound that they may not pass over; that they turn not again to cover the earth" (*Psalm* 104, v. 9, quoted in *En* 243 = NR 288).

16. *IP* 31 = IC 97. Cf. 2:158, 193 = N 2433, 266; *CS* 83 = F 133; *LR* 54 = GTG 127-28.

17. *CS* 168 = F 211; cf. *CS* 91 = F 140; 2:133 = N 228. See also 2:78 = N 192.

18. *CS* 225-26 = F 263, *IP* 69 = IC 129. "In our being God is torn apart. We are the crucifixion of God. My existence crucifies God" (3:230 = N 564).

19. Let us note that taking Weil's Kantian views on space and time as mere subjective, though universal, factors of our sensibility as a point of departure, one might perhaps resolve the apparently irreducible opposition between the texts that pose the material creation as obstacle between God and God, and those that attribute that role only to human autonomy.

20. 3:91 = N 471. The distinction was already known to Weil as a student: "The human mind is not made to understand that which exists, but rather that which is" (*OC* I.304). Cf. the paper "L'Existence et l'Objet" (*OC* I.80-88). However, even some mature writings forget or turn the distinction around, such as this note from New York: "God created me as *non-being* that appears to *be*, so that in renouncing out of love what I think my *being*, I leave *nothingness*" (*CS* 42 = F 96-97, my italics). Nevertheless, a great number of essential texts are clear: "existence" is the mode of being of the free human being; it is a condition only relatively true, apparent (*CS* 42 = F 96-97), or imaginary (*CS* 176 = F 218; cf. *CS* 226 = F 263, *PS* 109 = SN 184-85). Let us add that Weil seems to have recognized a certain similarity between her notion of existence and the use existentialists make of the term, but she vigorously reproaches the latter for having valorized a de facto state she never ceased denouncing (2:96 = N 203). On her critique of existentialism, cf. "Lettre à Jean Wahl," *Deucalion* 4 (1952):257 = SL 161. Yet also see 2:89 = N 199.

21. 2:202. Cf. 2:195 = N 272 and this text from her seventeenth year: "The good is therefore the very movement by which one uproots oneself from oneself as an individual" (*OC* I.71). In New York, she prays as follows: "Father. . .tear this body and this soul away from me. . .to make of them things belonging to you, and allow to subsist of me, eternally, only that wrenching apart" (*CS* 205 = F 244).

22. *AD* 174 = WG 224. Cf. *CS* 104–5, 165 = F 152, 209; *IP* 137, 153 = IC 177, 186–87.

23. For the young Weil the opposition me-I expresses that opposition between the noumenal self and the phenomenal self in Kant. Thus "in all circumstances, to be a human being is to know how to separate the 'I' and the 'me' " (*Leçons de Philosophie de Simone Weil*, 206 = LPxx). The distinction reappears in a passage of the *Cahiers* (2:326 = N 357–38), but in general in the mature writings "me" (3:10, 2:60, 2:205 = N 419, 180, 274, etc.) and "I" (1:198, 2:53, 2:59, 2:91, 2:331, 2:204, 3:8, = N 126, 175, 179–80, 200–201, 361, 274, 417 etc.) are equivalent.

24. *EL* 16 = SE 14. Cf. *EL* 30 sq. = SE 24, *CS* 136 = F 182.

25. *OC* I.282. For a more nuanced expression of this view, cf. *CS* 128 = F 174–75.

26. "As God, being outside the universe, is at the same time its center, in the same way each human being has an imaginary locus at the center of the world. The illusion of perspective situates the individual at the center of space; a similar illusion falsifies our sense of time; and still another similar illusion organizes the whole hierarchy of values around us. This illusion extends even to the awareness of existence, because of the close connection in us of the awareness of value and the awareness of being; being seems less and less dense as it is farther from us" (*AD* 117–18 = WG 158–59.)

27. *IP* 142 = IC 178; 2:292 = N 334.

28. *EL* 17 = SE 14. Cf. 1:198 = N 126. Cf. "Surprise is perhaps the special attribute of existence. Ideas do not astonish. . .the result of an addition surprises because existence appears naked" (*OC* I.300). Here "existence" has the same sense as "person" in *EL*.

29. 2:335 = N 364. Cf. *LP* 117 = LP 98.

30. Cf. *IP* 30 = IC 96. Cf. 3:218 = N 556.

31. 2:96–97 = N 204. Cf. 1:219 = N 140. See also 2:91 = N 200.

32. 2:117, 144 = N 218, 235.

33. 2:135 = N 229; *AD* 117 = WG 158; 2:132 = N 227.

34. 1:80; 1:97; 2:247; 3:280 = N, 48, 59, 302, 598; *AD* 159–60 = WG 205–6, etc.

35. *IP* 156 = IC 189. Cf. *CS* 234 = F 270. Whereas "supreme justice is the acceptance of the coexistence with us of all beings and all things that in fact exist" (*IP* 156 = IC 189). Cf. *IP* 137 = IC 173–74. The precondition of justice is thus the abandonment of perspective (1:37–38 = N 19; *CS* 31, 14 = F, 87, 70; 2:44 = N 299).

36. On personal existence insofar as due only to acknowledgment of us by others, see 1:189 = N 120; *EL* 35 = SE 27–28; *PS* 115 = SN 188–89; *AD* 109 = WG 109; *IP* 78 = IC 137–38; *EL* 27 = SE 21; *OL* 191 = OL 144–45. See also LP 203 = LP 161–62, and the essay "Caractère" (ms.).

37. 2:90 = N 200. Cf. *AD* 107–8 = WG 146–48; *CS* 264 = F 297; *AD* 136 = WG 179–80.

38. 3:193 = N 539. Cf. 2:115–16, 135, 220–21; 3:197 = N 216–17, 229, 284, 542. Cf. the influence of Alain on this idea of Weil's: Simone Pétrement, "Sur la religion d'Alain avec quelques remarques concernant celle de Simone Weil," *Revue de Métaphysique et de Morale* 3 (July–October 1955):306–30.

39. *CS* 170. Cf. *CS* 175 = F 213, cf. F 217–18.

40. *IP* 137 = IC 174. Cf. *IP* 44 = IC 108–9, *AD* 98 = WG 133–34. Cf. "God created me as a non-being who appears to exist, so that in renouncing this existence out of love, the fullness of being annihilates me" (*CS* 42 = F 96). Cf. "God gave me being in order that I may give it back to him. It is like one of those tests resembling traps that one sees in tales or stories of initiation. If I accept this gift, it is fatal and evil. Its virtue becomes apparent through refusing it. God allows me to exist being other than him. It is up to me to refuse this authorization" (3:110–11 = N 484–85). Cf. *CS* 132 = F 178.

41. 3:303 = N 614. Cf. *CS* 91 = F 140–41.

42. *CS* 232 = F 269. Cf. *CS* 169 = F 212. Here we take the liberty of quoting Claudel: "The creature / Seeing the being that had been given her, seized it, / Making of herself her end, and such was the first abduction and the first incest" ("Le Repos du Septième Jour," *Théâtre* [Paris: Pléiade, 1956], 1:824).

43. Cf. *IP* 48 = IC 112, 2:144 = N 234–35.

44. "It is enough to be without free will to be the equal of God" (*CS* 195 = F 226).

45. 2:187 = N 262. Cf. "Destruction is the extreme opposite of decreation" (2:303 = N 342). See also chapter 4. Cf. 1:98, 126; 3:130; 1:68 = N 60–61, 78–79, 498, 40; *IP* 148 = IC 183.

46. 2:196 = N 597. Cf. *CS* 40 = F 94–95. Will must deplete itself (2:336 = N 336–37, *CS* 195–96 = F 235–36).

47. 3:278 = N 597; *PS* 38, 115 = SN 154–55, 188–89; *AD* 27 = WG 59.

48. It is, moreover, the one free act granted us (2:295 = N 336–37). Grace gives its help (2:303 = N 342), but "God...does not undo creation; it is for creation to undo itself" (2:158 = N 243).

49. 2:185, 192–93 = N 261, 266. See also *IP* 141 = IC 177. Expressed in terms of Christian theology, this would mean that human beings have the vocation to develop their moral and spiritual faculties in this life and that, without original sin, the attainment of moral perfection would coincide with death. But death comes to the sinful human being like a thief in the night; it is thus found to be a break instead of a consummation, a pure maturation of humanity from within. Cf. K. Rahner, *Ecrits théologiques* (Paris), 3:139–40. See 2:357 = N 378, quoted in Chapter 6.

50. *CS* 175 = F 218. Cf. *CS* 43 = F 97. Cf. "For glass, nothing more is required than to be absolutely transparent. For a human being, nothing more is required than to be nothingness" (*CS* 326–27 = F 354). Cf. "Hell is to notice that one does not exist and not to consent to it" (*CS* 176 = F 121). *CS* 194 = F 234. See also the commentaries on the *Republic* 514a–516c in *SG* 98–103 = SN 106–111.

51. *OC* II.ii.253 = FW 225.

52. *OC* II.ii.234 = FW 211. Seven years later she wrote to Father Perrin of her factory experience: "What I underwent there marked me in such a lasting way that even today when a human being, whoever it may be, in whatever circumstances, speaks to me without violence, I cannot stop myself from having the impression that there must be some mistake and that the mistake will, unfortunately, probably be soon cleared up" (*AD* 36 = WG 67).

53. *CS* 42, 175, 48, 51 = F, 96–97, 217–18, 101–2, 132.

54. 2:206 = N 275. Cf. 2:134; 2:186 = N 229, 262.

55. There is a profound ontological distinction between existence, that is autonomy, and reality (cf. 2:406 = N 410). On the one hand, existence is opposed to the domain of the intelligible (3:52 = N 446), that is, of the necessary or of being (*SG* 118 = SN 122; 2:121–22 = N 220); on the other, to the good (*CS* 264 = F 297). Cf. Salvation means that "[w]e will be pure good. We will no longer exist. But in that nothingness at the limit of the good, we will be more real than at any moment of our earthly life" (*CS* 280 = F 311). Cf. *CS* 109, 224 = F 157, 262; 3:124 = N 494.

56. *IP* 160 = IC 192–93. Cf. *IP* 142 = IC 178.

57. However, "[w]hen a man turns away from God, he simply surrenders himself to gravity. Afterwards he thinks he desires and chooses, but he is only a thing, a falling stone" (*AD* 90 = WG 128).

58. *SG* 167 = SN 143; *IP* 61 = IC 123; *SG* 116–17 = IC 157–58; 2:214 = N 280; *SG* 97 = SN 105, etc.

59. *AD* 40–41 = WG 71–72. In a long letter to Joë Bousquet, Weil uses the symbolism of the "egg" (the "natural" world) to describe the process: "When the shell is pierced, when being has gone out of it, it still has for object that same world. But it is no longer inside.... The mind...is transported to a point outside space that is not a point of view, from which there is no perspective, from which this visible world is seen as it is, without perspective" (Simone Weil and Joë Bousquet, *Correspondance* [Lausanne: L'Age d'Homme, 1982], p. 38 = SL 136). Cf. *AD* 40–41 = WG 71–72. Still, it must be noted that she is not certain whether there exists a state from which the soul cannot fall back into an autonomous existence. Cf. *CS* 279 = F 310.

60. "It is given to very few minds to discover that things and beings exist," Weil writes to Bousquet. And she confesses to him: "From my childhood I have desired only to receive this revelation... evil actions are those that hide the reality of things and beings, or those that it would be impossible to do if one truly knew that things and beings existed" (*Correspondance*, p. 18 = SL 116). Cf. 1:84 = N 51; *AD* 69 = WG 101; *EL* 50 = PI 4.

61. *CS* 292, 249 = F 322–23, 283–84.

62. 2:243 = N 290. Cf. *CS* 35 = F 90; 2:236–37, 87, 223 = N 295, 198, 292. Perrin and Thibon, p. 128 = 115. "One must love one's enemies because they exist" (2:193 = N 267).

63. On the identification of love with consent, see *IP* 55 = IC 117–18; 3:59 = N 450; *IP* 163 = IC 145; *LR* 26 = GTG 112. "Where there is complete, authentic, and unconditional consent to necessity, there is the fullness of love of God" (*IP* 149 = IC 184). Other texts stress that the supernatural faculty in us is consent (*IP* 147 = IC 183, cf. *CS* 163 = F 206). Finally, one also reads that consent is always consent to the good, and, as such, it is the good itself (3:175 = N 527, *CS* 193–94 = F 234). On the other hand, see *CS* 131 = F 177–78. On supernatural assistance to consent, see *IP* 153, 11–15, 21 = IC 187, 3–6; 2:395 = N 404. The origin of the notion of "consent," moreover, is Stoic (*AD* 35 = WG 65), influenced also by Platonic elements (3:190 = N 558; *IP* 55 = IC 117–18).

64. *AD* 118–19 = WG 158–59. Cf. *EL* 56–57 = PI 9.

65. *AD* 93 = WG 130.

66. *AD* 91, 160 = WG 128, 206–7; *IP* 73 = IC 133–34.

67. "The aspect it presented to us earlier and that it still presents to almost our whole being, to the natural part of ourselves, is brutal domination. The aspect it presents after this operation to that

fragment of our thought that has passed over to the other side is pure obedience" (*IP* 153 = IC 189). Cf. *PS* 111 = SN 186; *IP* 154 = IC 187–88.

68. A note from London goes so far as to say: "The very power of God is also obedience" (*CS* 309 = F 338). Obedience to the good? Obedience to the laws he himself made and through which he consents to the existence of all that is (cf. *En* 223 = NR 263, *IP* 150 = IC 184–85)? We do not think we can or ought to insist on these questions.

69. *IP* 161 = IC 193. To the extent it means acceptance of the true place of each person in time and space, as well as of the coexistence of all beings and all things, the gift of decreation has its analogy in the material universe. Cf. *EL* 160.

70. Obedience is only love of the order of the world and, as such, it is an imitation of God (*AD* 117 = WG 158). Cf. *EL* 48 = PI 3–4, *PS* 35 = SN 153.

71. *AD* 17 = WG 47. Cf. *AD* 25, 43 = WG 56, 75; 2:206–207 = N 275; also 2:210 = N 277. But "the acceptance of hell out of respect for the will of God is good when the soul feels itself on the brink of damnation, evil when it feels itself on the brink of salvation, for then one accepts hell for others" (*CS* 69 = F 122).

72. *AD* 92 = WG 126; Cf. *En* 244–45 = NR 289–90; *CS* 225 = F 262–63. True freedom resides in obedience (*EL* 91–92).

73. On the absurdity of the notion of choice, see 2:341–42 = N 368; *AD* 33 = WG 69; 1:204, 2:359, 3:40–41 = N 130, 380, 438.

74. Still, from the "perspective of God," the soul does not see a different truth but a more complex one: "One must not, in the thought of the supernatural, in this life or after death, seek a loosening of the chains of necessity. The supernatural is more precise, more rigorous than the crude mechanism of matter. It is added to this mechanism and does not alter it. It is a chain upon a chain, a chain of steel upon a chain of brass" (*CS* 131–32 = F 178). Cf. 2:150 = N 239; *SG* 141; see also 2:21–22 = N 155–56.

75. *AD* 92 = WG 128–29.

76. Weil wrote of the young workers of Marseilles: "In the factory, matter weighs endlessly upon one's body and thoughts, and almost irresistibly forces one to descend. They are subject to matter more than others; but once they become aware of themselves, they feel more than others that they are so subject, and that is an immense superiority" ("A propos des jocistes," *Cahiers du Sud*, April 1941, p. 245, under the pseudonym Emile Novis).

77. 2:188 = N 263. Or "[t]o be as unconscious matter would be, if it were conscious" (*CS* 167 = F 211). Cf. *CS* 260 = F 294.

78. Cf. Perrin and Thibon, p. 41 = 33–34. Cf. *IP* 150, 167 = IC 184, 197.

79. "In order to achieve perfect obedience, one must exercise one's will, one must strive until one has exhausted in oneself the finite quantity of the kind of imperfection that corresponds to effort and to will. The effort of the will must wear down this imperfection in finite quantity in the way a wheel wears down a piece of metal. After this, there is no more effort or will. All that appears to be resistance to be overcome, inertia, fatigue, inferior desire on the level of will— all of that, when one has passed beyond a certain threshold, becomes suffering passively undergone; and movements are no more action than is immobility. When one is at that point, there truly is obedience" (2:336 = N 364). Cf. *CS* 296 = F 326.

80. *AD* 135 = WG 179; Cf. *CS* 37 = F 92. All human goods have their analogy in God, and among these obedience also: "It is the game he leaves in this world for necessity" (3:35 = N 434). Obedience is not only imitation of the God of Love, but also of God the Almighty: "The image of the indifferent power of God is the passive obedience of the creature" (*CS* 78 = F 130).

81. "The part of the soul located on the other side of the curtain" (2:186 = N 262). Pride means being proud of personal attributes (cf. *CS* 248 = F 283) on this side of the curtain (1:193 = N 123) and not noticing the divine spark in the soul: "To be proud," therefore, "is to forget that one is God" (1:200 = N 127); "the part of our soul that, like him, resides in the heavens" (*CS* 68 = F 120); "The supernatural point in our soul" (3:79 = N 463); "the immortal part of the soul" (2:163 = N 247); "the eternal part of the soul" (*CS* 252 = F 286); "the divine part of the soul" (2:369 = N 386), etc.

82. *CS* 248, 49 = F 283, 103.

83. 2:85 = N 196. Cf. 2:163 = N 247. Cf. "The Spirit...is the self of the perfect human being. It is the de-created self" (2:189 = N 264).

84. *AD* 116 = WG 159. See also 3:127 = N 496.

85. Cf. my paper on "Le mal selon Simone Weil," Akten des XIV. Internationalen Kongresses fur Philosophie, Vienna, 1969, 3:628–33.

86. "Evil is the distance between the creature and God. To abolish evil is to de-create" (2:303 = N 342). Note the identification of decreation with the suppression of evil! Cf. 2:184, 3:365 = N 261, 588; *CS* 263, 49 = F 296, 103; 3:13, 2:133 = N 486, 228. Evil comes

only from humanity (2:65 = N 183; cf. CS 176, 168 = F 218, 211). Another very striking formulation of evil as distance: "There are all scales of distance between the creature and God. A distance where love of God is impossible. Matter, plants, animals. Evil there is so complete that it destroys itself; there is no longer any evil; mirror of divine innocence." There is "the level where evil becomes innocence" (3:307 = N 616).

87. The good that is beyond being (cf. *Republic* 509b, quoted in *PS* 49) is the love of God in his perfect non-substantiality and humility. However, the necessity that is the other face of the real is also good, as pure and docile intelligibility (cf. CS 225 = F 263). Therefore, in a larger sense, the real and the good are ultimately identical (cf. CS 109–10 = F 157; 2:337 = N 365), even if their unity still remains a mystery (*OL* 229 = OL 174, quoted by R. Rees, *Simone Weil*, p. 95). See also note 68 above. Evil is that which is opposed to the two attributes of the real so conceived. In terms of inter-subjectivity, cf. 1:20 = N 8.

88. 2:295; 2:53 = N 336, 175.

89. 3:80 = N 464. Cf. CS 238 = F 274. One thereby becomes an intermediary between God and the material world, thus in the end between God and God (CS 81, 16 = F 132, 72; 2:335; 2:391–92; 3:16; 3:108 = N 363, 401, 422, 483.

90. We wish to quote at greater length a magnificent description of the decreative process: "The Holy Spirit is also the seed that falls on every soul. To receive him, the soul must become a simple matrix, a receptacle, something fluid, passive; water. Then the seed becomes an embryo, then a child; Christ is born in the soul. What I called I, me, is destroyed, liquefied; in place of that, there is a new being, grown from the seed fallen from God into the soul.... At the end of this process, 'I live no longer, but Christ lives in me.' It is another being that is engendered by God, another 'I.' ...it is the Son of God...as a parasite lays its eggs in the flesh of an animal, so God deposits in our soul a sperm that will, upon attaining maturity, be his Son.... Our soul ought to be uniquely a place of welcome and of nourishment for that divine germ. We must not give our soul anything to eat. We must give our soul to that germ to eat. After which it will eat, directly, everything our soul formerly ate. Our soul is an egg where that divine germ becomes a bird. The bird embryo is nourished by the egg...once it has become a bird, it breaks the shell, goes out, and pecks at seeds. Our soul is separated from all reality by a film of egotism, subjectivity, illusion; the germ of Christ

deposited by God in our soul, feeds upon it; when it is developed enough, it shatters the soul, causes it to burst, and enters into contact with reality" (*CS* 253–54 = F 287–88).

91. Dissolution of the human being is not at stake, for this unconditional "yes" that "bears truly into heaven, to the Father's breast, the part of the soul that pronounces it" (*IP* 58 = IC 120) is not "annihilation, but vertical transport into the reality superior to being" (3:196 = N 542). However, see also the passage cited in note 57 above.

92. Whereas to disobey implies not knowing that God is real (*CS* 87 = F 137).

2. Attention and Desire

1. Some of the major themes of this chapter are discussed in my paper on "Attention according to Simone Weil," Ecoute. . . (Sainte-Marie de la Pierre-qui-Vire, 1970), 7:49–55. An excellent analysis and description of most of the aspects of Weil's notion of attention can be found in the unpublished thesis of Dwight Harwell, "Fruitful Attention."

2. In her first surviving student paper one reads: "The only strength and the only virtue is to refrain from acting" ("Le Conte des Six Cygnes dans Grimm," *OC* I.59). A few months later she wrote: "If action were not preceded by attention, it would not be action" ("Que la seule action est la pensée," *OC* I.316). As a beginning teacher, she devoted a large part of her courses to problems of attention, and a note from this period states: "All the mind's strength is attention. The only power that is ours" ("Philosophie, Premières Années d'Enseignement" [1931–34], ms., f. 260).

3. *OL* 115 sq. = OL 85ff. Cf. *CO* 16, 166 = SL 15.

4. Cf. *AD* 71 sq. = WG 105ff.; 2:198 = N 269; "Philosophie, Premières Années d'Enseignement" (1931–34), ms., f. 260.

5. Cf. 2:291 = N 333, *SG* 116 = SN 120. "Wrong way to seek. Attention attached to the problem. . . . One must not want to find. As in the case of excessive devotion, one becomes dependent on the object of the effort. One needs an external reward, which chance sometimes provides, and which one is ready to receive at the cost of a deformation of the truth" (2:43 = N 169).

6. Defined in a very general way: "It is in desiring the truth in emptiness and without trying to guess its content in advance that one obtains light. That is the whole mechanism of attention" (*EL* 139). Cf. 2:168 = N 250.

7. *AD* 72 = WG 106. Cf.: "Attention must always be directed toward the object...never toward the self" (1:202 = N 128).

8. *IP* 61 = IC 187; *SG* 116–17, 167 = SN 120, 143.

9. *IP* 154–55 = IC 187–88. Cf. 3:175 = N 527.

10. 2:298 = N 338. Cf. *EL* 36 = SE 28.

11. R. Bourgeois, "La Spiritualité du travail selon Simone Weil," unpublished thesis, part I, chapter 4.

12. *CO* 270 = SWA 273. The first criterion of a good political and social order is its capacity to preserve the faculty of attention in the people (cf. *EL* 21 = SE 17), whereas the sole task of education is to develop it harmoniously (3:278 = N 597, *EL* 160, etc.).

13. Cf. 3:309 = N 618. Speaking of the hero of her unfinished play, *Venise Sauvée*: "The moment of Jaffier's meditation...is the moment when reality enters into him because he is paying attention" (3:214). Taken up again in *P* 47.

14. *IP* 155 = IC 188. Cf. *IP* 154 = IC 187.

15. Weil and Bousquet, *Correspondance*, p. 18. "We bestow as much of the fullness of reality as there is in us on the things and beings around us," (*IP* 155 = IC 188).

16. *AD* 109 = WG 149. "Creative attention consists in truly paying attention to what does not exist. Humanity does not exist in the anonymous and inert body by the roadside. The Samaritan who stops and looks nevertheless pays attention to that absent humanity" (*AD* 109 = WG 149). "That gaze is first of all an attentive gaze, in which the soul is emptied of all particular content in order to be able to receive into itself the being it gazes upon, such as it is in all its truth. Only a person able to give attention is capable of this" (*AD* 80 = WG 115).

17. Cf. 3:156, 174 = N 515, 527; *CS* 44 = F 99; 2:261, 3:278 = N 311, 597.

18. *AD* 76 = WG 111. We note that according to Saint Thomas, the sin of Lucifer was the lack of attention (*Summa Theologica* 1:63, 1–4; *Summa contra Gentiles* 3:110). See also chapter 4, note 18.

19. *CS* 274 = F 306. Cf.: "Attitude of supplication: I must necessarily turn toward something other than myself, since it is a question of being delivered from myself" (2:59 = N 179). Cf. 2:73 = N 188.

20. "Waiting is the passivity of thought in actuality" (*CS* 47 = F 101).

21. "One of the crucial truths of Christianity...is that it is the gaze that is saving" (*AD* 147 = WG 192). Cf. *PS* 41–42 = SN 157.

That gaze is the same thing as "the eye of the soul" in the *Republic*, identified elsewhere with attention (3:174 = N 527). It is the instrument of conversion, that is to say, of salvation (*AD* 148 = WG 193).

22. 1:150 = N 94. On patience and faithfulness in waiting, cf. *AD* 150-51, 78 = WG 195-97, 113-14; *PS* 76, 44-45 = SL 137, SN 159.

23. *CS* 91, 44 = F 141, 99.

24. "God is waiting like a beggar standing motionless and silent before someone who perhaps will give him a piece of bread...God is only the good. That is why he is there and is waiting in silence. Whoever steps forward or speaks uses a bit of force. The good that is only good cannot help but be present there. Beggars who have modesty are its image" (*CS* 91 = F 141).

25. A passage in the *Cahiers* identifies the Holy Spirit with attention (3:326 = N 628). The Spirit being the mutual love between the Father and the Son, one might express the link between the two aspects of God in terms of attention.

26. Cf. *CO* 261 = SWA 265, 3:89 = N 470.

27. It is interesting to note that nothing tends more precisely towards its goal than "blind desire." The very blindness of desire shows, in a paradoxical way, that the self has chosen a particular object it would like to appropriate to itself at any price. "Blind" desire is thus "directed" desire.

28. Cf. 3:125, 128 = N 494, 496; *OL* 209 = OL 173; *CS* 249 = F 284; *IP* 35 = IC 100; "Sur les responsabilités de la littérature," *Cahiers du Sud* 310 (1951):428 = SN 167; *PS* 43 = SN 158.

29. *Chandogya Upanishad* III, 14:1 in 1:237. Cf. *AD* 168 = WG 217.

30. 3:228 = N 562. Cf. *EL* 74 = SE 219.

31. *Symposium* 205d, 206a, quoted in *IP* 70 = IC 130. Cf. *SG* 92 = SN 101. Here Weil's translation of Plato constitutes part of her own theory of desire. Cf.: "The good is what every soul seeks and why it acts, intuiting that it is something real, but uncertain and incapable of grasping sufficiently what it is" (*Republic* 505e in *SG* 93 = SN 102). Cf. *SG* 96. See also the translation of *Chandogya Upanishad* VII, 1:5 = N 19-20 and the attached note in 1:231.

32. 3:14 = N 421. Cf. 2:96, 3:209 = N 203, 550.

33. "Here the object of our request is what is produced in time. But we ask for the infallible and eternal conformity of what is produced in time with the divine will. After having, by the first request, pulled desire out of time in order to apply it to the eternal, and after having transformed it in this way, we take that desire up

again, its having in a certain way become eternal, in order to apply it again to time" (*AD* 169 = WG 218).

34. *AD* 169 = WG 218. On the same process of formalization and purification applied to attention through the mathematical relation between the invariable and variations, see 3:308–9 = N 617.

35. 3:118 = N 489. Cf. 2:397; 3:207 = N 404, 548.

36. *CS* 285 = F 316. Cf. 3:120–22, 201–2 = N 491–92, 545; *CS* 109 = F 157; 1:200 = N 127.

37. The "literal" proof, if one be needed, is to be found in the lessons given by Weil in Roanne: "Kant: Act solely according to the maxim you can want at the same time to become a universal law." "Act as if the maxim for your action ought to be raised by your will into a universal law of nature." "(In other words, one puts oneself in God's perspective.)" (*Leçons de Philosophie de Simone Weil*, p. 181 = LP xx).

38. Moreover, Weil herself identifies or closely relates them in many texts. Cf. *IP* 62 = IC 123; 3:175 = N 527, *AD* 73, 75 = WG 107, 110; etc.

39. Cf. the text quoted in note 90 of the preceding chapter.

3. Energy, Motives, and the Void

1. 3:192–93 = N 539. Cf. *CS* 194 = F 234.

2. The expression "supplementary energy" appears for the first time in an early note on Freud (*OC* I.280). Cf. *CS* 252 = F 286. Cf. also the terms "animal energies" *CS* 178 = F 220) and "errant energy" (*CS* 189 = F 230).

3. *CS* 260 = F 294. Cf. *CS* 259 = F 293. See also *CS* 252 = F 286.

4. "Each earthly soul cries out 'I have had enough' when all its resources of supplementary energy have been exhausted, when vegetative energy, which serves to maintain life itself, is exposed and begins to be spent. . . . The will enabling one to resist has then disappeared. Living flesh is struck and devoured. . . . It is then impossible for the entire creaturely soul not to cry out: 'Enough.'. . . Then, if the eternal part of the soul answers, speaking to the true God, 'Forever, if it is your wish,' the soul is divided in two. What one feels as being the self is in the part that cries 'Enough,' and one still takes the part of the other interlocutor. That is truly to go out of the self" (*CS* 177–78 = F 220).

5. "A quarter-hour of this is truly equivalent to a perpetual duration of voluntary efforts, in such a way that after that quarter-

hour, the part of the soul that has refused to cry 'Enough' has crossed the indeterminate length of time and passed to the other side of time into eternity" (*CS* 178 = F 220). This ordeal is "[w]hen the sap itself flows out and the still surviving man becomes dead wood" (*CS* 178 = F 220).

6. At issue is an absurd consent not to exist, but "[c]onsenting not to exist is consenting to the privation of every good, and this consent constitutes the possession of total good" (*CS* 194 = F 234). It is a choice of which one is not even conscious at the moment one makes it (*CS* 180 = F 222).

7. Cf. the elaboration of the parable of the Prodigal Son (*CS* 181 = F 223).

8. *CS* 183, 254, 256–57 = F 224. 288, 290–91.

9. From time to time Weil uses the word "motif" simply as a synonym of "mobile" (*CS* 99–100 = F 148), but occasionally there is a real difference between their content. It is quite probably that they originate in translations of Kant, where "mobile" expresses "Triebfeder" and "motif" "Bewegursache" (cf. for example "Grundlegung zur Metaphysik der Sitten," *Sammtliche Werke* [1867] 2:290; in French, *Les Fondements de la Métaphysique des Moeurs*, trans. Delbos [Paris: Delagrave, 1954], p. 173). The German word "Triebfeder" suggests something carnal, whereas "mobile" suggests a force that desires and pushes. "Bewegursache" is a more general term used to express the reason, the cause of a movement or act, without at the same time specifying anything of the character for that reason or cause; it seems to be the most faithfully rendered by "motif." Nevertheless, it must be noted that Weil did not always closely follow the Kantian distinction, and her use of "mobile" refers above all to the personal goals of self-expansion and includes all representations that can incite the self to act, thus practically all representations that, naturally, that is to say, without relationship to decreation, can incite a human being to act.

10. See the long analyses on energy, motives, and the void in 2:9–14 = N 147–50, taken up again with few changes in *CS* 111–14 = F 159–61.

11. Weil goes so far as to say that "[t]he imagination is supplementary energy" (2:123 = N 221).

12. 2:55–56 = N 179. And Weil continues: "To make such an effort to help a wretched person one has never seen before; unless the vanity of 'doing good' intervenes, one can only be drawn to this by a view of justice and an effort of the imagination. But fatigue soon

puts an end to it, falsifies the balance, and invents sophisms. What remains present to the spirit when attention is released is base" (ibid.). Cf. *EL* 72 = PI1 97; 1:116–17, 192–93, 180, 62 = N 73, 122, 114, 36.

13. *CS* 249–50, 290 = F 284–85, 321. See also *IP* 135–36 = IC 172–73.

14. *CS* 194–95 = F 235–36. Cf. 3:124 = N 493. Weil compares these men to the giants of a Grimm fairy tale who had hidden their heart at the bottom of a lake and who, afterward, could not find it again (cf. *CS* 276 = F 308).

15. 2:220, 175 = N 283, 254.

16. *AD* 156 = WG 202; 2:233 = N 292.

17. *CS* 99–100 = F 148. Cf. 1:69, 214–15, 2:40 = N 41, 137, 167. The other favorite example in the *Cahiers* is Harpagon, who, having been robbed, lost his accumulated energy (2:55 = N 176). Cf. 2:94–95 = N 202.

18. *CS* 112 = F 160. Cf. 2:13 = N 150.

19. 2:13 = N 150. Cf. *CS* 112 = F 160.

20. 1:227 = N 145. Cf. 3:116; 2:313 = N 488, 348. Because of the necessities of life in the cave, the first duty is "to find the least evil idols" (2:13 = N 150). Cf. "The best institutions are those that lie the least" (2:116 = N 217).

21. 2:9 = N 147. Cf. "There truly is a void, for there is non-directed energy in the soul" (2:88 = N 198). Cf. 2:53 = N 175.

22. 2:13 = N 150. Cf. "the void-filling imagination" (1:227 = N 145). Cf. 2:21 = N 155. "What makes human beings capable of sinning is the void; all sins are attempts to fill up voids" (*CS* 113 = F 160). Cf. 2:12 = N 149.

23. Let it not be forgotten that for the early Weil, "error always means fault in the moral sense of the word" (*OC* I.282). Later, the identity will be nuanced into analogy (*CS* 128 = F 174), but it remains that "[w]rong actions are those the energy of which has been constituted by an error. All particular motives are errors. Only energy furnished by no motive is good" (2:148 = N 237).

24. *Leçons de Philosophie de Simone Weil*, p. 181 = LP xx. However, "[t]he moral law...is my very being" (*OC* I.66); there is therefore no question of a transcendent God.

25. *S* 29 = FW 43. Present author's italics.

26. We note that in the middle of a passage bearing on energy and motives, Weil seems to sum up her own itinerary from non-perspective toward the perspective of God: "N.B. Kant leads to grace" (2:94 = N 202).

27. Amid many sketches, perhaps the most systematic treatment is the one offered by "La théorie des sacrements" (*PS* 135 sq. = GTG 65–72).

28. 1:22 = N 135. *CS* 100 = F 149.

29. "There is a transcendent energy, its source in heaven, that flows in us once we desire it. It truly is a form of energy; it carries out actions through the intermediary of our soul and our body" (*AD* 172 = WG 221).

30. The "choice of Paradise" in the ordeal is possible only for those who are "rooted" in love (*CS* 178 = F 220; cf. 2:192–93 = N 266), whence the extreme importance of the right use of vegetative energy before the ordeal (cf. 2:321 = N 354).

31. 1:69; 2:16; = N 41, 152 etc.

32. 3:120 = N 491. It is only our "inverted condition" (*CS* 285 = F 317) that kept us from seeing that the void was "the supreme fullness" (2:11), whereas the life of the self unfolded in a "false fullness" (3:180 = N 531). The decreated person is from now on in the "free, breathable land" (*PS* 83 = SL 141).

33. *CS* 100 = F 149. "Obedience is the sole pure motive, the only one not including in any degree reward for the action and leaving all care for reward to the father who is in secret, who sees in secret" (2:13 = N 150). Matthew 6:18 is quoted immediately following.

4. Suffering and Affliction

1. *AD* 51 = WG 83. If one wished to indulge in cheap psychological reflections, it would perhaps be easy to "explain" the central role of suffering in Weil by reference to the "masochistic tastes" of this woman who knew herself to be "a badly cut-off piece of God" (J. Cabaud, *Simone Weil à New York et à Londres*, p. 88). However, on the level of *ideas*, the only one of interest to us, the image is quite different. Subject for years to terrible headaches, Weil wrote unequivocally: "I believe in the value of suffering provided that one does everything honestly possible to avoid it" (*Cahiers*, new ed. [1970], 1:11 = F 3). Cf. *CO* 145 = SL 41; *IP* 148 = IC 183. There is no question of a morbid quest for subjective sensations or of a selfish enrichment; cf. *PS* 121–22 = SN 192–93 and the analyses of M. Narcy, *Simone Weil, Malheur et beauté du monde*, pp. 20–29. At issue is the following: "Believing that reality is love, seeing it all the while exactly as it is. Loving what is intolerable. Embracing iron, pressing one's flesh against the hardness and coldness of metal. This is not a form

of masochism. Masochists are excited by the enactment of cruelty, because they don't know what cruelty is. But what must be embraced is not cruelty; it is blind indifference and brutality" (CS 222–23 = F 260).

2. A shorter exposition of a certain number of themes in this chapter is found in my article "Suffering in Simone Weil," *Thought* (1965), pp. 275–86.

3. "If, by an absurd hypothesis, I died without ever having committed any grave sins and on my death fell nevertheless into the depths of hell, I would all the same owe God an infinite gratitude for his infinite mercy because of my life on earth" (AD 59 = WG 90).

4. Except for an early note identifying original sin with the body (OC I.90), Weil distinguishes very clearly—in varying terms—between body and flesh (3:53, 77 = N 447, 462 etc.).

5. Stated in terms of energy, suffering is a process creating the void (2:132 = N 227). Compare: "In this world only physical suffering and nothing else is capable of imprisoning thought, provided that one likens to physical pain certain corporeal phenomena that are difficult to describe and rigorously equivalent to it. The apprehension of physical pain is notably of this type" (AD 82 = WG 118). See Perrin and Thibon, p. 146 = 132; PS 112 = SN 186.

6. CS 189 = F 230. "One part of the soul wants to fulfill an obligation, such as returning a deposit; another does not want to. They struggle. The body is the balance.... In a sense, it judges between the soul and the soul, as does the balance between weight and weight" (CS 256 = F 290).

7. CS 189 = F 230. Cf. CS 267, 271 = F 300, 303.

8. IP 167 = IC 198; CS 36 = F 91.

9. Cf. 3:122, 86, = N 492, 468 etc.

10. "We are nothing more than a place where the divine Love of God for himself passes through" (IP 166–67 = IC 197). Cf. AD 89–90 = WG 126; 2:391–92 = N 401; CS 27 = F 83; 3:192 = N 539. See also IP 149 = IC 184.

11. "[T]he growth of the seed in us is painful. In addition, by the very fact that we accept this growth, we cannot keep ourselves from destroying anything that might disturb it, pulling up bad grass, cutting weeds. Unfortunately, these weeds are part of our very flesh, so this gardening is a violent operation" (AD 95 = WG 133) Cf. IP 149 = IC 183.

12. AD 97–98 = WG 135. The entire process is described in a somewhat condensed form in 3:25–26 = N 428–29.

13. By "nearly infernal" suffering Weil understands the annihilation of the self; "if, before disappearing, the I has had the time, out of rebellion, to hate the good. . .that is the existence of hell" (2:305 = N 343). Cf. 3:25–26 = N 428–29.

14. The central text on this distinction is found in 2:303–05 = N 342–43. Cf. 2:304, 414, 137–38 = N 415–16, 230–31.

15. *AD* 94 = WG 131. Cf. *PS* 112 = SN 186; 1:210, 2:124 = N 134, 222.

16. 2:30 = N 160. Cf. *SG* 85–86 = IC 181–83.

17. 3:50 = N 444. Cf. 1:224 = N 143. The supreme choice for every soul is between truth and life (*OL* 226 = OL 172; *PS* 43 = SE 34; 1:86 = N 52; *AD* 163 = WG 210). Compare the following: "snow is immaculate, perfectly pure like death, cold and sterile. Blood is life itself, the carnal life principle of all stain" ("Folklore. Thème de la neige et du sang," Marseille [1941–42], ms.). "In this world, life, the vital impulse dear to Bergson, is only untruth, and death alone is true. For life compels us to believe what we need to believe in order to live. . . . But beings who despite flesh and blood have gone past an inner limit equivalent to death receive on the other side another life, a life which is not in the first instance life, but which is in the first instance truth. Truth come to life. True like death and alive like life" (*En* 211–12 = NR 249). "One does not enter into truth without going through one's own annihilation; without living for a long time in a state of extreme and total humiliation" (*EL* 34 = SE 27). Three weeks before her death, in her next-to-last letter, Weil wrote to her parents: "In this world, only beings who have sunk to the ultimate degree of humiliation. . .only they can possibly tell the truth" (*EL* 255 = SL 200). Cf. 2:366 = N 384.

18. 3:316 = N 623. Cf. *PS* 38–39 = SN 155–56, *IP* 71 = IC 130. Weil knows that very often the search for pleasure is only a pretext to avoid meeting God: "The soul, incapable of tolerating that lethal presence of God, that burning presence, hides behind flesh, uses flesh as a screen. In this case, it is not the flesh that causes God to be forgotten; it is the soul that seeks in flesh forgetfulness of God, that hides there" (*PS* 40 = SN 156). Cf. 3: 317 = N 623; *AD* 76 = WG 111; 3:314–15 = N 621. See also *CS* 294 = F 325, *PS* 45 = SN 159.

19. *Agamemnon*, 177, quoted in *SG* 44, *IP* 103 = IC 56–59, 68, etc. Weil notes that the word *pathos* evokes the idea of undergoing, rather than that of suffering or pain (*SG* 44 = IC 57).

20. 3:50 = N 444. CF. *IP* 104 = IC 69.

21. 2:146, 116 = N 236, 217. See also *CS* 250 = F 285; 3:38–39 = N 437.

22. "Belief in the immortality of the soul is harmful because it is not in our power to represent the soul as truly incorporeal. Thus this belief is in fact belief in the prolongation of life and takes away the use of death" (3:122 = N 492). Cf. 3:257 = N 582; SG 12 = IC 25; 3:86 = N 468. See also 1:163 = N 103.

23. 3:109 = N 483. Suffering must not be accepted with a view to spiritual consolation, because "counting on a spiritual advantage is under that name to give free rein to the animals that cry 'me' " (CS 192 = F 232). Cf. 1:204–5 = N 130.

24. 3:109, 2:297 = N 483, 337. It is true that Christ offered up his life, but at the precise moment that death neared, his suffering and death did not seem to him to be an offering. He was horrified by them and accepted them only because they were the Father's will (3:54 = N 447). Cf. 3:33, 2:413 = N 433, 415. Therefore, "[f]or whosoever is in affliction, evil can perhaps be defined as being above all that which procures consolation" (PS 83 = SL 142).

25. Suffering implies contradiction because it cannot be avoided (1:228 = N 146). Cf. 2:18 = N 153. But it is not only suffering we find impossible; everything that is impossible is suffering. And that impossibility—suffering—is everywhere in life (2:406, 409 = N 410, 412). This is so because "[e]ach thing we want stands in contradiction to the conditions and consequences attached to it; each affirmation we make implies the opposite affirmation; all our feelings are mixed with their opposites. This is because we are contradiction, being creatures, being God and infinitely other than God" (2:407 = N 411).

26. 1:23–24 = N 10. This is why the acceptance of death that exorcises fear of it is liberation from enslavement (CS 59 = F 112).

27. 2:369, 287, 342 = N 386, 329, 369. Cf. Chapter 5.

28. "Eve and Adam wanted to find divinity in vital energy. A tree, a piece of fruit. But it is prepared for us on geometrically squared-off dead wood upon which a dead body hangs. The secret of our relation to God must be sought in our mortality" (2:145 = N 235). See also 2:407 = N 411.

29. "Necessary link between the supernatural and suffering. Man being made of flesh, how could he not suffer when united to divine nature? God suffers in him from being finite" (2:132 = N 227). Cf. 2:195–96 = N 268. Or: "In our being God is torn. We are the crucifixion of God. My existence crucifies God. As we love an intolerable pain because God sends it, it is with this love, transposed from the other side of the sky, that God loves us. God's love for us is passion. How could the good love evil without suffering? And

evil suffers too in loving the good. The mutual love of God and man is suffering" (3:230 = N 564).

30. 3:225 = N 560. Cf. 3:192 = N 539.

31. 3:225 = N 560: Cf. "There is eternally and simultaneously in God perfect and infinite pain and joy" and "God is an eternal act undoing and repeating itself at the same time. . . . This opposition of the might and the love of God is supreme suffering in God. And the reunion of that power and that love is supreme joy, and that pain and that joy are one" (3:196–97 = N 540). See also *IP* 103 = IC 68; Perrin and Thibon, pp. 146–57 = 132ff.

32. *Philebus* 31d in *IP* 114–15, 164 = IC 156, 195; 3:191 = N 538.

33. 3:192 = N 538. Cf. 3:201 = N 545.

34. The first part of the essay is found in *AD* 81–98 = WG 117–36, the second part in *PS* 107–31 = SN 170–98 (both parts in SN).

35. Weil herself experienced affliction during her factory year (*AD* 36 = WG 66, *PS* 80–81 = SL 140). Curiously enough, the first description of the notion of "affliction," expressed by the word "misery," is found in one of the rare texts she wrote in English: "Misery is always metaphysical; but it can be brought home to the soul through the pain and humiliation suffered by the body. That I call real misery. It was not till Christ had known the physical agony of crucifixion, the shame of blows and mockery, that he uttered his immortal cry, a question which shall remain unanswered through all time on this earth: 'My God, why hast thou forsaken me?' " (SL 102–3). On the correspondence between affliction, the Dark Night of Saint John of the Cross, and the Cave of the *Republic*, see CS 203 = F 242; SG 103–4 = SN 110–11. See also 2:177 = N 256.

36. *AD* 82 = WG 118. In an early article on the *Electra* of Sophocles (1936): "an afflicted being" experiences "misery, and humiliation, and injustice, and the feeling of being all alone, of being given up to wretchedness, abandoned by God and men" (*OC* II.ii.340).

37. "Affliction is inseparable from physical suffering, and yet completely distinct. In suffering, all that is not tied to physical pain or something analogous is artificial, imaginary, and perhaps annihilated by a suitable disposition of thought. Even in the absence or the death of a loved one, the irreducible part of the sorrow is something like physical pain, difficulty in breathing, a vise around the heart, or an unappeased need, hunger, or the nearly biological disorder caused by the brutal liberation of an energy up until then oriented toward an attachment and which is no longer directed. . . .

Humiliation is also a violent state of the whole corporeal being that wants to leap up against the outrage but which must hold itself back, constrained by impotence or fear" (*AD* 81 = WG 117).

38. *AD* 83 = WG 119. The cause for this is that "everything that diminishes or destroys our social prestige, our right to consideration, seems to alter or abolish our very essence" (*PS* 109 = SN 184). Weil's definition of affliction seems to be directly inspired by the three abandonments of Christ spoken of by Saint John of the Cross (*La Montée au Carmel* 2:17 in *Oeuvres complètes* [Paris: Desclée de Brouwer, 1967], pp. 143–44).

39. *AD* 85 = WG 122. Cf. *CO* 112.

40. *AD* 85 = WG 122: "Affliction causes one to harden and despair because it imprints into the depths of the soul, like a hot iron, that contempt, that disgust, and even that revulsion for oneself, that sensation of guilt and stain, that crime ought logically to produce and does not. Evil resides in the soul of the criminal without being felt. It is felt in the soul of the wretched innocent one. Everything occurs as if the state of soul that by its essence is proper to the criminal had been separated from the crime and attached to affliction, and even that in proportion to the innocence of those afflicted." Cf. also 3:313–14 = N 621; *CS* 13 = F 69.

41. *AD* 85 = WG 122. Cf. 2:138, 26, 1:219 = N 231, 158, 140.

42. There can even be hatred against the benefactor who brings us out of affliction (ibid). Cf. 1:218 = N 139. See also *PS* 83 = SL 142. Cf. 2:296–98 = N 337–38.

43. On the relation between suffering and the perception of time, see Chapter 6 below.

44. 2:125–26 = N 223. Weil goes on to say: "Extreme affliction takes God, like all other objects of attachment, away from the sensibility. Life alone remains present to the sensibility. To accept death then is the fullness of the acceptance of death, the fullness of detachment" (2:126–27 = N 223). Cf. *En* 256 = NR 301.

45. Cf. *CO* 261–62 = SWA, 264–66; 3:203 = N 546.

46. The essay was originally to have been entitled "*L'Iliade* ou la Philosophie de la Force" (*OC* II.iii.304).

47. Might reduces people to things, either by truly killing them or by holding the threat of death over each moment of their lives (*OC* II.iii.228 = IC 25–26). "This thing aspires at every moment to be a man, a woman, and at no moment achieves it. This is a death that stretches out the whole length of a life, a life death has turned cold long before eliminating it" (*OC* II.iii.231 = IC 29). Cf.:

"Something in him wanting to exist is continually thrown back into nothingness, as if someone kept striking the head of a drowning man with renewed blows" (*PS* 118 = SN 190).

48. *Iliad* 20:115-16 in *OC* II.iii.229 = IC 26.

49. *OC* II.iii.236 = IC 34. Cf. *P* 93, 74; 168 = N 40.

50. *OC* II.iii.244 = IC 44-45. See also *OL* 94 = OL 65; *SG* 26 = IC 39.

51. *OC* II.iii.245 = IC 44-45. Cf. *IP* 54 = IC 117. See also 3:140 = N 505.

52. As Renaud says in *Venise Sauvée*: "Men of action and enterprise are dreamers; they prefer dream to reality. But through arms they force others to dream their dreams. The conqueror lives his own dream, the conquered lives another's dream" (*P* 77). Cf. 1:67 = N 39.

53. "Those to whom too much harm has been done cannot help becoming evil" (*Electra* 307-8 in *OC* II.ii.342). "No one ever pitied a slave; he therefore could spread around the harm he suffered only through wickedness, since he could not make anyone feel pity" (2:25 = N 158). Cf. 1:192; 3:313 = N 122; 621. See also 3:318-20 = N 624. Committing evil can also be envisaged under the aspect of "becoming richer": "doing harm to another is to receive something from it. . . . One has increased oneself—One has expanded oneself—One has filled some of the void in the self, having created it in someone else" (2:62 = N 181). Cf. 2:26 = N 156.

54. *Iliad* 21:106-14 in *OC* II.iii.244 = IC 44.

55. 3:132 = N 499. Cf. *OC* II.iii.233-34 = IC 31. See also *OL* 92-93 = OL 66-67.

56. 1:174; 2:28 = N 110; 160.

57. *PS* 75 = SL 137. Cf. *CS* 26 = F 82. Cf.: "might is on the level of appearances" (2:137 = N 230). See also 2:402-3, 305 = N 408, 343.

58. This is true to such an extent that the one in whom evil is incarnate must not be conscious of it (*PS* 118 = SN 190). Cf. *AD* 88 = WG 125; on the illusion of being in hell, 2:305 = N 343.

59. *CS* 306 = F 336, *EL* 14 = SE 11. Cf.: "humiliation always has for effect the creation of forbidden zones where thought does not venture and which are covered by silence or untruth. When afflicted ones complain, they complain almost always falsely, without evoking their true wretchedness. . . . In this way each condition of affliction among men creates a zone of silence where human beings are enclosed as if on an island" (*OC* II.ii.299 = SWR 64)

60. *EL* 35 = SE 27. Cf. *EL* 29 = SE 23; *PS* 75, 113 = SL 137, SN 187. "Attention flees from affliction as it flees from the true God, out of the same instinct of preservation; one and the other object force the soul to feel its nothingness and die while the body is still living" (*CS* 297 = F 327). "It is possible to look closely in the face of affliction with sustained attention only if one accepts the soul's death out of love for truth.... It is not really a question of the soul's dying, but of simply acknowledging the truth that it is a dead thing, a thing analogous to matter...what we think to be our self is a product of external circumstances as fleeting and as automatic as the form of a wave on the sea" (*PS* 114–15 = SN 188). Cf. note 18 above.

61. When Niobe lost her twelve children, she wept for nine days; but on the tenth, "she thought of eating, when she was exhausted from her tears" (*Iliad* 24:614 in *OC* II.iii.233 = IC 30–31). Cf. *CS* 292 = F 323.

62. *EL* 36 = SE 28; *CS* 297 = F 327; *CO* 241 = SWR 53–54.

63. "Natural pity consists in helping a wretch either in order to make it easier not to have to think of him, or in order to take greater pleasure in the distance between oneself and him. It is a form of cruelty opposed to cruelty strictly speaking only by the external effects" (*CS* 296 = F 327). See also *CS* 288 = F 319. Cf. *AD* 103–4 = WG 142–43; *EL* 13–14 = SE 11.

64. *AD* 105–8 = WG 144–45. Cf. *PS* 116, 119 = SN 189, 191; 2:216 = N 281; *CS* 297, 42–43 = F 327–28, 99; *EL* 36 = SE 28; *AD* 110 = WG 149–50. Real compassion is the kind felt by the "impassive" part of the soul when through the "sensible part" it is in affliction (*CS* 39–40 = F 94–95). It is basically the compassion of Christ for the self, at the moment when he said: "My God, my God, why have you abandoned me?" It is also the silent compassion of the Father. Consequently, "[t]he love that unites Christ abandoned on the cross to his Father across an infinite distance resides in every saintly soul. A point of that distance remains permanently with the Father.... In this soul, the dialogue of the cry of Christ and the silence of the Father echoes perpetually in perfect harmony" (*CS* 39 = F 95).

65. 2:22, 225, 234 = N 156, 287, 293; *CS* 50, 271 = F 104, 303; *AD* 107–8 = WG 147–48; *PS* 116 = SN 188–89.

66. 2:21 = N 155. Cf. "This irreducible I, which is the irreducible depth of my suffering, must be made universal" (2:234 = N 293). See also *CS* 287 = F 318.

67. 2:215 = N 281. The universalization of vulnerability involves more than a simple "placing under universal light" of vegetative

energy (2:221 = N 284). The passage from universal perspective to the point of view of God is explained by the close relation between perfect compassion and participation in the cross of Christ (2:216-18 = N 281-84). See also *LR* 38-40 = GTG 118-20.

68. *PS* 110 = SN 185; *EL* 34 = SE 27.

69. *PS* 110 = SN 185; *CS* 85 = F 136. See also *EL* 14-15 = SE 11-12.

70. Cf. *AD* 88 = WG 124; 2:414 = N 415.

71. 2:192 = N 266. Cf. *CS* 298 = 328.

72. 2:300 = N 340. Cf. 2:317 = N 352. Even those who have perfectly loved God retain the mark of affliction: "It is sometimes easy to deliver a wretch from his present affliction, but it is difficult to deliver him from his past affliction. Only God can do this. Even the grace of God itself does not heal irremediably injured nature. The glorified body of Christ bore wounds" (*AD* 86 = WG 123).

73. Indeed, Weil wonders whether there is "Hell (even after the destruction of the I?)" (2:305 = N 343). She seems not to be able to accept a supernatural option for evil.

74. "Affliction renders God absent for a time, more absent than a dead person, more absent than light in a completely darkened dungeon. A kind of horror submerges the entire soul. During this absence there is nothing to love. The terrible thing is that if, in these shadows where there is nothing to love, the soul stops loving, the absence of God becomes definitive. The soul must continue to love in a void, or at least want to love, be it only with an infinitesimal part of itself" (*AD* 84 = WG 120). Weil adds: "Then, one day, God comes to reveal himself to it" (ibid.). One must love in a void (3:257 = N 583; *CS* 89, 203, 292-93 = F 139, 242-43, 323-24). See also *Chandogya Upanishad* 8:3:1-2 in *CS* 286 = F 317, etc.

75. At issue is redemptive suffering through affliction: "When the human being is in the state of perfection; when, with the help of grace, he has completely destroyed the 'I' in him; if he then lapses into the degree of affliction in him corresponding to the destruction of the I from outside, were the I intact: that is the plenitude of the Cross" (2:203 = N 342). In other words: "When in the human being, nature, cut off from all carnal impulse, blind and deprived of all supernatural light, carries out actions in conformity with what supernatural light would impose, if it were present, that is the plenitude of purity. It is the central point of the Passion. Redemption takes place; nature has received its perfection" (2:354 = N 376). In general terms of energy: "The uprooting and direction upward of vegetative energy itself is redemptive suffering" (2:175 = N 255; cf.

2:321 = N 354). The essential thing still is the absence of God (2:303-4 = N 342-43), a notion that is necessarily very ambiguous. Weil seems to think that God remains always present in the uncreated, "impassive" part of the soul: "Only for souls in which God has already come down and become established, which have already experienced reality through contact with it—only for these can nothing take away the presence of God. But the feeling of that presence can be taken away from them. It was taken away from Christ" (3:229-30 = N 563-64). See also PS 37 = SN 154; 2:194 = N 267. Cf.: "Contact with God is given to us by the sense of Absence" (2:152 = N 240). Cf. 3:18 = N 424; CS 113 = F 160.

76. PS 122 = SN 193. See also IP 148 = IC 183. Cf.: "If there were no affliction in this world, we could think ourselves in paradise. Horrible possibility" (2:236 = N 294).

77. PS 123 = SN 193. Cf.: "Evil is the form the mercy of God takes on in this world" (3:125 = N 494). See also 2:394-95, 396 = N 403-4. These meditations lead Weil to state that "affliction is in a sense the very essence of creation" (PS 123 = SN 193).

78. We believe we have remained faithful to the spirit of Weil's metaphysics in identifying evil with autonomy. However, Weil herself uses the term "evil" rather often in a larger sense, encompassing the suffering caused by necessity (AD 145 = WG 189-90). Cf.: "Evil is neither suffering nor sin; it is one and the other at the same time, something in common with one and the other. For they are connected; sin makes one suffer, and suffering makes one evil, and this indissoluble mixture of suffering and sin is evil" (PS 14 = SN 149). Cf. 1:11-12 = N 2; PS 36 = SN 154.

79. In supernatural compassion, one loves through evil: "the most precious use of evil is to love God through evil as such.... To love God through the evil one hates, while hating that evil. To love God as the author of the evil one is hating. Evil is to love what mystery is to intelligence. As mystery compels the virtue of faith to be supernatural, so does evil for the virtue of charity" (2:301 = N 340). Cf. PS 36-37 = SN 154; 2:304 = N 342.

80. 3:173, 318-20 = N 526, 624-25.

81. In the essay giving its title to the collection Pensées sans ordre concernant l'Amour de Dieu, Weil explains that contact with a perfectly pure being dissociates sin and suffering in the other and opens the way to repentance, which will transform all the evil into suffering (PS 16-17 = SN 150). Elsewhere Weil seems to conceive of the abolition of evil as something taking place only in the Lamb of God

himself (3:142 = N 506; cf. 2:142 = N 234, *PS* 76 = SL 137). Cf. the profound reflection on the Redemption found in *CS* 105–6 = F 153–54.

5. The Experience of the Beautiful

1. Perrin and Thibon, p. 135 = 122. Cf. "Introduction," *La Pesanteur et la Grâce*, p. v. See also her comparison of Homer and Virgil; the author of the *Iliad* wrote with no intent to flatter or blame, but Virgil sold himself to Augustus, and "although he wrote charming poems, he did not deserve the name of poet.... Poetry is not bought and sold. God would be unjust if the *Aeneid*, composed under these conditions, were the equal of the *Iliad*. But God is just, and the *Aeneid* is infinitely removed from such equality" (*En* 198–99 = NR 233).

2. Most of the central ideas in this chapter are addressed in my article: "Le Piège de Dieu: l'idée du beau dans la pensée de Simone Weil," *La Table Ronde* 197 (1964):71–88.

3. *EL* 31 = SE 25; *En* 200 = NR 234, etc. She mentions also as "great" and "true" poets Maurice Scève, Agrippa d'Aubigné, Théophile de Viau, and Mallarmé. On Théophile de Viau, see *EHP* 110–13 = SE 79–85.

4. *EL* 16 = SE 13; Perrin and Thibon, p. 140 = 147; *En* 199–200 = NR 234–35, etc. She discovered Velasquez at an exhibition from the Prado in Geneva (1939). The preceding year, she had written to an Italian friend "of the few painters who speak to the soul: da Vinci, Giotto, Massaccio, Giorgione, Rembrandt, and Goya" ("Cinque lettere a uno studente e una lettera a Bernanos," *Nouvi Argomenti* 2 [1953]:101).

5. *En* 201 = NR 235; *CO* 256 = SWR 69, etc.

6. She also dismissed with contempt the idea of "personal achievement" in art (*EL* 16–17 = SE 13–14; 2:153–54 = N 241; *CS* 38 = F 93).

7. Cf.: "the beautiful is the real" (*CS* 21 = F 77). "Full existence and beauty are one" (2:256 = N 308). Cf. *CS* 212, 16, 45 = F 72, 98.

8. *En* 254 = NR 300. Cf. 3:280 = N 599.

9. *IP* 62 = IC 123; *AD* 91 = WG 128.

10. 3:42–44 = N 439–440; *CS* 312 = F 341; *SG* 139 = IC 175.

11. Cf.: "the beautiful is the real presence of God in matter" (3:48 = N 443). Cf. *SG* 146; 3:66 = N 455. Cf. also 3:135 = N 501; *CS* 21 = F 77. Indeed, "the beautiful...is God" (*IP* 87 = IC 145). Cf. *AD* 169 = WG 218; 2:72, 189, 365 = N 188, 264, 383; *En* 228 = NR 268; *IP* 37–38 = IC 101–3.

12. "What permits us to contemplate and love necessity is the beauty of the world. Without beauty this would not be possible. For even though consent is the function proper to the supernatural part of the soul, it cannot in fact work without a certain complicity with the natural part of the soul and even with the body" (*IP* 157 = IC 190). Cf. *CS* 35 = F 92; 2:343, 414 = N 369, 416.

13. *CS* 44, 149 = F 98, 194.

14. *IP* 158 = IC 191. Cf. *AD* 91 = WG 128.

15. *IP* 158 = IC 191. Cf.: "This unforced submission of necessity to loving wisdom is beauty" (*IP* 40 = IC 104).

16. *Homeric Hymns* V. Translation of part of this hymn is found in *IP* 9–11, commentary in *IP* 11–13 = IC 1–3 and *AD* 121–22 = WG 163. The term "God's snare" is in *CS* 316 = F 345.

17. *AD* 122 = WG 163; *IP* 11–12 = WG 3–4; 2:361–62 = N 381–82. Cf. 2:391 = N 401. For another explanation of the same myth, see 2:353 = N 375.

18. "The beauty of the world is Christ's tender smile to us through matter" (*AD* 123 = WG 164).

19. *AD* 126–27 = WG 168–70. The same text interprets the love for power as also having love for beauty in the background.

20. *AD* 129 = WG 171. Cf. *CS* 28 = F 83.

21. *AD* 129 = WG 171. Weil goes on to say: "Through error it thinks itself to be something else. The Incarnation alone can satisfy it. Therefore it is wrong to reproach mystics for using lovers' language. It is they who are its legitimate owners. Others only have the right to borrow it" (ibid.).

22. Cf.: "The part taken by things in the good...is beauty" (*CS* 188 = F 229). An early text says that it is through their order that things can belong to the mind (*OC* I.237). Cf. *IP* 157 = IC 190. "Beauty is to things what holiness is to the soul" (*CS* 89 = F 139).

23. *IP* 37–38 = IC 101; 2:189 = N 264. Cf. note 11 above.

24. *AD* 122 = WG 164.

25. *Mundaka Upanishad* 3:1:1 in 1:233 and *AD* 124 = WG 166.

26. 3:338 = N 637. Cf. *AD* 124 = WG 166; 3:76 = N 461. An early note on the story of Narcissus states: "his torment is to see in the water a wonderful youth he will never be able to touch; he only touches the water. But it is always this way.... What we see, we can never touch" ("Philosophie. Enseignement" [1931–34], ms., f. 181).

27. 3:339 = N 637. See also 2:241 = N 298; *AD* 124 = WG 166.

28. "Distance as the perceptible equivalent of the respect, the acknowledgement of things other than ourselves and no less real;

opposed to desire, the desire, the tendency to appropriate, enfold in myself everything I am going to eat. The feeling of distance comes to me while contemplating something I refuse to change even in the imagination (a cathedral, a beautiful statue), that is, the beautiful" (from a note written under the pseudonym Emile Novis in Joë Bousquet, "Conscience et Tradition d'Oc," *Cahiers du Sud* 28 [1943]: 387). Bousquet lived to see the publication of certain of Weil's writings, but he never indicated the exact origin of this quotation.

29. "The things of this world are like flowers that have no fragrance or beauty until someone picks them" (2:183 = N 260). Cf. 3:339 = N 637; *CS* 14 = F 70; *Cahiers*, new ed. (1970) 1:68.

30. 3:182 = N 533. Cf. 2:173, 240 = N 253, 297.

31. 3:76, 338 = N 461, 637. Cf.: "The eternal part of the soul feeds on hunger" (*CS* 252 = F 286). Cf.: "Be nourished by this universe through renunciation" (*Isha Upanishad* 1 in *CS* 250 = F 285). Cf. 1:233.

32. "Union over and above distance is the province of the beautiful. Staying motionless and becoming one with what one desires and does not approach" (3:304 = N 615). Weil continues: "One becomes one with God in this way" (3:305 = N 615).

33. 2:90, 292 = N 199, 334. The beautiful eliminates perspective also (2:140 = N 232).

34. On the evolution of her views, see *PS* 81 = SL 140. Cf. *OC* I.261–74. Cf. *LP* 187–89 = LP 149–51.

35. "Le Beau et le Bien," *OC* I.60.

36. *OC* I.62.

37. *OC* I.65. Cf.: the "beautiful, that is to say. . .the object as an object" (*OC* I.300).

38. *OC* I.66. Cf. *IP* 90 = IC 147; chapter 7 below.

39. "The beautiful is the movement by which one tears oneself away from oneself as an individual" (*OC* I.71).

40. *OC* I.72. Cf.: "This refusal is what makes matter the object" (*OC* I.72).

41. *OC* I.73.

42. *OC* I.73. Cf.: "we see the beautiful only through the act of becoming detached from it" (*OC* I.72). "Matter that was previously for us but feelings and affections of the body becomes an object perceived once art has taught us to see it as beautiful" (*OC* I.63).

43. *OC* I.73. Cf.: "Sin is sleep" (*OC* I.70), that is, subjectivity, error, lack of distance, refusal of renunciation.

44. One might note that this detachment is certainly valid for the experience of beauty in its visual manifestation, but how can it

be denied that seeing a tragedy by Shakespeare implies a conceptual judgment or a profound emotion engendered by the experience of intense participation? Still, it must be observed that there comes a moment when we are watching *King Lear* when we forget that conceptual judgment and are as it were swept away by necessity appearing exposed in the tragic truth of the human condition (cf. 2:413, 3:312 = N 415, 620). As for the feeling of participation, it is basically the expression of universal compassion where a person, while feeling the suffering of others, keeps a distance from their selves as well as from his or her own. Obviously, it remains to be determined whether a decreative compassion can be aroused uniquely on the strength of a momentary suspension of the self at the theater.

45. Weil mentions Kant on this subject in *AD* 124 = WG 165 and 3:172 = N 526.

46. *CO* 265 = SWA 269. Cf.: "The very essence of humanity is directed effort" (*EL* 99 = SE 211). "The spirit. . . is a striving toward a value" ("Quelques réflexions autour de la notion de valeur," ms.). See also *Chandogya Upanishad* 3:14:1 in 1:237. Cf. also my article "Uprootedness and Alienation in Simone Weil," *Blackfriars* 42 (1962):392-93.

47. 3:125 = N 495. Cf. 3:124, 202 = N 494, 545; *En* 181 = NR 211.

48. Cf. *PS* 19, 14, 34, = SE 15, 11, 27 etc.

49. *IP* 168 = IC 199; 3:208-9, 126-27 = N 549-50, 495-96. See also the confusion between "pure means," money or power, and absolute end (3:280 = N 598).

50. 3:301-2 = N 613. Cf.: "By thinking of ourselves. . . from the world's point of view, we achieve that indifference toward ourselves without which one cannot be freed of desire, of fear, of becoming; without which there is neither virtue nor wisdom; without which we live in a dream" (*S* 130-31 = SN 10).

51. 3:302 = N 613. Cf. 3:301 = N 613.

52. A brief description of the mechanism of this contemplation in music appears in the *Cahiers*: "The impression furnished by music of an expectation that the note about to come entirely fulfills and satisfies, all the while taking us entirely by surprise, is simply a reflection of the plenitude of attention wholly oriented toward the immediate" (3:289-90 = N 605).

53. *AD* 125 = WG 167. Cf.: "The value of the beautiful is being a purposiveness without a purpose" (3:210 = N 550). Cf. 3:202 = N 545.

54. *AD* 133 = WG 176. Cf. *IP* 40 = IC 104. Cf.: "The distinctive quality of the work of art is...to curb in us any desire to change it" (*OC* I.81). On inspiration, see also *En* 240–41 = NR 284–85.

55. 3:62 = N 452. Cf. *Timaeus* 28b in *IP* 22 = IC 89, *SG* 130 = SN 132, etc.

56. "There is one single case where human nature tolerates that the desire of the soul is drawn not toward what might be or will be, but toward what exists. This case is beauty. Everything that is beautiful is the object of desire, but we do not desire that it be different, we desire to change nothing in it, we desire the very thing that is. We watch the starry sky of a clear night with desire, and what we desire is simply the sight we possess" (*CO* 265 = SWA 268. Cf. 3:276, 216 = N 596, 554.

57. Cf. the magnificent commentary on the myth of the *Phaedrus* (*SG* 112–15 = SN 117–21) as "an attempt at a psychological and physiological theory of the phenomena that accompany grace" (*SG* 119–20 = SN 123–24).

58. *Phaedrus* 254d–e in SG 122 = SN 126.

59. "Death is in all beauty" (3:195 = N 541). Cf. 3:210 = N 551.

60. *CS* 16 = F 71. Cf. 2:240 = N 297.

61. 2:227 = N 228. See also 3:143 = N 507.

62. 2:180–81, 184 = N 258, 260; *EL* 37 = SE 29. See also 3:143 = N 507.

63. "To represent what is intolerable.... It is to bring the horror out of the shadows and into the light of attention. It is the work of decreation. Nothing is more beautiful, in the most precise sense of the word" (2:229 = N 290). Cf. "La fresque romane de l'église Sant'Angelo à Asolo," *Il Ponte* 7.6:612–14.

64. *AD* 109 = WG 149. As early as 1938, Weil wrote to an English friend: "the soul of genius is *caritas*, in the Christian signification of the word" (*SL* 104–5).

65. See note 44 above.

66. 2:180–81, 2:60 = N 258, 451. Cf.: "The *Iliad*, the tragedies of Aeschylus and of Sophocles bear the evident mark that the poets who made these did so in a state of holiness" (*En* 200 = NR 235). Cf. *SG* 130 = SN 132; 3:16 = N 423.

67. See "Commentaire d'une remarque de Kant pour faire partie d'une dissertation sur Poésie et Vérité," (*OC* I.94–98). This essay summarizes Kantian theory by saying that "beauty is defined by a miraculous harmony between necessity and finality" (*OC* I.94). Cf.: "The beautiful in nature: union of the perceptible impression and

of the awareness of necessity. That *must* be so. . .and in fact it is so" (2:49 = N 172). The coincidence of existence and necessity is also a form of joy (2:214 = N 416).

68. *IP* 157 = IC 190. Cf. *IP* 37 = IC 102; 2:329 = N 360.

69. 2:329, 192 = N 360, 266; *CS* 16 = F 72; 3:179 = N 530, etc.

70. 2:64, 124 = N 182, 222.

71. 1:137 = N 230. Cf. *Cahiers*, new ed. (1970), 1:18 = F 10.

72. 2:192 = N 266. Cf.: "It is a crime to make people sad" (ibid.). See also her severe judgment on modern anguish associated with sadness (*S* 232–33, 241 = SL 122,).

73. Cf. 1:163 = N 103. We must not even think of our nothingness as our own. Such a thought is very well capable of masking hidden pride: "the wrong kind of humiliation leads one to believe one is nothing as a self, as a particular human being. Humility is knowledge that one is nothing as a human being and more generally as a creature" (2:206 = N 275). Cf. my article "La Connaissance et la Mort," *La Table Ronde* (November 1965), 24–25.

74. 2:232 = N 291. Weil is still not completely sure of the grounding of her distinction and immediately adds: "The 'I' is also worn away by joy accompanied by intense attention" (ibid.). Cf.: "In intense and pure joy, one is also empty of the good, because all of the good is in the object. There is as much sacrifice and renunciation at the heart of joy as at the heart of pain" (*CS* 194 = F 235).

75. *IP* 168 = IC 199. Cf. *CS* 90 = F 139. See also *CO* 273 = SWA 276.

76. *AD* 58 = WG 89. Cf. *CS* 13 = F 69; 1:41 = N 22; *AD* 95 = WG 132; *En* 244 = NR 289. See also 2:276–77.

77. *AD* 58 = WG 89. Cf. *CS* 13 = F 69.

78. *PS* 123 = SN 193; *AD* 123 = WG 164.

6. Time and the Self

1. "Du Temps" (*OC* I.74–79). Cf.: "time. . .is existence itself" (*OC* I.299).

2. *OC* I.148.

3. *OC* I.144–45.

4. *Leçons de philosophie de Simone Weil*, p. 211 = LP 197. Cf. 1:63 = N 37. Time forms "the very fabric of human life" ("Enseignement. Philosophie," Bourges-Saint-Quentin [1935–38], ms. f. 325). Cf. 1:49 = N 27. "Everything that disturbs human beings disturbs us in our sense of time" (1:26 = N 12). The afflicted one is "torn in his or her

sense of time" (2:24 = N 157). Thus "[a]ll problems lead back to time" (2:115 = N 216); thus, "[c]ontemplation of time is the key to human life" (*CS* 137 = F 183).

5. *Leçons de Philosophie de Simone Weil*, p. 212 = LP 198.

6. On free rational activity, see my article, "Uprootedness and Alienation in Simone Weil," *Blackfriars* (1962), pp. 385–86.

7. *CO* 182, 246–47 = SL 56, SWR 58–60.

8. Whereas in the normal state of things, "the body lives in the present moment; the mind dominates, travels through, and orients time" (*CO* 182 = SL 56). Cf. *CO* 245 = SWR 57.

9. 3:279–80 = N 598. Cf. 3:128 = N 496.

10. Stated in terms of energy, the horrible kind of monotony means: "Having spent energy in order that everything is again in the previous state; intolerable" (2:47 = N 171).

11. *OC* II.ii.304 = SWR 69. Cf. 1:11 = N 2.

12. *CS* 178 = F 220. Cf. *CS* 92, 137 = F 141, 183.

13. 2:260 = N 311. The relation of the different components of a human being during the time of the process of decreation is explained by the supreme test of the soul during the "quarter-hour." "One part suffers beneath time, and each fraction of time seems eternity to it. One part suffers above time, and eternity seems to it a finite thing. The soul is divided in two, and between the two parts the totality of time is found. Time is the sword that divides the soul in two" (*CS* 182 = F 224).

14. 3:210 = N 551. Cf. 1:64 = N 37.

15. *PS* 79 = SL 139; 2:354, 201 = N 376, 271.

16. Cf. *CS* 73–75 = F 125–27. Cf.: "time proceeds from sin and did not precede it" (*CS* 75 = F 127). With respect to Adam: "It is obvious that there was no period of time when he was in a state of innocence" (2:196 = N 268).

17. 2:162, 359–60 = N 246, 380.

18. *CS* 91–92 = F 140–42. Cf. *CS* 68, 70–71 = F 120, 122–23.

19. *IP* 166 = IC 197; *AD* 89 = WG 126. Time is also the distance between God and human beings (2:390 = N 400). Cf. "The Son, separated from the Father by the totality of time and space, as a result of his having been made a creature; this time that is the substance of my life—the same being true for everyone—this time that is so weighed down in suffering is a segment of that line drawn by the Creation, the Incarnation, and the Passion between the Father and the Son" (*CS* 27 = F 83).

20. 2:289–90, 356 = N 330–31, 378.

21. 2:357 = N 378. Cf. 2:275 = N 321; *PS* 136 = IC 173.

22. *EL* 99 = SE 211. It is impossible also to situate absolute good in the present; as a result, "[a]theistic materialism is necessarily revolutionary, because in order to be oriented toward an absolute good from within this world, it must be placed in the future" (3:227 = N 562). Whereas it is essential "not to believe that the future is the location of the good capable of fulfilling us" (*PS* 13 = SN 148).

23. 2:65 = N 183. Cf. 2:118 = N 218; *CS* 291–92 = F 322–27.

24. *AD* 173 = WG 222. Cf. 2:159 = N 244.

25. 2:115 = N 216. Cf. 3:26–27 = N 429.

26. Weil connects the three times to the three divine persons, and in the outline of her meditation on the Our Father, she defines these relations. On the past she says: "Conceiving the relation of indefinite time to the Father, whose will is constituted by all events that occur, whatever they may be, one thinks of the totality of time under the aspect of the past" (2:259 = N 310).

27. The past itself has a certain appearance of eternity: "The past, when the imagination is not taking pleasure in it. . . is time with the color of eternity. The sense of reality there is pure" (3:16 = N 423). Cf. 3:49–50 = N 443–44; *EHP* 75–76 = SE 44–45.

28. *AD* 172 = WG 222. Cf. 2:209 = N 276

29. "Our personality depends entirely on external circumstances, which have an unlimited power to crush it. But we would rather die than acknowledge this. The balance of the world is for us a course of circumstances that leaves our personality intact and seems to belong to us. All past circumstances that have harmed our personality seem to us an upsetting of balance that one day or another must inevitably be compensated for by phenomena going in the opposite direction. We live in the expectation of these compensations" (*AD* 174 = WG 224).

30. *AD* 175 = WG 225. Cf.: "Conceiving the relation of indefinite time to the Spirit, who cuts roots planted into time, who comes down into souls to save them and transplant them, give them root in eternity, place them in the fullness of perfection, one thinks of the totality of time illuminated by hope, under the aspect of the future" (2:259 = N 310).

31. *CS* 91 = F 141. Cf.: "Humility is inevitable when one knows one is not sure of oneself for the future" (*CS* 137 = F 183). According to an unpublished work dating from before 1940, the Christian virtue of humility consists in knowing that our character (personality) is not sheltered from change ("Caractère," ms.).

32. 2:159, 1:15, 104 = N 244, 5, 64. Cf. *Timaeus* 28b.

33. Cf. *LP* 29–30 = LP 37.

34. 2:67 = N 184. Numbers "fill" the void and as a result reinforce the self. Cf. 2:93 = N 202; *CS* 323–24 = F 351.

35. Let us recall that one does not look for sin with a view to pleasure but in order to avoid the sight of God (chapter 4, note 18).

36. Similarly the disappointment one feels after a pleasure or even while still enjoying it is due to the fact that when a pleasure is attained, the future one desired in and through that pleasure is lost (3:310 = N 619).

37. "Time strictly speaking does not exist...and yet we are subject to it. Such is our condition. *We are subject to that which does not exist....* But our subjection exists" (1:114 = N 71). Cf. 1:42 = N 23.

38. 1:200 = N 127. Cf. *CS* 248 = F 284.

39. Cf.: "Conceiving the relation of indefinite time to the Word, organizing, spreading over all things the light of beauty and immortality, one thinks of the totality of time under the aspect of the present" (2:259 = N 310). Cf. *CS* 90 = F 140; *AD* 168 = WG 217.

40. *AD* 172 = WG 221. Cf.: "Supernatural bread is the bread of this day; it is therefore the food of the humble soul" (*CS* 47 = F 102).

41. *AD* 168 = WG 217. Cf.: "Joy is our escape out of time" (*CS* 154 = F 199).

42. *AD* 82 = WG 118. Cf. 2:122 = N 221.

43. *AD* 174 = WG 224. Upon the death of others, we feel a horror similar to the loss of compensations (1:214 = N 136).

44. *CS* 154 = F 199. "Pain nails us to time, but the acceptance of pain transports us to the end of time, into eternity. We exhaust the indefinite length of time, we cross through it" (*CS* 154 = F 199). "We escape time by remaining below—the flesh gives us the means— or by passing over, into eternity. But in order to pass over, we must go through all of time, in its infinite length, we who live only an instant. God gives the means to those who love him" (*CS* 298 = F 328). Cf.: "Eternity is found at the end of an infinite amount of time. Pain, fatigue, hunger give time the color of the infinite" (*CS* 165 = F 208). Cf.: "the passage of time into the eternal through the intermediary of the perpetual" (*CS* 58 = F 111). Cf. *CS* 47 = F 102; 2:217 = N 282.

45. *CS* 258 = F 292. On the identification of the "part of the soul that is at the level of time" with the part that measures, see *CS* 258 = F 292, 2:67 = N 184, and *EL* 164. See also *OC* I.299–300.

46. Cf.: "A candle is the image of a human being who at each moment offers God the internal combustion. . .of all the moments constituted by vegetative life. This is offering time to God. It is salvation itself" (*CS* 322–23 = N 350).

47. *CS* 178 = F 220. Another text in *La Connaissance Surnaturelle* sums up the process in this way: "One must have crossed through the perpetuity of time in a finite time. For this, a contradiction, to be possible, the part of the soul at the level of time, the discursive part, that part that measures, must be destroyed. For the part of the soul located beneath time, a finite duration is infinite. . . . If by the destruction of the discursive part the layer of the soul underneath is exposed, if in this way in a finite time perpetuity is crossed, if during this perpetuity the soul remains turned toward eternal light, in the end the eternal light will perhaps have compassion and enfold the entire soul in its eternity" (*CS* 258–59 = F 292).

48. Cf. 2:142, 137 = N 233, 230. Cf. the poem of Milarepa in Evans and Wentz, *Tibet's Great Yogi, Milarepa* (Oxford University Press, 1951), p. 214.

49. 2:292 = N 334. On the role of time and space in art: "Space and solitude in painting. Space is solitude, indifference to all things. No events have more importance than others; even the crucifixion of Christ is no more important than a pine needle falling. God equally wants everything that is. Time and space make that equality perceptible. The body of Christ took up no more space, did not take up space in a different manner, than any tree trunk, and did no less disappear through the effect of time. The arts have as their subject space and time, and as their object representing that indifference" (2:389–90 = N 400). Cf. 2:287, 3:44 = N 329, 440. See also 2:215 = 280.

50. 2:211 = N 278. See also 1:173–74 = N 110. Time also makes the distinction between the divine and the diabolical. Those not "rooted" in love (*CS* 178 = F 220) succumb to the temptations of evil after more or less long tests of suffering and emptiness; this is symbolized by the different destinies of the seed in the parable of Christ on the wheat and the tares (*CS* 313 = F 342). Cf. *CS* 15 = F 71.

51. 1:49 = N 27. The horror of time is mitigated in this life by flashes of eternity, but in hell there is only time; we are endlessly drawn toward something we cannot tolerate: "We live here on this earth in a mixture of time and eternity. Hell would be pure time" (*CS* 154 = F 198). Here Weil, very probably without knowing it, is expressing a Thomist position: "In inferno non est vera aeternitas, sed magis tempus" (I a Q. 10, a. 3, Resp. 2).

52. "Should I be condemned to death, I will still not be executed if, in the meantime, time stops" (1:51 = N 28).

53. 1:51 = N 28. Cf. 3:301 = N 612.

7. Non-Acting Action

1. Cf. *CS* 182, 228 = F 224, 265 etc.

2. Cf. 2:170, 211, 274 = N 251, 278, 320.

3. Cf. *CS* 182, 238 = F 224, 274. There is, however, a possibility that supplementary energy reemerges in the decreated person (*CS* 181 = F 222).

4. The imperfect comes from the perfect, and not the opposite (3:194 = N 540). Cf. 2:404 = N 409; *OL* 113 = OL 83.

5. However, Weil often attributes non-acting action to Chinese spirituality (*EHP* 76 = SE 45; see also *IP* 30–31 = IC 96). Among her writings from Marseilles is a seven-page typed text containing quotations from Taoist sages, many of which are on non-acting action.

6. *Bhagavad Gita* 4:18, 20–21 and 5:25 in 2:418.

7. 2:228 = N 289; *PS* 143 = GTG 70; *CS* 131 = F 177. Cf. *CS* 37–38 = F 92–93.

8. *Laws* 10:897–98a. The heavenly voyage of the soul when it "contemplates and eats the truth" is also a circular movement: *Phaedrus* 217d–e in *IP* 92 = IC 149 and *SG* 114 = SN 119.

9. *Timaeus* 47b in *IP* 29–30 = IC 97–98. Cf. also *Timaeus* 90c–d.

10. *IP* 177–79 = IC 206–7. Weil goes so far as to connect circular movement to the Cross (3:159 = N 517).

11. "Movement itself must be seen as an upsetting of equilibrium. The notion mediating between rest and movement can only be uniform circular movement. For this movement changes nothing. If one imagines a circle that is pure, homogeneous from all sides, if it turns, nothing changes" (2:399 = N 406).

12. *IP* 27 = IC 93. Cf.: "The Trinity being an act with itself for subject and object is perfectly represented by circular movement" (2:395 = N 403). Cf.: 3:311 = N 619; *CO* 268 = SWA 271; *IP* 159–60 = IC 191–92; *En* 246 = NR 291–92.

13. The second "birth" of the soul is another expression for decreation, and it is a "circular process": "New birth." Instead of the seed serving to create another being, it serves to create the same being a second time. Return upon oneself, closed circuit, circle" (*CS* 154 = F 199).

14. 3:75 = N 461. Cf. *Symposium* 189d–190b in *IP* 43–44 = IC 108–9. See also 2:85 = N 196.

15. 3:64, 89 = N 453, 470. Cf. 2:162 = N 246.

16. *IP* 30 = IC 96. Cf. *AD* 134 = WG 177.

17. 1:169 = N 107. Cf. *CO* 248 = SWR 60. See also 2:235 = N 294.

18. In Weil's description of the activity of the athlete, there is an interesting image of decreation: "in long-distance runners, after a breathlessness growing to the point of becoming nearly intolerable, a new system of respiration is established that allows the race to be finished without pain. General law of all transformation" (2:41 = N 168). The second form of respiration is an image of the activity of the decreated state reached after long suffering. The individual has endured the test of the quarter-hour, and his or her body is then perfectly obedient.

19. 1:169 = N 107. See also 2:22 = N 156.

20. *OC* II.ii.296 = SWR 60. Cf.: "Moment of stopping. Contemplation. Distinctively human moment" ("Philosophie. Enseignement" [1931–34], ms., f. 187); 1:152 = N 95.

21. Weil herself considered her major works to be "Réflexions sur les Causes de la Liberté et de l'Oppression Sociale" and *L'Enracinement* (cf. *EL* 237 = SL 186), two great studies devoted above all to the problems of labor; the nine years separating them did not change her judgment on the central role of labor in the human condition (cf. *OL* 137 = OL 104; *En* 256 = NR 302). Evidently, the meditations on the perspective of God relativize the claim of labor to be the finest example of essential human virtues (cf. *OL* 140; *CO* 142 = SL 38; *OC* I.274). At the same time, humanity is enriched by the possibility of participation in obedience, the experience of the void, and redemptive suffering.

22. At that time, for example, she gave some classes at a sort of people's university for railroad employees (Cabaud, *L'Expérience vécue de Simone Weil*, p. 36). Later she wrote two essays on *Antigone* (*OC* II.ii.333–38 = IC 18–23) and *Electra* (*OC* II.ii.339–48) for a small factory publication.

23. *OC* I.125–26.

24. *OC* I.327. "Labor contains all human greatness. . .without any return upon the self. One thinks only of the object, in the form of a necessity" (*OC* I.373).

25. *CO* 19 = SL 20. Or, as she would write in London about modern factories: "Human beings need a warm silence, and they are given an icy tumult" (*EL* 22 = SE 17).

26. *CO* 18, 21 = SE 19–20, 22 etc.

27. Weil's views on Marx are discussed in Simone Pétrement, "La critique du marxisme chez Simone Weil," *Le Contrat Social* (1957), pp. 230–36. Let us note that, unlike Marx, Weil had experience in working on machines, which is evident in her insistence on the practical problems of factory work.

28. *CO* 124 = SWA 265–66; 2.173 = N 252–53

29. *OC* II.ii.79 = OL 92. Cf. *CO* 256 = SWR 68.

30. Weil is of course aware of the impossibility of this overview, an ideal that can never be attained (*OC* II.ii.82 = OL 95). However, it might be noted that this whole theory identifying freedom and rationality with this human version of continuous creation implies to a certain extent the condemnation of the act of learning from experience and its accumulation, and might also logically imply the condemnation of the continuity of a human being. What strange manifestation of the self-destructive war the rational wages against the empirical!

31. Cf. *S* 34 sq. = FW 45ff. For a comparison with the Platonic doctrine of the *Epinomis*, see *S* 122 = SN 4.

32. 1:52 = N 29. See also 1:54 = N 30–31.

33. 2:180 = N 258. Cf. 1:87 = N 53.

34. Cf. 3:140; 2:228, 321 = N 504, 288, 354.

35. 1:195 = N 124. Cf. 1:93, 153 = N 57, 96. See also 3:37–38 = N 436.

36. "The pure and simple completion of prescribed acts. . .that is, obedience, is to the soul what immobility is to the body" (*CS* 306 = F 336). Cf. 2:336 = N 364; "prescribed acts follow automatically from a soul in the state of motionless waiting" (*PS* 143 = GTG 70). In other words, "what one does expresses exactly what one is" (1:77 = N 46). Cf. 3:37 = N 436. See also 3:55 = N 448.

37. *CS* 16 = F 72, or "As the arrow to the target through the archer" (2:329 = N 360). This metaphor comes from the *Bhagavad Gita* 11:33 in 2:423.

38. 2:327 = N 358. "One's neighbor must not be helped for Christ, but through Christ. Let the self disappear so that Christ, through the intermediary constituted by our soul and our body, may help one's neighbor" (ibid.). Cf. *CS* 103, 96 = F 152, 141.

39. 2:238 = N 359. None other than the true incarnation of the will of God can be seen in the person who helps a sufferer: "A good act is what in a given situation would be done by an incarnate God" (3:147 = N 509).

40. *CS* 181 = F 223. In another passage of *La Connaissance Surnaturelle*, the parable symbolizes the whole configuration of creation and decreation; the father is God, the prodigal son is humanity, the share of inheritance is autonomy, and the obedient son is matter (*CS* 326 = F 354). Cf. *CS* 168 = F 211.

41. 2:235 = N 293; *CS* 162 = F 206. Stated in terms of the void: "Renouncing the fruits is having a life entirely composed of efforts in the void" (2:132 = N 227).

42. Cf. *CO* 244–45, 262 = SWR 56–58, SWA 265.

43. *En* 255 = NR 300. Cf. 3:278 = N 597.

44. 2:44 = N 170. This means experiencing our subjection to time and space (2:45 = N 170). Work makes us understand the reality and irreducibility of the external world: "A stone is hard only to someone who wants it to yield" (*OC* I.366).

45. "Habit, second nature; better than the first" (2:44 = N 170). Habit acquired through work is in some way an image or approximation of the new existence one receives upon achieving decreation. In an early note habit is considered as perfect control over the body by thought: "It is a matter of making the body penetrable to thought in the same way it is to nature" (*OC* I.276).

46. 2:44 = N 170. Cf. *OL* 137, 140 = OL 104, 106; *AD* 127–28 = WG 169–70.

47. Letter to Xavier Vallat, Commissioner of Jewish Affairs in Vichy, quoted in Cabaud, *L'Expérience Vécue de Simone Weil*, p. 236.

48. We have said above that in non-perspective I certainly do not count for more than others, but at least I count for as much, whereas in God's perspective I live in sacrifice and abnegation (see Chapter 1). Indeed, we see that the *state* of non-perspective is only an abstraction, and even the acceptance of the equality of others implies the supernatural.

49. *En* 254 = NR 299. Therefore, one of the major consequences of original sin is the refusal of humankind to consent to the order of the world. But "[l]abor is consent to the order of the universe" (*CS* 331 = F 358).

50. 2:40 = N 167. Cf.: "Physical labor is a daily death" (*En* 255 = NR 300). Cf. 1:157 = N 99.

51. "Labor is not an imitation of the Creation, but of the Passion" (2:347 = N 372). It is an imitation of the creation only insofar as it implies decreation, the imitation of God emptying himself of himself in the form of the Incarnation (2:196-97 = N 269).

52. Cf.: "One who labors unaware does not imitate the cruci-fixion" (3:271 = N 592).

53. The goal is "[t]hat eternal light give, not a reason for living and working, but a plenitude that exempts one from seeking that reason" (3:277 = N 596).

54. 3:214 = N 553. Detachment is the orientation of all our energy toward God, after the test of the quarter-hour: "Any attachment to an object is a sending out of energy. . . . Detachment is a sending out of the totality of energy to God" (3:92 = N 472). Cf. *CS* 252 = F 286.

55. 2:271 = N 318. Cf. 2:264 = N 313.

56. 3:214 = N 553. Cf. *CS* 239 = F 275. On the substitute for detachment caused by biological reasons, see Perrin and Thibon, pp. 152–53 = 137–38.

57. The "explosion" of signs is probably the central notion of Weil's social thought; see especially "Réflexions sur les Causes de l'Oppression et de la Liberté Sociale."

58. *OC* I.66.

59. 2:280 = N 324. Cf. 2:262 = N 312; *IP* 34 = IC 99. One is reminded here of the "reckless leaps" of the unjust man in *Laws* 716b.

60. "Philosophie. Enseignement," Bourges-Saint-Quentin (1935–38), ms., f. 292.

61. ". . .if mystical ecstasy is something real in the soul, there must be corresponding phenomena in the body that do not appear when the soul is in another state" (*En* 226 = NR 267).

62. She wants "a war in the image of peace" (1:107 = N 66). Cf. 1:56 = N 32.

63. 1:153 = N 96. The literal meaning of "dharma" is balance, followed by order of the world, justice (right, duty), and the obligation belonging to each human being (vocation). Cf. 2:428.

64. Cf. *Bhagavad Gita* 11:33 in 2:423.

65. *Bhagavad Gita with Sri Ramanujacharya's Visistadvaita Commentary* (Madras: 1898), p. 30. Cf. ibid., p. 97.

66. *CS* 306 = F 336. Cf. 2:280 = N 324.

67. 1:92 = N 56. Cf. 1:89 = N 54. See also 2:79–80 = N 192–93.

68. 2:236 = N 294. Cf. 1:88, 92, 186 = N 53, 56, 118. But also see *CS* 162 = F 206.

69. However, "it is necessary to be very pure to commit evil" (1:139 = N 87).

70. "However just the cause of the conqueror, however just the cause of the defeated, the evil done by either victory or defeat is none the less inevitable. Hoping to escape it is forbidden" (1:46 = N 25).

71. 1:90 = N 55. Cf.: "One is not corrupted by actions from which one is absent in this way. . .even though they are mixed up with evil" (1:93 = N 57).

72. 2:261-62 = N 311-12. Cf. *SG* 32 = IC 44-45. However, "just" punishment has a purifying and curative role (*AD* 112, 115 = WG 152, 155; *EL* 41 = SL 32, etc.).

73. Cf. *The Ramayan of Valmiki*, book 6, songs 117-20.

74. Weil desperately seeks the criteria of a situation in which one is forced to commit injustice against an individual for the good of the social order. She thinks they are to be found in a state in which one is prepared to act in the same way toward those one loves the most, or: "In the case where the life of a certain person is bound to one's own to the point that the two deaths would be simultaneous, would one still want the other to die? If the body and the whole soul aspire to life and if yet, truthfully, one can answer yes, then one has the right to kill the other" (1:57-58 = N 33). Of course, even here the norm ultimately remains subjective. . . . On the evolution of her views on pacifism see *EHP* 248-49, 273-79 = FW 257f, 264-49; *CS* 317 = F 345. See also *CS* 311 = F 340.

75. 1:46 = N 25. Cf. *EHP* 80 = SE 49; 3:212 = N 552. Cf.: "Impossible to handle that piece of iron without abruptly reducing the infinite within the human being to a point of the tip, a point of the handle, at the cost of rending pain... The whole being is struck in the instant; no room for God remains. . . . The whole being becomes privation of God" (1:47-48 = N 26). Cf. 3:128-29 = N 497.

76. Cf.: "God making evil pure is the idea of the Gita" (3:136 = N 502). Elsewhere Weil compares Christ to Rama and Arjuna (2:223-24 = N 286; 1:153 = N 96).

77. *EL* 77 = SE 221. Cf. *En* 12-13 = NR 6-7; *AD* 116 = WG 157

78. 2:328 = N 359. Cf. *AD* 13-14 = WG 43-44; 2:181-82 = N 259-60. On passivity in the assistance of others, see 2:228 = N 288 and *PS* 37-38. "For the things within our power. . .Read obligation as a necessity" (1:68-69 = N 40-41). However, she confesses in a letter to Father Perrin that she always finds a reason to help someone: "For any particular human being whatsoever, I always find reasons to conclude that affliction is not right for him or her, whether the individual seems to me too mediocre for so great a thing, or on the contrary too precious to be destroyed. One cannot fail more gravely in the second of the two essential commandments" (*AD* 50-51 = WG 83). And in the same letter: "I wish you all possible good except the Cross, because I do not love my neighbor as myself" (ibid.).

See also a conversation mentioned by Thibon in Perrin and Thibon, p. 130 = 117, and a letter from Weil to Thibon, *La Pesanteur et la Grâce*, vii.

79. *AD* 110-11 = WG 150.

80. *AD* 105-6 = WG 146. Cf. *AD* 61 = WG 92; 2:238, 338-39, 16-17 = N 295, 366, 152; *CS* 223 = F 261. See also *CS* 170 = F 213. God also needs my cooperation so that he may love a creature (2:290 = N 333). Cf. also: "That wretched person lies on the road, half-dead from hunger. God has mercy on him or her, but cannot send bread. But I who am there, fortunately I am not God; I can give the person a piece of bread. That is my sole superiority over God" (*CS* 281 = F 312). After this, one is not astonished to read: "Whoever suffers unjustly must pity first of all God who is forced to permit the injustice. The same for the sufferings of others" (*EL* 165).

81. *AD* 156 = WG 205. Cf. *EL* 155.

82. *AD* 158 = WG 205. Cf. Weil's article on "Otto Rühle: *Karl Marx, Critique Sociale*" (*OC* II.i.354).

83. This impersonal character of friendship is found even in conjugal love: "As for conjugal love, if the two spouses are saints, it is friendship between saints; if only one of them is, the anonymous love of neighbor is the only stable factor in their relationship" (*CS* 76 = F 128).

84. *AD* 159-60 = WG 206. Cf. *AD* 66 = WG 98.

85. *AD* 161 = WG 208. Cf. *IP* 127-29 = IC 166-68. God is also "the friend par excellence. For something like equality to exist between him and us across infinite distance, he willed placing in his creatures an absolute, the absolute freedom to consent or not to the orientation he gives us toward him" (*AD* 166 = WG 214).

Conclusion

1. Martin Buber, implacable critic of Simone Weil, says of this struggle: "Reality had become unbearable to her, and God was the power that delivered her from reality. . . her soul was in flight from reality" (*An der Wende: Reden uber das Judentum* [Cologne and Olten: J. Hegner, 1952], pp. 75-76).

2. Let us not forget that "[s]in is related to the individual" (2:195 = N 267).

3. *IP* 71, 163 = IC 130, 195. Cf.: "a perfect human being is God" (*CS* 263 = F 297). Cf. *AD* 175 = WG 225.

4. On this subject see my article "La Connaissance et la Mort," *La Table Ronde* (November 1965), pp. 13–27.

5. *CS* 40, 263 = F 94, 296.

6. Cf.: "God must be impersonal to be innocent of evil, personal to be responsible for the good" (*CS* 59 = F 112).

7. Cf. 2:287, 368 = N 329, 386; see also *CS* 58 = F 111.

8. Note that the most important and systematic formulation of her views on the structure and the philosophical and theological sense of the central doctrines of Christianity is found in the great study "A Propos de la Doctrine Pythagoricienne," *IP* 108–71 = IC 151–201.

9. "Folklore: Thème de la neige et du sang," Marseilles (1941–42), *CSW* 15.1 (Mars, 192), 88–89.

10. She appears to have read passages of the *Summa Theologica* of Saint Thomas. It is likely that she knew Abélard and some of the Church Fathers; she read Meister Eckhart. But she has only contempt for contemporary Thomism (*En* 207, 235 = NR 243, 277), and her judgment on Saint Thomas himself is very severe (*EL* 142–43).

11. Péguy, "Note sur M. Bergson et la philosophie bergsonienne" in *Oeuvres en Prose* (Paris: La Pléiade, 1961), p. 1331.

Chronological Table

Presented below are only the most important events and writings in the life of Simone Weil. A complete table, established by Florence de Lussy with the assistance of André Weil and Géraldi Leroy, may be found in each of the volumes of Simone Weil, *Oeuvres complètes*, eds. André-A. Devaux and Florence de Lussy (Paris: Gallimard, since 1988).

3 February 1909	Birth of Simone Weil in Paris.
1925–1928	Preparation for the Ecole Normale Supérieure. She is a student of Alain. "Le Beau et le Bien" (February 1926).
1928–1931	Ecole Normale Supérieure and the Sorbonne. Weil continues to take courses with Alain. First publication: "De la Perception ou l'Aventure de Protée" (May 1929).
1931	Weil passes the *agrégation*.
1931–1932	Teaches at the *lycée* in Le Puy. First contacts with syndicalism.
1932	Travels to Germany (summer).
1932–1933	Teaches at the *lycée* in Auxerre. Syndicalist activity.
1933	Meeting of the C.G.T.U. (July). She violently criticizes the German communist party and the Soviet Union. "Allons-nous vers la révolution prolétarienne?" (summer).

1933–1934   Teaches at the *lycée* in Roanne. Syndicalist activities at Saint-Etienne. "Réflexions sur les causes de la liberté et de l'oppression sociale" (1933).

1934–1935   She works in several factories (4 December–22 August). "Journal d'usine."

September 1935   Vacation in a small Portuguese fishing village. Experience of "Christianity as the religion of slaves."

1935–1936   Teaches at the *lycée* in Bourges. "Lettres à un ingénieur d'usine" (January–June 1936).

1936   She is in Barcelona and later on the Aragon front with Durutti's anarchists (August–September).

1936–1937   She has a year's leave for health reasons. She begins participating in meetings of the circle of the *Nouveaux Cahiers* (continued until 1940). "Ne recommençons pas la guerre de Troie" (spring of 1937).

1937   Travels to Italy (spring). Religious experience in Assisi at Santa Maria degli Angeli. "Cinque lettere a uno studente."

1937–1938   Teaches at the *lycée* in Saint-Quentin (October–January).

1938   On leave for health reasons (beginning in January).

1938   Solesmes (from Palm Sunday until Easter Tuesday).

1938	Trip to Venice and Asolo (June–July).
1938	First experience of Christ (autumn).
1939–1940	Improvement of headaches. "Réflexions en vue d'un bilan" (February). "Quelques réflexions sur les origines de l'hitlérisme" (1939–1940). "L'*Iliade* ou le poème de la force" (1940).
June 1940	She leaves Paris.
1940	Vichy (July or August to October). First versions of *Venise Sauvée. Cahiers.*
1940–1942	She is in Marseilles (October 1940–May 1942). Contacts with the group of the *Cahiers du Sud* (autumn and winter 1940). "Dieu dans Platon" (October 1940–November 1942).
1941	She attends a meeting of the *Jeunesse Ouvrière Chrétienne* (March 30). "Conditions Premières d'un Travail non-servile" (spring or summer).
June 1941	She meets Father J. M. Perrin.
1941	She works at Gustave Thibon's farm and later picks grapes at another farm (7 August–October). "A Propos du Pater" (autumn 1941).
1941–1942	Meetings with Father Perrin and his circle (winter). Letters to Father Perrin and Gustave Thibon. "Réflexions sur le bon usage des études scolaires en vue de l'amour de Dieu" (spring). "L'Amour de

Dieu et le malheur" (spring). "Formes implicites de l'amour de Dieu" (spring). "Réflexions sans ordre sur l'amour de Dieu" (spring). "Descente de Dieu" (November–26 May).

1942   Meets Joë Bousquet at Carcassonne (Easter). Letters to Joë Bousquet.

1942   She leaves for North Africa (14 May). Seventeen days in Casablanca. Letters to Father Perrin and Gustave Thibon. *Cahiers d'Amérique* (May–November).

1942   New York (end of June–10 November). *Lettre à un religieux.*

1942–1943   She works in London for the Free French (November–April). Enters the Middlesex hospital in London (15 April). Is taken to the Grosvenor Sanatorium, Ashford, Kent (17 August). *L'Enracinement. Notes Ecrites à Londres* in *CS*. "Théorie des sacrements." *Ecrits de Londres et dernières lettres.*

24 August 1943 Death of Simone Weil.

Suggested Reading

A comprehensive reference for primary and secondary works is J. P. Little, *Simone Weil: A Bibliography* (London: Grant and Cutler, 1973; supplement, 1979). Readers new to Simone Weil may wish to begin with the following works available in English (compiled, with several additions, from Little and McLellan, below).

Works by Simone Weil

First and Last Notebooks. Tr. Richard Rees. New York: Oxford University Press, 1970.

Formative Writings, 1929–1941. Ed. Dorothy Tuck McFarland and Wilhelmina Van Ness. Amherst: University of Massachusetts Press, 1987.

Gateway to God. Ed. David Raper. Glasgow: Collins, 1974.

Gravity and Grace. Tr. Arthur F. Wills. New York: Putnam, 1952.

Intimations of Christianity. Tr. Elizabeth Chase Geissbhler. London: Routledge & Kegan Paul, 1957.

Lectures on Philosophy. Tr. Hugh Price. Cambridge: Cambridge University Press, 1978.

Letter to a Priest. Tr. Arthur F. Wills. New York: Putnam, 1954.

The Need for Roots. Tr. Arthur F. Wills. New York: Putnam, 1952.

The Notebooks of Simone Weil. Tr. Arthur F. Mills. 2 vols. New York: Putnam, 1956.

On Science, Necessity and the Love of God. Tr. Richard Rees. Oxford: Oxford University Press, 1968.

Oppression and Liberty. Tr. Arthur F. Wills and John Petrie. London: Routledge & Kegan Paul, 1958.

Selected Essays (1934–1943). Tr. Richard Rees. London: Oxford University Press, 1962.

Seventy Letters. Tr. Richard Rees. London: Oxford University Press, 1965.

Simone Weil: An Anthology. Ed. Siân Miles. London: Virago, 1986.

The Simone Weil Reader. Ed. George A. Panichas. New York: David McKay, 1977.

Waiting on God. Tr. Emma Crauford. New York: Putnam, 1951.

Works on Simone Weil

Allen, Diogenes and Eric O. Springsted. *Spirit, Nature and Community: Issues in the Thought of Simone Weil.* Albany: SUNY Press, 1994.

Anderson, David. *Simone Weil.* London: SCM, 1971.

Bell, Richard, ed. *Simone Weil's Philosophy of Culture.* Cambridge: Cambridge University Press, 1993.

Blum, Lawrence and Victor Seidler. *A Truer Liberty: Simone Weil and Marxism.* London: Routledge, 1989.

Cabaud, Jacques. *Simone Weil: A Fellowship in Love.* New York: Channel, 1965.

Coles, Robert. *Simone Weil: A Modern Pilgrimage.* Reading, MA: Addison-Wesley, 1987.

Davy, Marie-Magdelaine. *The Mysticism of Simone Weil.* Boston: Beacon, 1951.

Fiori, Gabriella. *Simone Weil: An Intellectual Biography.* Atlanta: University of Georgia Press, 1989.

Little, J. P. *Simone Weil: Waiting on Truth.* Oxford: Berg, 1988.

McLellan, David. *Utopian Pessimist: The Life and Thought of Simone Weil.* New York: Poseidon, 1990.

Pétrement, Simone. *Simone Weil: A Life.* New York: Pantheon, 1977.

Rees, Richard. *Simone Weil: A Sketch for a Portrait.* Carbondale: Southern Illinois University Press, 1966.

Springsted, Eric O. *Simone Weil and the Suffering of Love.* Cambridge: Cowley Publications, 1986.

Winch, Peter. *Simone Weil: "The Just Balance".* Cambridge: Cambridge University Press, 1989.

Author Index

Subject Index